INDIA IN PORTUGUESE LITERATURE

INDIA IN PORTUGUESE LITERATURE

BY

Ethel M. Pope, M.A., D. LITT.

L.R.A.M., A.R.C.M., F.R.S.A., M.R.A.S.

Socio Correspondente da Associacao de Arqueologos, Lisbon. Member of the British Institute of Philosophical Studies. Member of the Council of the Osmania University, Hyderabad-Dn. Principal, Osmania University College for Women, Hyderabad-Dn.

GYAN

Published by

Gyan Publishing House
5, Ansari Road
Daryaganj, New Delhi-110002
Phone: 011-47034999, 9811692060
E-mail: books@gyanbooks.com

Distribution Network
gyanbooks.com
India, USA, Canada, UK, Australia, France

ISBN : 978-81-212-3589-1 (PB)
First Published, 1937

2nd Impression 2020

Printed at: Gyan Press, Delhi.

India in Portuguese Literature
Author: Ethel M. Pope

INDIA IN PORTUGUESE
:: LITERATURE ::

BY

Ethel M. Pope, **M.A., D. LITT.,**

L.R.A.M., A.R.C.M., F.R.S.A., M.R.A.S.

Sócio Correspondente da Associação de Arqueólogos, Lisbon.
Member of the British Institute of Philosophical Studies.
Member of the Council of the Osmania University, Hyderabad-Dn.
Principal, Osmania Unversity College for Women, Hyderabad-Dn.

PRINTED AT
"TIPOGRAFIA RANGEL"
BASTORÁ—PORTUGUESE INDIA

"Thus (in Portugal) India invaded and absorbed the interest of the social life of the higher classes, as well as of the common people. This is felt in the literature. The great national epic poem was written in India, by a soldier of India... And in those forms of literature which give expression to the most intimate feelings of a people, the Indian touch is never wanting."

Conde de Ficalho

"Garcia da Orta e seu tempo"
Lisbon, 1886.

To my dear Mother

who

inspired me to do this work

and

to my revered friend

Colonel Froilano de Mello

who

made it possible.

CONTENTS

querque, (Bras de Albuquerque), Dom João de Castro, Antonio Galvão, João de Lucena, Antonio de Castilho, Antonio Tenrreyro, Garcia de Orta, Francisco de Andrade, Damião de Goes, Lopo de Sousa Coutinho, Father Gastão, Father Fernando de Santa Maria, Belchior de Moraes, Fabiam da Motta, Diogo Botelho Pereira, Father Pedro Martins, Francisco Rodrigues, Balthazar Dias, Father Luis Froës, Father Luiz de Gouvêa, João Nunes Barreto, Father Ayres Brandam, Father Jorge Caldeyra, Father Gaspar Villela, Father Amador Rebello, "Chronica de Guzerate". (Anonymous).

CHAPTER II :— The Gongoric School, 1580-1706.

Political and literary decadence.

Influence of the Jesuits on the literature about India.

Epic Poets :

Francisco Sá de Menezes.

Historians and travellers :

Antonio Bocarro, Jacinto Ferreira de Andrade, Antonio Pinto Pereira, Antonio Rodrigues de Costa, Francisco de Pinho e de Mello, Manuel Jacome Mesquita, Father Antonio de S. Miguel, Salvador de Couto de Sampaio, Dom Constantino de Sá e Noronha, Cosme Lafeta, Father Antonio Monserrate, P. Manuel Barradas, Capitão Barreto de Resende, Antonio de Andrade, Gaspar Ferreira Reyman, Antonio Gil Preto, Manoel Godinho, P. Fernando Guerreiro, Father Antonio de Gouvêa, Father Domingo do Espirito Santo, Simão Torrezão Coelho, Cosme da Guarda, Mosseh Pereira de Paiva.

Language and Poetry :

João Franco Barreto, Father Diogo de Sancta Anna, Father Antonio Pereira, Father Fernando de Queyroz, Father Antonio da Silva, Father Antonio da Trindade, Father Diogo Monteiro, João da Costa, Father Antonio

João de Frias, João Ribeiro, Domingos Affonso, Antonio de Fonseca Osorio, Father Francisco de Sousa.

Religion :

Father Agostinho de Santa Maria, Father Antonio Pereira, Father Fernando de Queyroz, Father Antonio da Silva, Father Antonio Trindade, Father Diogo Monteiro, João da Costa, Father Antonio João de Frias, João Ribeiro, Domingos Affonso, Antonio de Fonseca Osorio, Father Francisco de Sousa.

CHAPTER III:—The French or Arcadian School, 1706-1826.

Continuation of literary decadence.

Establishment of Academies for literary reform. Poets of the 18th century who wrote on India :

Bocage, Father José Agostinho de Macedo.

Effect of the disastrous wars with the Marathas on the literature.

Prose writers who wrote on the wars :

Diogo da Costa, Jacinto Machado de Sousa.

Poems by Antonio de Meirelles on the victories over the Marathas.

Prose account by the same author.

Instructions of the Marquis of Alorna and the Marquis of Pombal.

Indian languages.

CHAPTER IV:—The Romantic School and Contemporary writers.

Literary position of Portugal with reference to India.

Indologists and Historians : Cunha Rivara.

PREFACE

> **Não tornes por detrás; pois é fraqueza**
> **Desistir-se da cousa começada.**
>
> ***Camões, E. 40. v. 3. & 4.***
>
> **Don't turn back; for it is weakness**
> **To give up something which is begun.**

More than one psychologist of modern times has laid stress on the part which chance plays in the events of human life. While turning over in my mind the plan for the present work, to which I have tried, as far as I was capable, to give a sequence not devoid of logic and harmony, I was more than ever convinced that chance has many times played an important role in the production of a work.

The work of an author is like the work of a people, a synthesis of various organic factors: some, inherent, constitute the personal and characteristic ego in the individual, and in the people, form a homogeneous whole, called race; other factors, external, concern the social life of the individual, and in peoples contribute to the inter-relation of the races; other factors again are occasional which in the individual, produce the moment and in the race the epoch.

My readers may be interested to know the circumstances which led me to take up this study. While a student in London, I was thrown in the constant society of some Portuguese families. Through them I learned to appreciate the beauty of their language, their art and the cult of their heroes. I became familiar with their everyday life, with the charm of their popular songs and even with their slang and their subtle wit. And one day when I resolved to dedicate my services to India, it was chance again which enabled me to revive, in a little country which is the reproduction of Lusitanian civilisation, my knowledge of the culture, art and literature of the Portuguese. Thus when, in the course of my intellectual studies, I sought the advice of an eminent scholar in the University of Benares who is interested in Portuguese culture, the subject he suggested for this thesis was accepted by me with the greatest satisfaction as a natural sequence of my Portuguese associations and my predilection for Portuguese history, art and literature.

"India in Portuguese Literature" was the subject chosen for my research work. Portugal was the first nation to give to Europe in the Middle Ages a knowledge of the legendary countries of the Orient. As the Portuguese were the pioneers of modern civilisation in India and as such promoted the intercourse between the West and the East, it would naturally be interesting to Indologists to know what can be found in the various branches of Portuguese literature concerning India, its peoples, customs, ethnology and its religions.

To English people Portuguese literature is not as well known as it should be, in spite of the learned works of Edgar Prestage, Aubry Bell and others. With the exception of the immortal strophes of Camões, it is seldom that the writings of a Portuguese author are seen on the shelves of our libraries. Luiz de Camões, though incontestably the greatest of all the Portuguese writers, is

not the only one. The fleets of the conquerors were accompanied by scribes and chroniclers who have left most expressive and vivid documents relating to the evolution and history of the India of their time. Whether we examine the Classic or the Gongoric period, the Arcadian or the epoch of Contemporary Romanticism, we find that many Portuguese writers have left documents of great value for the history of the East in general and for that of India in particular. To unearth from the dust of libraries those valuable records and offer them to Indologists in a short review together with my modest personal criticism is the aim of the present work.

It is necessary to state clearly the lines on which I have proceeded in this study. By literature I do not mean only literary composition, whether in verse or prose, but I use the term in its widest conception: namely, the written expression of human thought. Whether this expression of thought in the works of the writers of different periods of Portuguese literature be in verse or in prose, whether about history, sociology, religion or language, the politics of the Indian States or their folkore, natural sciences or medicine, I have searched in those writings for the passages which speak about anything pertaining to India. Moreover literature is one of the forms of Art, and, in order to understand and analyse the art of a people as the comprehensive result of its active and emotional life, Taine teaches us: "Nous sommes obligés de considerer le peuple qui l'a faite, les moeurs qui la suggeraient et le milieu où elle est née. (1)

India would not have been a reality for the Portu-

(1). TAINE, "Philosophie de l'Art", Librairie Hachette, 1895. Quatrième partie, "La Sculpture en Grèce.", p. 86, vol, ii, 20th odn.

guese people if it had not first been an aspiration. And that aspiration would never have been born in Portuguese breasts, if the indomitable warlike sons of the mountains who resisted the legionary Roman hosts, had not been filled with the sentiment of independence and the spirit of adventure which led them to the shores of the Atlantic. Then came the Crusaders who helped them to conquer Lisbon. The conquest of Algarve and the love of adventure led them to look towards the African coast. And it is at that point that a chance cause, the infusion of the rational blood of an English princess in the royal family of Portugal ([1]) transformed the maritime adventure into a school of systematic exploration which was called the School of Sagres.

The discovery of Vasco de Gama was not merely the result of a fortunate adventure. It was preceded by daring attempts and bold discoveries on the African coasts and by the wresting of its secrets from the Sea of Torments. In truth, one cannot separate Portuguese literature from its history. The Lusiadas would have not existed, if the century of the discoveries in the Atlantic had not had as its corollary the voyage of Vasco de Gama and the Empire of Affonso de Albuquerque.

The chapters of this work are dependent on the natural divisions of the literary history of Portugal, and in them

---

([1]) D. João I of Portugal married D. Filipa, the daughter of John of Gaunt, Duke of Lancaster, and sister of Henry IV of England. They had a son, Henry, known as Prince Henry the Navigator, who established the school of exploration, called the School of Sagres. For 40 years, from the time of the discovery of the island of Maldive till 1460. he was busy making discoveries by sea. He died in 1460 at the age of 66. He lies buried in Batalha.

Cf. BARROS, Decada I, Liv. I, Cap. XVI.

the historical events which influenced the development of the race are dealt with briefly. For example we cannot find in Gongorism, which in Portugal is contemporaneous with the loss of independence and the breaking up of the Empire, the magnificence of the culture which marks the Manueline period and culminates in the classic of which Portugal is so justly proud: the Lusiadas of Camões.

The book begins with an introduction in which are described the characteristics of the Portuguese race, the birth of their nationality, their warlike and adventurous qualities, and their culture. This is followed by four chapters comprising respectively the Classic Epoch, its genesis and its results, the Gongoric, Arcadian and Romantic Schools, each containing a brief historical resumé, and a bibliographical and critical review of the works in any branch of written thought, which have any reference to India.

In the last chapter I have tried to sketch the Indo-Portuguese movement which had its origin in India itself. Any one who travels through the Orient will be convinced that the Portuguese influence was deep and widespread as is proved by the Portuguese names and designations which have found their way into the Indian languages, and by the Portuguese dialects which even today prevail among the Sinhalese and Malasian families who came in contact with Lusitanian civilisation.

To collect material I visited the principal countries of Europe, including Portugal, France and England, where I found many precious literary documents which in great part have been utilised for this work and in Portugal, in the Libraries and Archives of Lisbon, Ajuda and Evora, I discovered a mine of unused material for my proposed works on India.

I cannot conclude these lines without expressing my sincere thanks to Professor Seshadri of Government

College, Ajmer, for important suggestions, and to Father Hosten who in reviewing this work, made many valuable annotations and corrections. I am grateful also to Lt-Colonel de Costa Veiga Director of the National Library, Lisbon, and to the Government and the authorities in Goa as well as to the scholars resident there for the facilities afforded me in consulting their libraries, and above all for the use of the abundant documents contained in their old and unpublished Archives,—now under the able supervision of the learned Indologist Professor Pissurlencar,—a source not yet thoroughly examined, which can be recommended to Indologists.

INTRODUCTION.

"Inclyta geração, altos Infantes."
(Illustrious race, noble Princes.)

Camões—E. 50 a. v. 8.

"O' gente forte, e de altos pensamentos,
Que tambem della hão medo os elementos!"
(Strong people with noble thoughts,
Of whom even the elements are afraid!)

Camões—E. 47 a. v. 7 & 8.

A short description of the characteristics of the Portuguese race, their political organization and culture before the discovery of India.

On the west of Europe, there is a little country, part of the Iberian peninsula, whose shores are washed by the wild Atlantic. This country, so small and insignificant in itself, was the cradle of heroes who played an important part in the history of the world, gaining immortal fame through the discoveries that they made, both in the Orient and in the New World. "Abrindo ao mundo novos mundos," (Opening to the world, new worlds), they revealed to the astonished eyes of Europe new fields of exploration and established the first bases of social intercourse in modern times, between the East and the West. It is to Portugal that we owe our first real knowledge of the East—that East which was sung about and speculated about, around which legends had gathered and whose sparkling riches and seductive glories formed the theme of many a fireside dream in the centuries which had passed, while Europe was still in her early growth.

What was the origin of this little nation which was to become so celebrated through great deeds of dauntless bravery?

The origin of the Portuguese Monarchy.

The early history of Portugal erroneously called Lusitania [1], is the history of the peninsula of which it forms a natural

---

(1) The name "Lusitania" only recently came to substitute the name Portucalensis, as is shown by Alexandre Herculano ironically in his "História de Portugal", but this idea has become a popular one. See:—Oliveira Martins' "História de Portugal", page 2, Morse Stephens' "Portugal", pages 6 & 8, Introduction to Fortunato de Almeida's "História de Portugal", Volume I.

The primitive Lusitania had for its boundaries on the south, the Tagus; on the west and north, the Ocean; on the east, the Carpentanos, Vettaes, Vacceus and the Gallaicos; according to some Greek geographers, the inhabitants of these areas were called the Lusitanians. Some give as the limit of the east the lands of the Astures and Celtiberians. See:—Geographia III, iii, 3 (Ed. de C. Muller, Paris, Didot).

Ancient Lusitania was within the limits of Galliza, Entre Douro-e-Minho, and the Portuguese region between the Douro and the Tagus and Traz-os-Montes. Lusitania of Roman times embraced all the Portuguese region between the Douro and the Guadiana.

"Only the ancient Lusitanians dwelt, as we saw, north of the Tagus; this is what gave in the Roman epoch, the name of Lusitania to all that region situated south of the Douro, to which was afterwards added also the south of the Tagus. This should be attributed to the fact that the Lusitanians had gone to live in the meridional region, brought, as Strabo says, (Geography III, i, 6.) from the right of the Tagus, by the Romans. Seeing that the north of the Douro had received, according as is noted above, the name of Callaccia, the name of Lusitania thus very naturally stuck to all the country situated south of the river."—J. Leite de Vasconcelos, "Religiões de Lusitania", Volume I.

part. It was originally inhabited by the pre-historic cave-dwellers, signs of whose existence are traceable even to-day all over Portugal. These people made room for a combination of Celts with a non-Aryan race (1), known as the Iberian nation, and they formed the five different tribes mentioned by Greek writers. Then, Greek colonies were established at the mouths of the Douro, Minho and Tagus. When the rule of the Greeks gave way to that of the Roman Empire, this part of the Iberian peninsula with the rest of Europe, was gradually taken possession of by the Romans. Their inroads, however, met with obstinate resistance in guerrilla wars, and though these wars indicated merely the germ of independence in the nation, they caused much Roman blood to flow and diminished Roman prestige. Among the various chiefs of that period who stand out as symbols of revolt against foreign aggression, it is but just to mention the shepherd-warrior, Viriathus; his brave resistance for ten years has surrounded his name with a legendary halo and he is regarded as the first great hero of Portugal. In course of time, the entire peninsula became Romanised. And such was the lasting influence of Rome upon the conquered people, that not only is their language derived from the language of the Roman conquerors, their laws based on the old Roman code, but they also acquired from Rome their religion, the religion of Christianity, which was to be such a powerful factor in spurring them on to conquests in the East.

After the fall of Rome, the Visigoths established their empire in the peninsula; but their influence on Portugal was very slight, as, being representatives of a lower stage of civilisation, they became assimilated and merged into the higher, accepting the language and

(1) Cf. Morse Stephens' "Portugal", page 5.

the religion of the people they had conquered. Their peaceful empire was in time overthrown by the Muslims who fought and killed Roderic, the last of the Visigothic kings, in the battle of the Gaudalete, in the year 711 A. D. Under the Arabs, the Christian religion was protected, and, for some time, peace reigned in Iberia. But in the tenth century the Muslim power gradually grew weaker as the people became more luxurious ; and then Bermudo II, the Christian king of Galicia of Visigothic origin, by taking Oporto from the Moors, began that struggle which was to result in the formation of the Kingdom of Portugal and the Portuguese race.

The wars which followed the breaking up of the Moorish Empire in the peninsula at the beginning of the eleventh century, forced the inhabitants to give up their hitherto tranquil existence and to take an active part in them; and this contributed to the development of the spirit which breeds heroes and warriors, and which, later on, was to find its outlet in the East.

The formation of Portugal, 1128-1279.

Portugal of the present day was established in 1095 A. D. when Affonso VI of Leon gave his daughter, Theresa, in marriage to Count Henry of Burgundy, with a dowry of the counties of Oporto and Coimbra and the title, Count of Portugal. After Count Henry's death, his widow, Theresa encouraged her subjects to regard themselves as Portuguese and not as Galicians, thus fostering a spirit of national independence. Her son, Affonso Henriques, was the first king to conquer the Moors. In 1140 he took the title of King with the tacit consent of Pope Innocent II who, imbued with the crusading spirit, wished to reward him. This was later ratified by Alexander III and the succession secured to Affonso Henriques' heirs. It was not only the victorious struggle with the Moors but it was also the conflict of one Christian king with another—Affonso Henriques with his cousin Affonso

VII—which gave the former his throne and his independence, and made Portugal an independent kingdom.

In 1147, Lisbon, Olyssipo or "the city of Ulysses", was taken by Affonso. This city which had remained in the possession of the Moors for over four hundred years, was destined to be of great importance in the future history of the country, for Portugal owes her maritime life to Lisbon. Without this city, Portugal could never have resisted the movement towards unification with the peninsula. Lisbon became the maritime, geographical and historical capital of Portugal. Affonso was assisted in his enterprise by a band of Crusaders, mostly Englishmen, who had put into Oporto on their way to Palestine; and this is interesting as the first instance of amicable relations between the two countries, relations which were never broken off, but became consolidated, as time went on, in conventions and alliances which continue to the present day (1).

The strength of Affonso Henriques had now made Portugal an independent kingdom; it was distinct from the rest of the peninsula in language, literature and national customs, but it had not, till then, attained geographically its present limits. The Moors were still firmly established in the south, and it was in the attempt by the Portuguese to drive out the enemy of the Christian

---

(1) The first commercial treaty which we know of, dates from October 1308, in the time of king Dom Diniz. This treaty which presupposes a previous agreement between Portuguese and English merchants, appears to have been for a long time the basis of commercial relations between England and Portugal. Vide:—Pinheiro Chagas, "História de Portugal", Volume II, page 114.

New conventions ratifying the treaty were signed in 1353, 1372, 1373, 1380, 1386, 1387, 1404, 1642, 1654, 1660, 1661, 1703, 1815 (Treaty of Vienna), 1825, 1826, 1873 and 1898. Vide:—Schoeffer's "História de Portugal"—"Sessões do Congresso da República", Diário de Câmara, Série 1914 & 1926.

peoples of Europe and to widen their dominions, so necessary for the expansion of the people, that the idea of a country was born. The succeeding kings of Portugal continued to war against the Moors, driving them further and further south till Affonso III was eminently successful in his conquest of the Algarves. In 1263, he became the sovereign of that coveted territory and for the first time the king of Portugal used the title of "Rei de Portugal e dos Algarves" (King of Portugal and the Algarves). The country was now determined geographically and the separation from the Peninsular Government settled.

Consolidation of the Kingdom, 1279-1383.

None of the systems of government, definitely known and practised to-day in the cultured world, prevailed in Portugal. The government was a hereditary monarchy, but it was neither absolute nor limited. It had a mixed character, with diverse powerful elements, as was the case with many other countries in Europe. It was more or less theocratic, because all the powers were, within certain limits, subjugated by the national clergy and by the great authority of the Pope. It also showed some aristocratic tendencies, because the nobles and the military orders divided between them the greater part of the kingdom. Democracy was, however, beginning to be popular through the importance that, day by day, the municipalities acquired, and through the growing power of the "Cortes" which soon obtained notable preponderance. The system was monarchical and hereditary, because, ever since the time of Count Henrique, the royal power was transmitted by inheritance to one individual alone, whom all recognized as the supreme, administrative, judicial, political and military head.

In the reign of Dom Diniz, the power of the nobility was held in check, and reforms were introduced in the administrative Courts of Justice. Officers, called "corregedores" (1), were appointed in every town and city where there were Crown lands, and these constituted the judges of appeal, both of the district as well as of the city courts. Dom Diniz also carried out reforms in the military orders of the country, and left to future generations another means for the accomplishment of the great deeds of Portugal (2).

The country was now divided into five large provinces: Alemtejo, Algarve, Estremadura, Beira, Entre Douro e Minho and Traz-os-Montes, divisions which satisfied the administrative necessities of the kingdom. The principal cities were Evora, Lisbon, Coimbra, Guimarães and Bragança. Dom Diniz followed the administrative policy of his father, promoting in every way the internal progress of the nation.

To put down robbers and highwaymen, he populated lonely districts and brought them under agricultural cultivation. He built new towns and beautified the old ones. He scattered all over the kingdom, chapels, convents and churches, institutions prompted not only by the religious feeling of the time, but also by the thought that a church would be the beginning of a village in a lonely place. Civilization progressed and he instituted the most efficacious means of hastening it by the development of labour in all its manifestations— agriculture, commerce and industry—, and above all by raising to a high standard the administrative and social status of property and people. His great reform was established by the laws of "Mortmain" (3). Their far reaching and salutary effect brought honour to the

---

(1) "Corregedores" were chief civil magistrates appointed by the king.

(2) Cf. Pinheiro Chagas' "História de Portugal", Vol. I, Chap. XIX, page 135.

(3) P. Chagas' "História de Portugal", Vol. I, Chap. XVIII, page 125.

kingdom; moreover, by the repression of extortion and robbery which the rich privileged classes exercised over the poor, Dom Diniz hastened the great evolution which was taking place in the Portuguese people.

It was then that the production of wine, vegetables and fruit was developed; and so abundant was the produce of cereals that it was possible even to export them. At the same time, the mining industry expanded and, besides the mines of iron, mercury and gold already known, many others of silver, lead, copper, and sulphur were opened. The principal branches of mining, industry and commerce were in the hands of the Jews and Moors, of whom there was a large number in the country. Dom Diniz sent to Genoa for someone to instruct his people in the art of shipbuilding (1), the taste for mercantile pursuits and maritime exploits having been awakened in the people by the voyages of Marco Polo, the Genoese, between 1253 and 1295. History recognized and gave to this king of the first dynasty, the title of "Rei Lavrador e Pae da Patria" (The Peasant King and Father of the Country).

The development of education in Portugal.

During Dom Diniz' reign, a great impetus was given to the development of education. In the early days of the monarchy, education was confined principally to the ecclesiastical orders and even among them, many could not write. In the other classes of society, it was rare to find the least mental culture. Those who were educated were foreigners or those who had been educated in Italian or French schools.

There were, however, some schools in Portugal where one could obtain instruction in Latin, Theology,

(1)—P. Chagas' "História de Portugal", Vol. I, Chap. XXII, page 150.

Canonical Laws and Scholastic Philosophy. In this period classes were started in the metropolitan church for the instruction of the clergy. D. Domingos Jardo, Chancellor of Dom Diniz, founded the school of St. Paulo in Lisbon in 1291. This example was afterwards followed in other cathedrals and monasteries, and small libraries and public places of study were also opened. Thus, little by little, the taste for science and letters began to be developed, and doctors, jurists and poets appeared. The reign of Dom Diniz was a brilliant period of intellectual work, which did great honour to the Portuguese.

As Portugal was connected with France through the medium of education, with Italy on account of its marine service and its pontifical importance, with England through commerce, and all these countries had universities of their own, Dom Diniz was filled with the desire of having a university in his country, and, accordingly, he founded the University of Lisbon, which was afterwards removed to Coimbra, where it is still a centre of literary influence of no small importance. It was the first, and for a long time, the only establishment for higher secular education in Portugal, and, notwithstanding its defects, it is the greatest legacy, the most lasting and beneficial monument which Dom Diniz left to posterity.

Literature of early Portugal.

The mediæval period of Portuguese literature belongs to what is known as "Escola dos Trovadores" (School of the Troubadours). One may say that Portuguese literature was born in Provence. There we find the origin of the first poetical productions which reveal the soul of the people. Provençal poetry left a stamp on Portuguese literature which will never be effaced. It was transplanted from Provence through the alliance of Dom Affonso Henriques with a daughter of the Count of Savoy, and it is supposed that she brought with her the taste for the poetry of the troubadours. The characteristics of this School was the spacious liberty of thought of the feudal times. Glory, independence and love were the themes of their songs as the troubadours passed from castle to castle, spreading the doctrine of love, equality and fraternity. This poetry was developed by Dom Diniz, who brought his "Courts of Love" and the poets from Provence to give inspiration to Portuguese verse; and this love poetry, so full of romantic sentiment, struck a responsive chord in the hearts of his courtiers and people. Himself a poet of no mean merit and the greatest of his court, he spared no pains to embellish the literature with beautiful verses which are still read and appreciated. His court became the centre of an intense literary life, poets coming from Galicia, Leon and Castile, to bask in the sunshine of his patronage. Through his encouragement of education and literature, he brought such influence to bear on the tongue that he raised it from a mere dialect to a most beautiful and expressive language. He is rightly regarded as the maker of the Portuguese language and the founder of Portuguese literature.

At the same time, prose was also not neglected and a number of tales and legends, histories and chronicles appeared, amongst which the most famous is the "Livros das Linhagens" (Books of Descent or Pedigree), being accounts of aristocratic families and their doings, which form interesting reading and constitute a precious document for the study of the ethnology and philology of the Portuguese in their early stages.

The invention of printing in 1456 brought hitherto expensive books within the reach of the many; this greatly stimulated education and thus the number of authors increased. To this period belongs the poet Garcia de Resende, 1470-1536, who organized the "Cancioneiro" and wrote his Miscellany, which touched on all the subjects of his time, including the invention of printing to which he refers in the following lines :—

E vimos em nossos dias
A letra de forma achada,
Com que a cada passada
Crescem tantas livrarias,
E a sciencia é augmentada.
Tem Allemanha louvor
Por d'ella ser o auctor
D'aquella cousa tão dina ;
Outros affirmam na China
O primeiro inventador.

(And in our time printing was discovered, which step by step caused so many libraries to grow and science to increase. Germany has the credit of being the author of such a worthy thing. Others affirm that the first inventor belonged to China).

Condestavel D. Pedro, 1429-1466, another exponent of the same school, is known by his "Satyra de felice e infelice vida" (Satire on Happy and Unhappy Life) and "Tragedia de la insigne Reyna Dona Isabel" (Tragedy of the Great Queen Dona Isabel). Prose writers include Dom João I, 1365-1433, who was the author of "Livro da Montaria (Book about Hunting on Horseback), recently published by the great Portuguese Orientalist, M. Esteves Pereira, for the Lisbon Academy of Sciences ; the Infante Dom Pedro, Duke of Coimbra, 1392-1449, celebrated for his book on Moral Philosophy entitled "Da Virtuosa Bemfeitoria", in six volumes ; Fernão Lopes, 1380-1450, who was the first great Portuguese historian ; Gomes Eanes de Azurara, ?-1474, who succeeded Fernão Lopes as Chief Chronicler of the Portuguese Kingdom, and Librarian of the "Torre do Tombo"; Ruy de Pina, 1440-1521, who was the successor of Vasco Fernandes de Lucena, besides many other biographers and religious writers.

Amongst these authors, we do not find any who

have mentioned anything about India. It is true [1] that ideas about India existed in the form of legends, tales and wonderful stories which could be found in translations from Greek authors, the Greeks having been from the time of Alexander in contact with India, and having invented stories about the country in their own mythology even before that time ; but in the literature of Portugal of this period, there is no trace of such influence.

Portuguese Discoveries.

It was in the beginning of the 15th. century that the mind of the people of Portugal grasped the idea of widening their dominions and expanding their nation, though the population of Portugal at the time was merely a million and a half. After the battle of Aljubarrota, 1385, the spectre of Spanish domination was dispelled and national independence established.

In the spirit of the Portuguese people, essentially Catholic, was impressed not only the hereditary gratitude for the help which the Crusaders had given, but also the hatred which the Christian peoples of Europe felt for the Saracens, who, when established in the Peninsula, had invaded France and whose advance was checked by the battle of Poitiers (Tours) in 732 A. D.

As the Portuguese were confined to a strip of land between hostile Spain and the alluring Atlantic Ocean, their attention was naturally directed towards the latter. To inspire their adventurous spirit, legends of the ancient geographers idealised by the Breton imagination, were not wanting. They had created the "Mar Tenebroso", the Gloomy Sea, with green isles where were

---

(1)—Cf. H. G. Rawlinson's "Intercourse between India and the Western World", Professor Pissurlencar's "A Antiga India e o Mundo Externo", and G. de Vasconcellos-Abreu's "Summario das Investigações em Sanscritologia desde 1886 até 1891."

cities with resplendent walls. (1) The Arab tradition was not so glowing. It represented the Gloomy Sea as a vast stretch full of fogs, where there was no inhabited country and where the sailors would get lost without recall, for the sea was bounded only by the sea. (2)

Besides these influences there was the ambition for the commerce with the Orient which had been awakened in Europe and especially in the Peninsula, by the intermediary of the Crusades and by the contact established by Arab rule in Spain during the Middle Ages.

The first dream of the Portuguese was the conquest of the flourishing Muslim Empire developed in the North of Africa. The expedition, though successful in the conquest of Ceuta, 1414, terminated in a disaster at Tangiers, where Dom Fernando remained a prisoner and ended his life rather than yield to the Moors on the field of battle. It was the martyrdom of their Prince that gave birth to the dreams of Dom Sebastião some hundred and fifty years later.

The first voyages of exploration under the guidance of the School of Sagres began in 1412, though maritime expeditions had already been sent out from Portugal in 1341, and even as early as 1336 the discovery had been made of the Canary Islands which by the treaty of 1480, were given to Spain.

Two Portuguese travellers, (3) who, following the path of the caravans, had set out to seek the kingdom of Prester John (4) had not, till then, shown any sign

---

(1)—Cf. Oliveira Martins' "História de Portugal", Vol. I, page 164.

(2)—Cf. Oliveira Martins' "História de Portugal", Vol. I, page 165.

(3)—Pero da Covilhan and António da Paiva.

(4)—From very early times the popular imagination had been captivated by the legendary tales of a Christian kingdom in the East. The stories of the kingdom of Prester John had excited on all sides the curiosity of the Christians in Europe, not

of their return. So the Portuguese launched out decisively by way of the sea. The School of Sagres prepared cosmographers and pilots; information was taken from the sailors feeling their way across the seas in different directions and therefore, in the third

---

only on account of religious affinities, but also because it was said that the dominions of this Prince were "Paraizos, carregados de ouro e encantos" (Paradises laden with gold and charms). The legend of Prester John was so widespread in Europe that the Papal Legate of the Church in Armenia talked to the Pope Eugene III, about this Prince whose dominions were beyond Armenia and Persia, saying that he was a warrior and a conqueror and that he united his secular power with his sacerdotal sway, being Pope of the extreme Orient.

As this legend, which had taken such a hold on the imagination of the Portuguese people, may be considered as the immediate factor of influence in the discovery of India—it was actually one of the explorers sent by João II in search of Prester John's dominions, who arrived at Calicut and was thus the first one to set foot on the soil of India—it would not be out of place here to dwell a little on this legend which contributed so much towards opening for Europe the gates of the Orient.

Before the voyage of Pero da Covilhan, the name of Prester John, or Presbyter John, as he was accustomed to be called, represented a king, intangible and visionary, about whose person and whose dominions there were the most contradictory and conflicting reports. All agreed that he was a Christian, but according to the theory which the Bishop of Armenia had promulgated in conversation with Pope Eugene III, Presbyter John was a Prince of the Khitan Dynasty, who had fled from China in 1125, when that dynasty was defeated in China by the Kin. With a numerous following, he pushed his way to Turkestan and founded a new empire of Kara-Khitay, taking the title of the "Universal Khan" or Gur Khan. The weak point in this theory was the difficulty of explaining a Christian name in an Asiatic potentate, but even this point was waived by the explanation that Prester John had been a Buddhist and had become a Nestorian Christian.

According to the second theory, Presbyter John was John Orbeliano, a General-in-Chief of the Christian kingdom of Georgia having almost kingly powers. There was actually a person of that name who commanded the armies of Georgia against the Per-part of the fifteenth century the Portuguese pilots recognised the following points : (1)

1. The nearest way to India should be by the African Coast.
2. To the west should lie either a great continent

---

sians and who took a city in Armenia from the Turks in 1124, though he belonged to the Greek Church and not to the Nestorian sect. But it is not easy to understand how rumour converted him into a sacerdotal king whose dominion was in the extreme Orient.

The third theory was based on the description of Marco Polo whose book was widely read in Portugal where it had been translated about 1500. He described him as Uang-Khan, Chief of a powerful Mongol tribe, allied to Chengiz Khan by whom he was beaten and killed in 1203. A Syrian writer, Abul Faradj, speaking of the same tribe said that with their king they had been converted to Nestorianism and he was called John. This report was confirmed by the Persian Muslim writer, Raschid-ud-din, who stated that the tribe was Christian from the time of Chengiz Khan. Marco Polo affirmed that when he passed through the country of the Yellow River, he found a Christian king who was a descendant of the great Prester John, though very little remained of the greatness of his ancestor. Thus the legend of Prester John clung to Uang Khan or King John.

However, though the legendary king had been described as already dead, rumour was loth to part with him, and his dominions were now reputed to be no longer in Tartary but in India ; this was again delightfully vague, for no one knew exactly where India was. In fact, the general acceptation was that there were three divisions of India, (*) and Prester John became spoken of as "Prester John, Emperor of all the Indies." By 1440, Prester John, the Christian King, was supposed to be in Ethiopia and no doubt that was the Prester John whom Pero da Covilhan sought and found.

(1) Norton de Matos' "Primeiro Congresso de Medicina Tropical da Africa Ocidental, Loanda, 1923."—Revista Médica de Angola, Vol. 1, No. 4, Lisboa, 1924.

(*) Conde de Ficalho's "Viagens de Pero de Covilhan", page 26.

or a large group of islands.

3. In this last direction, the way to India should be impossible, or much longer.

Now began a series of discoveries: in 1418, Porto Santo and Madeira; in 1431, the Azores; in 1433, some islands of Cape Verde. In 1434, Gil Eanes passed the Cape of Bojador; in 1435, the Gold River was discovered; and from 1421 till 1460, the date of the death of the Infante, exploration went on as far as Sierra Leone.

In 1471, the Portuguese took Arzila and Tangiers. The Portuguese fleets, masters of the Straits of Gibraltar, could then go without hindrance to continue their discoveries. Thus in 1471 the Equator was crossed and they discovered the Isles of S. Thomé, Anno Bom and Principe. In 1482, Diogo de Azambuja founded in Guiné, the Castle of S. Jorge de Mina, in order to defend the Portuguese commercial interests. Between 1482 and 1483 Diogo Cão discovered the river Zaire; in 1485, he arrived at Serra Parda and Cross Point—21°. 48' South. In 1498, Bartholomew Dias doubled Cabo das Tormentas (Stormy Cape), which name was changed to Cabo da Boa Esperança (Cape of Good Hope) by Dom João II.

Here ended the first Canto of the epic poem of exploration of the Portuguese race whose magnificent discoveries marked for them a place of honour in the history of the civilisation of humanity.

CHAPTER I.

The Classic Epoch, 1498-1580 (1)

The accounts of Pedro da Covilhan's discoveries on his memorable journey, which he had sent to the King through a Jewish traveller whom he met in Cairo, incited Dom João II to action and he immediately occupied himself with preparations for the expedition to India. A far-sighted and cool-headed king who never acted on impulse, or from purely sentimental feelings, his interest in solving the mystery surrounding this mythical personage, Prester John, was not a mere poetic whim. He was prompted by political and religious motives which arose from the isolated position of western Christians and the growing power of Islam. Moreover, the desire to rival Venice in her monopoly of the trade in spices and pepper with the Levant, made him feel that a bona-fide Christian ally in the East would be of real assistance to him. But death cut short his plans.

Discovery of India by the Portuguese.

His successor, Dom Manuel, found the enterprise

(1) In his "História da Literatura Portuguesa", Mendes dos Remédios makes the Classic period extend from 1521-1580. But in consultation with Sr. J. Leite de Vasconcellos, Dr. José Maria Rodrigues and other eminent Portuguese scholars, I have placed the Classic epoch from 1498 to 1580, to include all the writings on India from the time of the discovery of the way to India, till the beginning of the Spanish domination.

well begun and had nothing to do but complete the project of his predecessor. After examining the writings of Pero da Covilhan and listening to the story of Bartholomew Dias' experiences on the sea, he had the vessels constructed and he chose Vasco da Gama to lead this new attempt at the discovery of the sea route to India.

Amidst profound emotion, so eloquently described by João de Barros (1), on the part of the onlookers who were stirred to the depths at the thought of the dangers these brave men were about to confront to satisfy kingly ambition, the expedition set sail from Portugal on the 8th. July 1497. It consisted of the ship "S. Gabriel", 120 tons, in which were the Admiral Vasco da Gama, and the pilot, Pero de Alemquer; the ship "S. Raphael", 100 tons, commanded by Paulo da Gama, having as pilot, João de Coimbra; and the "Berrio" (2), whose captain was Nicholau Coelho, and pilot, Pedro de Escobar, besides a transport ship with reserves which sailed under Gonçalo Nunes, the servant of Vasco da Gama.

After a voyage full of perilous incidents, an account of which has been left us in the "Roteiro de Viajem de Vasco da Gama MCCCCXCVII" (Log-book of the

---

(1) João de Barros' Decada I, Book IV, Chap. II, pp. 278-279. cf.—Castanheda's "História da India," Book I, Chap. II, p. 7.

(2) (a) "Os Navios de Vasco da Gama" by João Braz d'Oliveira—Tenente de Armada—Typographia da Academia das Sciencias, 1892, Lisboa, Bibliotheca Nacional, page 6.

(b) João de Barros' Decada I, Book IV, Chap. II. fol. 62 states that the ship under Nicholau Coelho was the "Berrio". But there is a difference of opinion, for the "Registo dos Reis", Collecção Pombalina", fol. 121, No. 265, about "As armadas que foram a India desde o seu descobrimento que foi no anno de 1497" contains the information that the ship under Nicholau Coelho of the first expedition was the "San Miguel".

Voyage of Vasco da Gama, 1497), written by Alvaro Velho, one of the sailors, Vasco da Gama and his men arrived at Melinde, on the east coast of Africa, and received from the King of that place a pilot (1) who accompanied them to Calicut where they arrived on the 20th. May 1498 (2) after a journey of ten months and eleven days, to India, the land of golden dreams, the land of wealth and spices. Here their astonishment reached its height when they found people worshipping the image of a goddess, the Virgin Mary as they wrongly thought. This confusion, combined with their ignorance of the language, gave rise to many comical scenes. "Here they took us" (3), writes Alvaro Velho in his

---

(1) The pilot was called Ahmed ibn Majid who was sent on the 22nd. of April. (Pinheiro Chagas, História de Portugal, Vol. III, p. 226).

Vide the article of P. Pissurlencar entitled "Piloto Indiano de Vasco da Gama" in the "Heraldo" de Nova Goa, 9th. January, 1925.

(2) On the question of the date there are diverse opinions. Oliveira Martins, in his "História de Portugal", gives the date as 19th. of May; Pinheiro Chagas says it was on the 17th. of May; Morse Stephens in "Portugal" and M. J. Gabriel de Saldanha in his "História de Goa", 1925, give the date as 20th. May 1498.

(3) "Aquy nos levaram a hũa grande Igreja em a quall estavam estas cousas seguintes:

Primeiramente ho corpo da Igreja ha da grandura du mosteiro toda lavrada de quantaria, telhada de ladrilho, e tinha a porta principal e hũ padram darame daltura de hũ masto e em cima deste padram esta hũa ave que parece gallo e outro padram daltura de huũ homem e mujto groso. E em o meo do corpo da Igreja esta huũ Corucheo todo de quanto e tinha hũa porta quanto huũ homem cabia, e hũa escada de pedra perque sobiam ha esta porta, a quall porta hera darame, e dentro estava huũa ymajem pequena a quall elles diziam que era nossa Senhora, e diante da porta principall da Igreja ao longo da parede estavam sete campaas pequenas. Aquy fez o capitam mor oraçam e nos outros com elle, e nos nom emtramos dentro em esta capella porque seu costume he em nom entrar nella senam homens certos que servem as Igrejas aos quaes elles chamam quafers. Estes quafers trazem hũas linhas per cima

"Roteiro", "..............to a large church in which the following things were noted: first, the body of the church was of the size of a monastery, worked in stone and paved with tiles, and had at the principal door a bronze monument of the height of the mast of a ship (1), and on top of this monument was a bird (2), which appeared to be a cock and another huge monument of the height of a man. And in the middle of the body of the church was a spire all of stone and it had a door in which a man could enter and a flight of steps leading to this door which was of bronze. And inside was a small image, which they said was of Our Lady, and in front of the principal door of the church, along the length of the wall, were

---

onbro lançadas (e onbro he ho esquerdo) e por debaixo do onbro do braço direito asy como trazem os Creligos davangelhos a estolla. Estes nos lançaram agoa benta; dam hũ barro branco que os Xrstãos desta terra acostumam de poor em as testas e nos peitos e derredor do pescoço e em os buchos dos braços. Toda esta cerimonia fezeram ao capitam e lhe davam aquelle barro que posese, e o capitam o tomou e o deu a guardar dando a emtemder que depois o pomria. E outros mujtos santos estavam penhados pellas parredes da Igreja os quaes tinham diademoas, e a sua pimtura hera em diversa maneira porque os dentes eram tam grandes que sayam da boca hũa polegada, e cada santo tinha quatro e cinco braços, e abaixo desta Igreja estava hũ gram tanque lavrado de quantaria asy como outros mujtos que pello camjnho tinhamos visto."

Roteiro da Viajem que Em Descobrimento da India Pelo Cabo da Boa Esperança fes Dom Vasco da Gama Em 1497.

Published by Diogo Kopke and Dr. António da Costa Paiva, Porto, 1838.

(From the manuscript which is in the Bibliotheca of Porto, formerly in the collection of manuscripts belonging to the Monastery of Santa Cruz of Coimbra).

(1) Apparently this was the *Dwaja Stamba* of the Hindu temples, which is used for cocoanut sacrifices. Sometimes the pillar has receptacles for lamps.

(2) The Garuda of Hindu worship. The Garuda is a legendary bird which is supposed to have released Rama from snake bondage.

seven small bells. Here the Chief Captain prayed and we also with him. And we did not enter inside the chapel, because it was their custom that only certain men should enter who were in the service of the church, and whom they called Quafers (1). These (Quafers) wore some twisted threads over their left shoulder (2) and under the shoulder of the right arm, just as the priests of the Gospel wear the stole. They sprinkled us with holy water and gave us a white clay (3) which the Christians of this country use to put on their foreheads and on their chests, around their necks and in the crevices of their arms. All these ceremonies they performed to the Captain, and gave him that clay which he took and kept, making them understand that he would use it afterwards. And many of the saints were painted in different ways and their teeth were so great that they protruded about an inch from their mouths. And each saint had four or five arms, and below the church there was a large tank made in masonry, just like many others which we had seen on our way."

After a stay of some months, Vasco da Gama decided to return; he arrived on the 29th. August 1499, bringing with him thirteen Indians and one Arab (4) from Calicut and these were the first Indians to be taken to Portugal as the authentic proof that the expedition had attained its object.

---

(1) "Quafers" is a corruption of the Arabic word *qafir* which means pagan. Evidently here "qafers" refers to Brahmans.

(2) The Yajnapavit of the Hindus.

(3) The Vibhuti of the Hindus.

(4) (a) Besides thirteen Indian prisoners, he took with him the Arab, Abu Said, who fled to Vasco da Gama's ship, because his co-religionists accused him of being a traitor. (Pinheiro Chagas, História de Portugal, Vol. III, p. 237).

(b) "As Chronicas de Dom Manuel", by Damião de Goes, Vol. I, Ch. 43, Fol. 41, Ed. 1566.

This achievevement so filled with enthusiasm the hearts of the Portuguese people (1) that the King, Dom Manuel, communicated the fact of the discovery to the King of Castile, and to the Court of Rome, through

---

(1) "História da Colonização Portuguesa do Brasil", Vol. II, Chapter V, by Dr. Jaime Cortezão :

" Good chance ! Good luck ! Many rubies ! Many emeralds ! We are in the land of spices, of precious stones, of the greatest riches that there are in the world ! Thus cried Monçaide on the right of Gama at the entrance to Calicut. That cry of triumph, those thrills of astonishment and emotion which drew tears from the eyes of the sailors, they carried in their hearts till they anchored in Lisbon, and communicated them to the entire nation. At once in the city they had bull-fights and sports and the bells rang all day in sign of joy ". (a)

" The King hastened to communicate to all the cities and notable towns of the Kingdom, the arrival of Gama, the great deeds which he had done and the importance of the discovery, ordering them to prepare many processions and feasts. The picture of India and her riches, transmitted through the first voyagers who were dazzled by the unfamiliar sights, fired their imaginations. And, in the letter of Dom Manuel to the King of Castile, giving him the news of the discovery, the triumph and the joy of the King, his delight and astonishment overflow in each phrase : (b)

" What a torrent of stones has India !
She has rubies ! such diamonds !
Which have neither price nor count !
Emeralds absolutely royal !
And pearls of very great value !
Spinel rubies and besides carbuncles,
Amethysts, turquoises and chrysolites,
Sapphires, cats-eyes, brilliants of the richest kind,
And many others whose names are given." (c)

" One can imagine the wonder which the news about India

(a) Barros' "Decada I da Asia", Book IV, Chapter XI.
(b) See King Dom Manuel's letter quoted on page 23.
(c) Miscellanea de Garcia de Resende e variedades de historias, costumes, casos e cousas que em seu tempo acontecerão, quoted by Jaime Cortesão, História da Col. Port. do Brasil, p. 9.

the following interesting letters, authentic documents whose historical value no one disputes and which till today have not been published in English :

King Dom Manuel's letter to the King of Castile.

" Very high, very excellent Princes and Powerful Lords—Your Highnesses know how we had sent on a voyage of discovery by sea, with four ships, Vasco da Gama, a nobleman of our house, and with him Paulo da Gama, his brother, who had set out already more than two years ago; and as the principal reason on the part of our ancestors for this undertaking was glory to God our Lord and benefit to ourselves, He showed us His mercy in so guiding them, according to the message which we have received from one of the Captains who has just now arrived in our city, that they found and discovered India and other Kingdoms and dominions adjoining ; and that they entered and navigated the Indian Sea, found large thickly populated cities with fine buildings and rivers where is carried on all that traffic in spices and precious stones which ships, in great number and of great size which were seen and met by the said discoverers, carry to Mecca and thence to Cairo, whence it is spread all over the world. They have now brought a quantity of those spices, such as, cinnamon, cloves, ginger, nutmeg, pepper, and other kinds of spices and even the woods and leaves of the same, and very fine precious stones of different kinds, as for instance, rubies and others. They even found land where there are gold mines of whose products and of the said spices and precious stones, they did not carry away as much as they could have, because they had not taken (with them) merchandise (enough to buy more). And because we know that yonr Highnesses are bound to receive great pleasure and satisfaction from this, we thought it good to give you news of this. Your Highnesses may

---

augmented by the fantasy of the sailors and by recounting the news from mouth to mouth, must have caused in the hearts of the people. The first chroniclers and historiographers relate this fact.

From that atmosphere, which the nation breathed, were to issue forth the imposing figures of the first captains of India, men of the temperament of Pacheco, of Dom Francisco de Almeida, or of Albuquerque." (a)

(a) Hist. da Colonização do Brasil by Jaime Cortesão, p. 12.

well believe that as we know by these what it is possible for us to do, there is no doubt, according to the state of the Christian people who are found there, even though they are not so fixed in the faith nor have such a complete knowledge of it, that there will follow and be done service to God in their being converted and entirely confirmed in their sacred faith with great exaltation thereof; and that after being thus confirmed, they will be the occasion of the destruction of the Moors of those parts. Besides we hope in our Lord that the principal trade of which all the Moorish people of those parts took advantage and carried on themselves without the aid of other persons or races, will be completely changed by our agreements with the natives and by the ships of our Kingdom, so that henceforth all the Christians of this part may be largely provided with the said spices and precious stones, which, with the help of the same God, Who in His mercy ordains it so, will rouse in us greater resolution and determination to employ ourselves more fervently for His service in the war against the Moors in our conquests in these parts, in which Your Highnesses have so much interest, and we so much devotion. Very high, very Excellent Princes, and Very Powerful Lords, may Our Lord God always have your persons and Royal Estates in His Holy keeping. (1)

Written in Lisbon, July 1499."

---

(1) Note of the letter which went to the King and Queen of Castile with the news of the discovery:

" Muyto altos, Muito excellentes Principes e Muito poderosos Senhores. Sabem Vossas Altesas como tinhamos mandado a descobrir Vasco da Gama fidalgo da nossa casa, e com elle Paulo da Gama, seu irmão, com quatro navios pelo oceano, os quaes agora já passava de dous annos que eram partidos; e como o fundamento principal desta empreza fosse por nossos antepassados de serviço de Deus Nosso Senhor e proveito nosso, prouve-lhe por sua piedade assy os encaminhar; segundo o recado que por hum dos capitães que a nós a esta cidade ora he chegado ouvemos, que achárão e descobrirão a India e outros Reynos e Senhorios a ella comarquaãos; e entraram e navegaram o mar della, em que acharam grandes cidades e de grandes edificios e rios e de grandes povoações, nas quaes se fas todo o trauto de especiaria e pedraria que passa em naus, que os mesmos descobridores virão e acharão em grande cantidade e de grande grandesa, a Meca e d'hy ao Cairo de honde se espalha pelo mundo, da qual trouxerão logo agora estes cantidade, a saber, de canella, cravo, gengivre, nós moscada e pimenta e outros modos de especiarya e ainda os lenhos, e folhas

"Most Reverend Father in Christ, whom we love as a brother. We, Dom Manuel by the Grace of God, King of Portugal and of the Algarves, of both sides of the African sea, Lord of Guiné and of the Conquest, Navigation and Commerce of Ethiopia, Arabia, Persia and India, send to give to Your Most Reverend Paternity great news... Our Lord giving us the completion of our work regarding the investigation of Ethiopia and India, other lands and the Oriental Islands...with pleasure we inform you,... and in order that you may know the process of this case about which we write to the Holy Father, we send you in this the draft of his letter, besides what we write to His Holiness. Your Most Reverend Paternity will know that those persons, who have just now returned from the said investigation and discoveries, have been, among other ports of

King Dom Manuel's letter to the Cardinal Protector.

---

delles mesmos, e muita pedraria fina de todas sortes, a saber, Robys e outras ; e ainda acharão terra em que ha minas d'ouro, do qual e da dita especiaria e pedraria não trouxeram logo tanta soma como poderam, por não levarem mercadoria. E por que sabemos que Vossas Altesas disto ham de receber grande praser e contentamento, ouvemos por bem dar lhe disso noteficação ; E cream Vossas Altesas, que segundo o que por estes sabemos que se pode fazer, que nam ha hy duvida que, segundo a disposição da gente christaam que acham, posto que tão confirmada na fee não seja nem della tenham tam inteiro conhecimento, se nam sigua e faça muito serviço de Deos em serem convertidos inteiramente confirmados em sua santa fee, com grande eixalçamento della ; e depois de serem assim confirmados, ser azo da destroyção dos mouros daquellas partes ; alem de esperarmos em Nosso Senhor, que o trauto principal, de que toda a mourama daquellas partes se aproveitava e que por suas mãos se fazia, sem outras pessoas nem linhageens nisso entenderem, por nossas ordenanças com os naturaes e navios de nossos Reynos se mudar todo, para daquy se largamente poder prover toda a christandade desta parte da Europa das ditas especiarias e pedrarias, que será, com ajuda delle mesmo Deos que assy por sua merce ho hordena, mais causa de nossas tençoens e propositos com mais fervor se exercitarem por seu serviço na guerra dos mouros de nossas conquistas destas partes, para que Vossas Altesas tem tanto proposito, e nos tanta devoçam. Muyto altos, muito excellentes Principes y muito poderosos Senhores, Nosso Senhor Deos haja sempre vossas pessoas e Reales Estados em sua santa guarda. Escrita em Lisboa, de julho 1499."

India in a city called Quolicut (Calicut) from where they brought us cinnamon, cloves, &c. &c... The King considers himself Christian as well as the greater part of the people... One finds there all the year round cucumbers, oranges, lemons and citrons......There are great fleets......The island of Taprobana, which they call Ceilam (Ceylon), is 150 leagues from Quolicut. Our men brought five or six Indians from Quolicut,....besides a Moor from Tunis....and a Jew converted to Christianity, a merchant and lapidary, very learned in the knowledge of lands of the coast from Alexandria to that side, and of the lands of India, towards the interior, and Tartary up to the Greater Sea.....We, as soon as we heard this news, at once gave orders for general processions to be made in all our kingdoms, giving many thanks to Our Lord ; and His Holiness and Your Reverence must show publicly not less joy and give great praises to God. Besides, although we hold very amply by apostolic donations the lordship and dominion of all we have found so that it appears little necessary, yet, because it will please us much we ask you affectionately that, after having placed our letters before the Holy Father and the College (of Cardinals), you will be pleased speaking of this as coming from yourself, at least as a proof of some fresh satisfaction for us, in something so new and of such great and novel merit, to obtain from His Holiness a renewed approval and grant thereof, in the form which seems best to Your Most Reverend Paternity, whom may Our Lord keep as you desire.

Written in Lisbon, the 28th, August 1499. (1)

---

(1) Copy of the letter written to the Cardinal Protector :

" Reverendissimo em Xpto. Padre que como irmão muito amamos. Nós, D. Manuel por graça de Deus Rei de Portugal e dos Algarves daquem e d'alem mar em Africa e Senhor de Guiné e da Conquista, da navegação e commercio da Ethiopia, Arabia, Persia e da India, nos enviamos encommendar a V. Rma. P...da mui grande nova......dando nosso Senhor fim ao nosso trabalho acerca da investigação da Ethiopia e India, terras outras, e Ilhas Orientaes;... com praser vollo noteficamos...e para saberdes o processo deste caso pelo que escrevemos ao Santo Padre vos enviamos dentro nela a minuta de sua carta...alem do que a S. Santidade escrevemos, saberá V. Rma. P. que estes que ora tornaram da dita investigaçam e descobrimento entre outros portos da India estiveram em uma cidade chamada Quolicut donde nos trouzerão canela, cravo (&c. &c.)...... O rei se tem por christão e a maior parte do seu povo ... ha lá por todo o anno pipinos, laranjas, limões e cidras ... ha grandes frotas, ...A ilha Taprobana, á qual lá se chama Ceilam,

In commemoration of the voyage of Vasco da Gama, Dom Manuel ordered to be constructed the Monastery of S. Maria of Belem and the "Jeronymos", a noble resting place for the remains of Luiz de Camões and the tomb of Dom Sebastião, the hero of the African expedition.

Dominion of the Portuguese in India.

In 1500, the year immediately after the return of Vasco da Gama, Pedro Alvares Cabral ([1]) was given the command of an expedition to Calicut. The expedition consisted of thirteen ships, well-furnished and well-armed, for Dom Manuel wished to overwhelm the

---

he 150 leguas de Quolicut...Trouxeram os nossos 5 ou 6 indios de Quolicut ... e mais um mouro de Tunis ... e um judeu tornado christão mercador e lapidario muito sabedor das terras da Costa des Alexandria para lá e da India para o Sertão e Tartaria até ao mar maior ... Nós tanto que esta nova soubemos, logo mandamos fazer geraes procissões por todos os nossos reynos dando muitas graças a nosso Senhor e deve S. Santidade e V. Rma. mostrar publicamente nom menos alegria e dar muitos louvores a Deus. Outrosy como quer que por doações apostolicas mui largamente tenhamos o senhorio e dominio de todo o por nós achado, de guisa que pouco necessario pareca mais nada, porem muito nos pracerá e affectuosamente vollo rogamos que, depois de dadas nossas cartas ao Santo Padre e ao collegio, queiraes, fallando n'isso como de vosso, ao menos por mostra de algum novo contentamento para nós em cousa tão nova e de tão grande e novo merecimento, aver de S. Santidade nova approvação e outorja dello, na melhor forma que parecer a V. Rma. P. a qual nosso Senhor prasa conservar como ella deseja. Scripta em Lisboa a XXVIII d'agosto de 1499. REY".

(Archivo Nacional da Torre do Tombo, Collecção de S. Vicente, Liv. III, fol. 513 e Liv. XIV, fol. i.)

Extract from "Descripção general e Historica das Moedas Cunhadas em Nome dos Reis, Regentes e Governadores de Portugal", by A. C. Teixeira de Aragão, Bibliotheca Nacional de Nova Goa, Lisboa, Imprensa National, 1880.

([1]) "A Expedição de Pedro Alvares Cabral e Descobrimento do Brazil", by Jaime Cortezão, 1922, pp. 27–28.

Indians with the magnificence of this second expedition, in order to obtain the greatest prestige possible in the seas of India. Cabral left Lisbon with the avowed purpose of going to India, but by chance or intention, (1) he went further west and reached in 1500 a place called Vera Cruz, which is to-day in the republic of Brazil.

A third fleet of four ships followed in 1501, under João da Nova, and a fourth, consisting of twenty ships, sailed in 1502 with Vasco da Gama as Admiral. The fifth (2) squadron left Portugal in 1503 under Affonso d'Albuquerque and Duarte Pacheco. Affonso d'Albuquerque conceived the magnificent plan of an oriental Portuguese empire. He extended the dominions in India and in other parts of Asia. He took Goa in 1510, thus securing Malabar; his conquest of Ormuz gave him the key to Persia and Central Asia, while the possession of Malacca secured for him the commerce with the Extreme Orient, and thus he founded the Lusitanian Empire in India. (3)

In 1505, Dom Manuel nominated Dom Francisco d'Almeida, a valiant admiral with exceptional ability as a statesman, to be the first Viceroy of India; and the first trading station was established in the factory at Cochin. The factories of Cannanore, Quilon and Angediva (4)

---

(1) Manoel Xavier in his "Compendio Universal de todos Viso Reis, Governadores, Capitães e Geraes", p. 4, says that Cabral went to Brazil "fogindo de Guiné" (running away from Guiné) probably owing to the weather.

(2) "Breve tratado ou Epilogo de todos os visoreis que tem havido no Estado da India, successos que tiuerão no tempo de seus governos, armados de naus, etc."

Barreto de Rezende, Sec. do Conde de Linhares, 1635.

(3) "Portugal nos Mares", Oliveira Martins, Appendix B, page 66.

(4) The island of Angediva is situated to the south of Goa in Latitude N., 14° 58′ and Longitude east of Greenwich 74° 49″ It is mentioned in the "Roteiro da primeira viajem de Vasco da Gama a India", of Alvaro Velho.

were founded during the rule of Dom Francisco de Almeida. Dabul was taken by him in revenge for the death of his son. He also took Diu after a bloody battle.

Discoveries.

The navigation and conquests of the Portuguese in the East increased the number of maritime discoveries day by day. In 1506, João Homem found the islands of Maria da Garcia, S. Jorge and S. João, off the coast of South Africa. In the same year, Tristão da Cunha found the islands of his own name and Ruy Pereira Coutinho touched the island of Madagascar. In 1507, Lourenço de Almeida reached the Maldive Islands; the next year, Tristão da Cunha found the island of Ascenção, not to be confused with the one [1] discovered in 1501 by João de Nova near the coast of Brazil. Diogo Lopes de Sequeira occupied Malacca in 1509, and explored the island of Sumatra; three years later, Francisco Serrão discovered the Moluccas; in 1512 or 1513, the island of Bourbon or Reunion, east of Moçambique, was claimed for the Portuguese crown by Pedro de Mascarenhas. In 1515-1518, during the government of Lopo Soares de Albergaria, Fernão Peres de Andrade constructed a fortress in Pacem, went to Cochin-China and Canton, made peace with the Mandarins and established relations between Portugal and China. In 1520, Fernão de Magalhães, a Portuguese sailor in the Spanish service, passed through the Straits of Magalhães

---

(1) Goes ("Chronica de Dom Manuel", 1 p. C. 63 i, p. 84) writes: "Na qual viagem (de Lisboa a Moçambique; 5 Março 1501 e Agosto), sendo já da banda do sol acharam uma ilha á que pozeram nome Conceição. É Ascenção."

(In that journey from Lisbon to Moçambique, 5th. March 1501 to August, being already on the south side, they found an island to which they gave the name of Conception. It is Ascension).

and entered the Pacific Ocean, while his companions, after his death, completed the circumnavigation of the world, touching at Borneo on their return. In 1542, the way to Japan was discovered by Antonio da Motta; Portuguese colonies were established in 1556 in Formosa, and in 1557, the Portuguese obtained the territory of the island of Macao in recompense for aid given to China against pirates (1). Such was the rapid extension overseas of the Portuguese power which exercised lasting influence on her art, literature and social life.

Religious Influence.

As the object of Portugal was not only conquest but conversion, her missionaries accompanied the troops wherever they went and Goa became the metropolis of Christian education and civilisation. This work was accomplished by the Portuguese missionaries, not always by persuasive measures but many times by violence, pardonable when judged according to their times as all historical facts cannot be criticised only according to our light and actual experience.

It was thus natural that the fleet should be followed by an army of missionaries and in those times it was a common thing to find the Cross and the Sword in permanent alliance with the same objectives of conquering lands for the King of Portugal and winning souls for the King of Heaven. The influence of religion in bringing about closer relations between the West and the East, was by no means small. Amongst numerous missionaries who took up this role, the most important without doubt, was St. Francis Xavier, 1497-1552, (2)

---

(1) Cf. "Portugal nos Mares", Oliveira Martins, part 2, pages 131–142.

(2) Compendio da vida de S. Francisco Xavier, Apostolo do Oriente. (1497–1552).

to whom the following lines of Camões could be well applied :

> " O bom religioso verdadeiro,
> Gloria vã não pretende, nem dinheiro."
>
> (The good and true monk desires neither vain glory nor wealth).

Having laboured as a missionary from India to Japan, he sleeps to-day in the Convent of Bom Jesus in Old Goa, where his body is venerated by thousands of Orientals, both Catholics and non-Christians.

The engrossing desire of the first discoverers and conquerors was to expand the temporal and spiritual confines of the kingdom of Portugal and to unite the East and West with ties of affection. The captains and viceroys followed in the footsteps of the great Affonso de Albuquerque, who used to address as "daughters" the Hindu and Muslim women of Goa whom he converted and married to his soldiers and sailors.

The mercantile monopoly remained in the hands of the Portuguese till 1595, before which time there were no European competitors. Their commercial programme obliged the creation of factories along the coasts under the jurisdiction of the respective captains and governors.

The colonial institutions invented by the Portuguese and reproduced by the nations which followed them in the East, were the means of the colonization of the Asiatic Islands, Africa and Brazil.

The influence which the Portuguese had in India, resulted from several causes: viz, their direct government over the people ; their commercial intercourse with the different races ; the political influence which they exercised in their relations with the various Indian potentates ; the nearness of the Portuguese possessions to the Indian States, and the religious propaganda which they carried out.

The colossal fortresses which were scattered all over the East, massive monuments of Portuguese glory, and the Portuguese surnames which may be heard in all parts of India, testify eloquently to Portugal's meteoric passage, which, although ephemeral in various parts, exercised powerful influence and left lasting traces on the whole of India.

As it is not within the scope of this work to treat of Portuguese history at length, for that would require several volumes, it is enough to say that the dominion of the Portuguese in the East was of short duration. Her imperial sway was never firmly established. To quote Oliveira Martins: " It was an epic adventure." Even as early as the reign of Pedro II, 1683-1706, the Portuguese standard was no longer waving on the borders of the Hugli, or in the city of Bombay, (1) on the coast of Coromandel, or in Ceylon, Malacca and Ormuz. Of the immense empire that was founded, as if by enchantment, by the strong arm of the terrible Albuquerque and the able Castro, now only a few fragments remain.

The literary movement in Portugal during the Classic Epoch.

The reigns of Dom João III, 1521-1557, Dom Sebastião, 1557-1578, and Dom Henrique, 1578-1580, correspond to the period of the full development of the Classic Epoch or the Italian School. This epoch is the most brilliant in Portuguese literary history.

The fall of Constantinople had caused the exodus of the Greek scholars of that place into Italy, where they carried the treasures of their learning. The invention of gunpowder which changed the politics of the European

---

(1) See "Tratados e concertos de Pazes", by J. Biker, pages 18 to 95.

See also I. Gracias, " Notes " to Saldanha's "Historia de Goa" about this subject.

nations, the art of printing which cheapened and increased the circulation of books, the accumulation of wealth owing to the discoveries of the East, all combined to produce the Revival of Learning which spread to Portugal through the medium of Spain which set the example, and also to Italy, with which country the Portuguese people had already much literary intercourse. From the classic lands of Italy came educationists as well as religious teachers, and besides the clerical school a secular one was established. It was for Portugal the golden age of learning.

As we have previously noted, in Portuguese literature, we find that the early writers did not deal with subjects relating to India, but, after the discovery of the way to India by sea and the establishment of Portuguese rule in the East, familiarity with the East, especially India, produced a number of brilliant writers. both in poetry and prose, who show intimate and enthusiastic knowledge of the country.

The riches which had come from the overflowing Orient, were eclipsed by the more precious treasures of learning which embellished the kingdom of Dom Manuel and his successors. It was enough to have produced an epic poet like Camões, a dramatist such as Gil Vicente or a historian like Goes, to make any epoch glorious.

Poets of the Sixteenth Century, Camões 1524?–1580.

The superhuman deeds of bravery accomplished by those intrepid early explorers, aroused the loudest enthusiasm and admiration among the writers, whose minds had already been developed by their contact with the Italian learning, and the world was startled by the memorable production of the great epic poem of Camões, dealing with the discovery and conquest of India by Vasco da Gama.

"Cesse tudo o que a musa antigua canta,
Que outro valor mais alto se alevanta."

(Camões, E. 5A. Verses 7 & 8)

(No more will ancient heroes arouse poetic fire,
For now a worthier theme awakes my tuneful lyre).

"Camões", says Schlegel, "by himself alone, is equal to an entire literature." As in his epic and lyrical poetry he has dealt more fully with subjects pertaining to India and the Orient, it will not be out of place to dwell for a while on the life and works of this most illustrious of the sons of the Renaissance in Portugal.

Of his birth we know very little. There is even some doubt about the date, though most chroniclers give it as 1524. There is equal dispute over his birthplace, some saying it, among other places, to be Coimbra, but the majority accept Lisbon as the most probable.

His early education was obtained in Coimbra, and, judging by his mastery of the classics and his familiarity with the literatures of Spain, Italy and his own country, it must have been a very thorough one.

As a youth he was at the court of Dom João III and then his life began to be so full of sorrow and adventure. There he fell in love with a lady-in-waiting to the Queen, called Catarina de Ataíde, who had accompanied the Queen from Spain, and this lady has been immortalised in his poem "Natércia"; but his marriage with her was prevented by his banishment from the court. His parting with her is commemorated in his sonnet beginning: "Aquella triste e leda madrugada." (That sad and smiling dawn), and her death inspired in him the never-to-be-forgotten exquisite lines: "Alma minha gentil que te partiste", which have been so beautifully translated by Southey. In 1547 he enlisted as a private soldier for Africa, where he fought during two years, having the misfortune to lose his right eye in an encounter with the Arabs. Returning to Lisbon, he was imprisoned for nearly a year on account of a quarrel in the street.

In 1553, he embarked for India. Elizabeth Barrett Browning sees in her " Vision of Poets ":

> Camoens, with that look he had
> Compelling India's genius sad
> From the wave through the Lusiad ;
> The murmurs of the storm-cape ocean
> Indrawn in vibrative emotion
> Along the verse. (1)

His prolonged stay there has made his wonderful poem so valuable ; for he saw with his own eyes the places which he described in his Cantos, often having to lay aside the pen, for he had begun his great poem already in 1544 or 1545 (2), to take up the sword. He arrived in Goa in September 1553, after a severe storm encountered off the Cape of Good Hope, an account of which is found in his elegy, " O poeta Simonides fallando." He lived in the Portuguese colonies till 1556, when he went to Malacca. Thence he proceeded to the Molucca Islands, returned to Malacca in 1558, and went to Macao. There he wrote the greater part of his ' Lusiadas ', so tradition says.

On his return to Goa, he was shipwrecked off the coast of Cambodia, south of Annam, in the China Sea ; he saved his precious work by swimming to shore with it in his mouth :

---

(1) The poetical works of Elizabeth Barrett Browning from 1826-1844, pp. 400. Ward Lock & Co., Ltd., London.

(2) Mendes dos Remedios' " Historia da Literatura Portuguesa ", Çoimbra, p. 141.

"In his embrace the song that swam to land
From sad and piteous shipwreck dripping wet,
'Scaped from the reefs and rocks that fang the strand." (1)

Canto X, Est. CXXVIII.

This incident reminds us of a similar occurrence in the life of Julius Caesar so graphically told by Plutarch, when he saved his manuscripts in an engagement off Pharos, by holding them in one hand and swimming with the other. (2)

The story of the succeeding years is not known. We know that he went to Moçambique and returned to Lisbon in 1570 in company with Diogo de Couto whom he met on the way and who mentions the meeting in his "Decada" VIII, Chapter 28. (3) He got back bringing with him from the East, only a sense of failure and profound discouragement in his heart, to find his country devastated by plague, his friends gone, his beloved dead. His old mother alone remained to take a natural pride in the poem he had written. "Os Lusiadas", the work of twenty-five years, was concluded and printed in 1571. It was dedicated to Dom Sebastião, the youthful sovereign of Portugal. The battle of Alcacer Qebir foreshadowed the domination of Spain over Portugal. Camões, being a true patriot, was most distressed by this, "as beseemed the aged soldier whose sword had often vindicated his country's honour", and he wrote to his friend, Dom Francisco de Almeida: "At last my life will end and all will see that I was so

---

(1) Translation from "Os Lusiadas".

(2) Plutarch's "Caesar", Everyman's Library, p. 567.

(3) "Historia da Literatura Portuguesa", by Mendes dos Remedios, has cited Decada VII, Chapter 28, while in "Studies in Portuguese Literature", Aubrey C. Bell makes it appear in his Notes that the quotation comes from Decada VIII, Chapter 26. The quotation is from Decada VIII, Chapter 28.

devoted to my country that I was not content merely to die in her, but with her."

On the 19th. of June 1580, this noble patriot and glorious singer of his country's brave deeds, breathed his last in a hospital in Lisbon, attended by a priest to whom he gave his copy of the 'Lusiadas.' He was buried in the little Franciscan church of St. Anna. His bones were afterwards removed and reverently placed by the side of other heroes in 'Jeronymos,' where he sleeps in the shadow of the building erected in memory of the discovery of the way to the contemplative East.

Camões is just as perfect in his lyrical poems as he is in his great epic. Wordsworth in his immortal "Sonnet on the Sonnet", refers to Camões' power in the well-known lines: "With it Camões soothed an exile's grief."

Many of his sonnets describe experiences of the East. His celebrated "Redondilhas", "Babel e Sião" were probably composed during his voyages from Goa to Malacca. The seventy-five verses of these "Redondilhas" are the expression of Camões' grief at his exile, as the following selection shows:

> "Que se vida tão pequena
> S'accrescenta em terra estranha;
> E se amor assi o ordena
> Razão é que cansa a penna
> De escrever pena tamanha,
> Porém, se para assentar
> O que sente o coração,
> A penna já em cansar,
> Não canse para voar
> A memoria em Sião."

(How life which is so short seems long drawn out in a strange country, and if Love ordains it thus, the reason is that the pen gets tired of writing of so much sorrow. But if my pen should be tired of writing what my heart feels, let my memory not tire to fly to Sion.)

His "Auto de Filodemo", or "The Play of

Filodemo", which was written to celebrate the occasion of the investiture of Francisco Barreto as Governor of Goa, contains allusions to Goa and the East.

His "Disparates de India" or "The Vagaries of India", satirises the evils of the administration of the Governor Francisco Barreto, whose name unfortunately became celebrated owing to his persecution of Camões, whom he sent into exile for having written the satire.

This is how one of the biographers of Camões narrates the facts: "In order to celebrate afterwards the succession of the new Governor, Francisco Barreto carried out in Goa grand feasts, games and other amusements, in which debauchery and intemperance reigned supreme ; and even some of the most distinguished citizens were not loth to take part in such a repulsive show. Camões, who was a severe critic of such vices and indignant at such shameless and scandalous proceedings, wrote a satire in which he mercilessly scourged those who joined in the orgies. It was a satire which roused the anger of those against whom it was written and defied the superior power of the famous Governor who arbitrarily banished the poet to the Molucca Islands." (1)

A bronzed daughter of India, Barbara the Slave, awoke the tender harmonies of the Camonean lyric in a lament entitled "Endechas de Barbara Escrava", which a century after, Frederic Mistral, the immortal author of "Mireille", a poem of the people of the South, translated into Provençal. The following lines from the "Lament" show how his passionate temperament was influenced

---

(1) F. E. Leoni, "Camões e Os Lusiadas", p. 131. Cf. Visconde de Juromenha, "Obras de Luis de Camões", Volume I, p. 70.

by the Orient:

Aquella captiva,
Que me tem captivo,
Porque nella vivo,
Já não quer que viva.
Eu nunca vi rosa
Em suaves molhos,
Que para meus olhos
Fosse mais formosa.

Nem no Campo flores,
Nem no Ceo estrellas,
Me parecem bellas,
Como os meus amores.
Rosto singular,
Olhos socegados,
Pretos e cansados,
Mas não de matar.

Uma graça viva,
Que nelles lhe mora,
Para ser Senhora
De quem é captiva;
Pretos os cabellos,
Onde o povo vão,
Perde opinião,
Que os louros são bellos.

Pretidão de amor,
Tão doce a figura
Que a neve lhe jura
Que trocara a côr;
Leda mansidão,
Que o sizo acompanha,
Mas barbara não.

Presença serena,
Que a tormenta amansa;
Nella emfim descansa
Toda minha pena.
Esta é a captiva
Que me tem captivo:
E pois nella vivo,
E' força que viva.

(That captive, who has made me captive, for in her I live, does not now care that I should live. I never saw a rose in its soft bunch of leaves, that seemed more beautiful to my eyes.

Neither the flowers of the field nor the stars of heaven seem to me as beautiful as my love. Uncommon face, quiet eyes, black and weary, but not (weary) of killing.

But containing a lively charm to be the mistress of him whose slave she is. Her black hair makes fickle people change their opinion that light hair is beautiful. The blackness of Love—so sweet is her face—that snow swears to her it will exchange its colour for hers.

She is smiling suavity accompanied by good sense. Indeed, she appears a foreign beauty, but not barbarian. She has a serene presence which stills my passions, and in the end takes away all my sorrow. This is the captive that has enslaved me, and since in her I live it is necessary that she should live).

The poem "Os Lusiadas" (1) is the epic poem

---

(1) Dr. José Maria Rodrigues, Professor of the Faculty of Arts, Lisbon University, discussed with me the question of "Os Lusiadas" being feminine. He referred me to his own book, his edition of "Os Lusiadas" entitled, "Re-impressão Facsimilada da verdadeira primeira edição dos Lusiadas de 1572", preceded by an introduction and followed by a criticism by the said author as well as "Os Lusiadas de Luis de Camões," Edição Nacional Camoneana, 569 B. N. L., the same edition with the spelling and punctuation reformed and revised by the "Mestre Camonista", Dr. José Maria Rodrigues.

"A palavra "Lusiadas" é da autoridade de André de Resende que a derivou de "Luso", por imitação de Virgílio, que de Aeneas formou o património Aeneades. Os Lusiadas são os descendentes de Luso, os Lusos, os Lusitanos, os Portugueses. Embora de data recente, foi êste vocábulo escolhido para o título do poema, por causa do cunho épico que o caracteriza. E para lhe dar todo o realce, Camões só o empregou no frontispício da Epopeia. O artigo também pertence ao título, de que na grafia se não deve desligar. Intoleráveis são as alterações que já se tem feito para "Lusiada" e "As Lusiadas".

(The word "Lusiadas" is authorised by André de Resende, who derived it from "Luso", in imitation of Virgil who formed the patronymic Aeneades from Aeneas. The Lusiadas are the descendants of Luso, the Lusos, the Lusitanos, the Portuguese.

of the Portuguese Fatherland, the autobiography of the poet and an encyclopaedia

"........................... transunto reduzido
Em pequeno volume........................."

(................ transcript compressed
into a small volume..........................)

of all the knowledge of the period, of the discovery and conquest of India, of the traditions peculiar to the sixteenth century in Europe and of those which at that time had come from the Orient.

"The Lusiadas"—a poetic historical record so aptly expressed by Oliveira Martins as "an epitaph of the nation,"—describes the memorable voyage of Vasco

---

Though of recent date, the name was chosen for the title of the poem on account of the epic nature which characterises it. And in order to give it all its value, Camões used it only in the frontispiece of the "Epopeia". The article (os) also belongs to the title, and should not be separated from it. The alterations which have already been made from "Os Lusiadas" to "Lusiada" and "As Lusiadas" are intolerable.

p. XLV, Notas filológicas, históricas, geográficas, e cosmológicas.

The work entitled "A obra monumental de Luis de Camões" by Brito Aranha contains, as Dr. José Maria Rodrigues put it, "todos os disparates que teem feito os traductores," all the nonsense which the translators have made, for example:

P. 197. "La Lusiada de el famoso poeta Luys de Camões. Traduzida en verso Castellano de Portugues, por el Maestro Luys Gomez de Tapia Vezino de Sevilla Salamanca.

P. 201. La Lusiade du Camoens by M. Duperron de Castera a Paris.

P. 201. 2.° La Lusiade du Camoens by M. Duperron de Castera.

P. 206. La Lusiade de Louis Camoens.

P. 207. La Lusiade de Camoens by M. de la Harpe, Londres. Lusiada Italiana de Carlo Antonio Paggi.

This is enough to show that many mistakes have been made. The great authorities say that the word was never feminine at allda Gama and his discovery of the way to India with all its hardships and maritime incidents, in ten Cantos, each Canto comprising eight "estancias" or divisions. The apparent hero of the poem is Vasco da Gama; the real hero is the spirit of the nation. Brave himself, the bravery of others attracted Camões and brought forth from him undying strains of music. He lives to inspire every Portuguese in his wonderful lines, so full of art, beauty and pathos. Till the last strophe, Camões is as thoroughly conversant with his subject as he is sublime in his music and is as ardent in genius and as vigorous is his phrases as he is in his daring, heedless bravery. (1)

The bitter and heartfelt reasons for the complaints to which sometimes Camões gave utterance, did not make him forget what he saw, what he read and what the classic Renaissance had taught him, or bias his judgment of the men with whom he had to deal, or cause him to exaggerate the difficulties and dangers which he encountered. The disasters and misfortunes into which fate led him wandering

"Com pobreza aborrecida
Por hospicios alheios degradado" ......

(With hateful poverty
Exiled to distant inns ......)

Canto VII. LXXX.

did not break his spirit nor prevent him from recounting the tales heard in the country of Aurora, or of gathering from the natives themselves a faithful interpretation of them, till then not known to the West.

The poem is not only the thrilling story of the realisation of the dreams of all Europe in the discovery of the way to the land of India, shrouded in mystery and

---

(1) Cf. "Passos dos Lusiadas", Vasconcelos de Abreu.

myth, which had attracted the known world since earliest times. It is also the description of the founding of a vast empire in the romantic East.

The determination of Dom João II, "the second of the name, the valiant John" and "thirteenth monarch," to find the elusive kingdom of Prester John, is referred to in Canto IV, Est. LX :

" Este, por haver fama sempiterna,
Mais do que tentar pode homem terreno
Tentou, que foi buscar da roxa Aurora
Os terminos, que eu vou buscando agora."

(But as thro' gathered shades of night eterne
Afonso sped to realms of endless joy,
The Prince who rose to rule our realm in turn
Was John the Second and the thirteenth Roy.
This, never-dying glory's meed to earn,
Higher than ventured mortal man to fly,
Ventured, who sought those bounds of kindly morn,
Which I go seeking, this my voyage-bourne.)

(Richard Burton's Translation,
Vol. I, Canto IV., P. 159, Est. LX.)

And about the departure of the great explorers, Pero de Covilhan and Affonso de Paiva in obedience to the King's behest, he says : "Manda seus mensageiros" (Selected messengers his will obey), and then the countries through which they pass are described :

" ....que passaram
Hespanha, França, Italia celebrada
E lá no illustre porto se embarcaram
Onde já foi Parthenope enterrada,
Napoles, onde os fados se mostraram,
Fazendo-a a varias gentes subjugada ;
Pola illustrar no fim de tantos annos
Co'o senhorio de inclitos Hispanos.

Pelo mar alto Siculo navegam
Vão-se, as praias de Rhodes arenosas,
E dali ás ribeiras altas chegam,
Que co'a morte de Magno são famosas,
Vão a Memphis e as terras, que se regam
Das enchentes Niloticas undosas;
Sobem a Ethiopia sobre Egypto,
Que de Christo lá guarda o sancto rito.

Passam tambem as ondas Erythreas,
Que o povo de Israel sem náo passou;
Ficam-lhe atras as serras Nabatheas,
Que o filho de Ismael co'o nome ornou;
As costas odoriferas Sabeas,
Que a mal do Bello Adonis tanto honrou,
Cercam, com toda a Arabia descoberta,
Feliz, deixando a Petrea e a Deserta.

Entram no estreito Persico, onde dura
Da confusa Babel inda a memoria;
Ali co'o Tigre o Euphrates se mistura,
Que as fontes onde nascem tem por gloria.
Dali vão em demanda da agua pura,
Que causa inda será de larga historia,
Do Indo, pelas ondas do Oceano,
Onde não se atreveo passar Trajano.

(Canto IV, Est. LXI-LXIV.)

(Through Spain and France they hold their vent'rous sway.
Through Italy they reach the port that gave
The fair Parthenope an honour'd grave;
That shore which oft has felt the servile chain,
But now smiles happy in the care of Spain.
Now, from the port the brave advent'rers bore,
And cut the billows of the Rhodian shore;
Now reach the strand where noble Pompey bled;
And now, repair'd with rest, to Memphis sped;
And now, ascending by the vale of Nile,
(Whose waves pour fatness o'er the grateful soil),
Through Ethiopia's peaceful dales they stray,
Where their glad eyes Messiah's rites survey;
And now they pass the famed Arabian flood,
Whose waves of old in wondrous ridges stood,

While Israel's favoured race the sable bottom trod ;
Behind them, glistening to the morning skies,
The mountains nam'd from Ishmael's offspring rise ;
Now, round their steps the blest Arabia spreads
Her groves of odour, and her balmy meads ;
And every breast, inspir'd with glee, inhales
The grateful fragrance of Sabaeas gales ;
Now, past the Persian gulf their route ascends
Where Tigris' wave with proud Euphrates blends ;
Illustrious streams, where still the native shows
Where Babel's haughty tower unfinish'd rose ;
From thence, through climes unknown, their daring course
Beyond where Trajan forced his sway, they force.)

"Viram gentes incognitas e estranhas
Da India, da Carmania e Gedrosia,
Vendo varios costumes, varias manhas
Que cada região produz e cria ;
Mas de vias tão asperas, tamanhas,
Tornar-se facilmente não podia ;
Lá morreram em fim e lá ficaram,
Que à desejada patria não tornaram."

(Canto IV, Est. LXV.)

(Carmanian hordes, and Indian tribes they saw,
And many a barb'rous rite, and many a law
Their search explor'd ; but to their native shore
Enriched with knowledge, they return'd no more.)

(Translation by Mickle.) (1)

---

(1) From the description, one would be inclined to conclude that both travellers, Affonso de Paiva and Pero da Covilhan, had travelled together continuously; but according to Die Kirche der Thomas Christen, 1877, p. 314, Pero da Covilhan separated from his companion at Aden, went to Malabar on Arab ships, and returned by Soffala and Madagascar to Cairo ; here he found that Affonso de Paiva was dead, and he met two Jews on the way to Ethiopia with new errands ; one of the Jews was sent back with Covilhan's news to the East. Covilhan then returned to Ethiopia, where he was kept a prisoner. He was alive in 1520. (See Conde de Ficalho, *Viagens de Pero de Covilhan.*)

The poem contains the vision of the King Dom Manoel, when he sees the Indus and the sacred Ganges, which addressed him :

"Eu sou o illustre Ganges, que na terra
Celeste tenho o berço verdadeiro ;
Est' outro é o Indo, Rei, que nesta serra
Que vês, seu nascimento tem primeiro.
Custar-te-hemos com tudo dura guerra,
Mas, insistindo tu, por derradeiro,
Com não vistas victorias, sem receio,
A quantas gentes vês porás o freio."
Não disse mais o rio illustre e sancto,
Mas ambos desaparecem n'hum momento ;
Acorda Manuel...... ....

(Canto IV, Est. LXXIV & LXXV.)

("I am the illustrious Ganges, who begin
my real source on celestial ground :
This brother is King Indus, who, within
This serra thou dost see, his first birth found :
Hard warfare we shall cost withal to win ;
But, if thy courage to the last be sound,
With victories unseen, and without fear,
Thou shalt lay bonds on all thou seest here."
No more the illustrious holy river said,
But both within a moment disappear ;
Manuel awakes......

(Translated by J. J. Aubertin.)

The journey having been decided upon, Vasco da Gama was chosen to lead the way :

"Eu vos tenho entre todos escolhido
Para huma empresa, qual a vós se deve ;
Trabalho illustre, duro e esclarecido,
O que eu sei que por mi vos será leve."

(Canto IV, Est. LXXIX.)

("For this dread labour, to your valour due,
From all your peers I name, O Vasco, you,
Dread as it is, yet light the task shall be
To you, my Gama, as performed for me.)

(Translation by Mickle.)

Then followed the departure from Lisbon, attended by "a woeful, weeping, melancholy throng", "a scene so solemn" with "the tender woe of parting friends". They sailed on their adventurous path along the coast of Africa towards the East till they reached the shores of Melinde "where India's ocean laved the orient shores of gold." Camões has given the reasons for the journey:

"Comendo alegremente perguntavam
Pela Arabica lingua, donde vinham?
Quem erão? de que terra? que buscavam?
Ou que partes do mar corrido tinhão?
Os fortes Lusitanos lhes tornavam
As discretas respostas que convinham,
"Os portugueses somos de Occidente
Imos buscando as terras do Oriente."

(Canto I, Est. L.)

(A feasting cheery all the guests inquired
in Arab language, whence had come their hosts?
Who were they? Where their land? What they desired?
What seas their keels had cut and conn'd what coasts?
The valiant Lusians answered with required
discretion and eschewing foolish boasts,
"We are the Occidental Portuguese,
And seeking Orient lands we sail the seas".)

(Translation by Richard F. Burton).

Great was their joy when the pilot whom they had brought out from Melinde, as they drew near Calicut, cried out: "Behold, O Chief, the shores of India rise!"

" Esta é por certo a terra que buscais
Da verdadeira India, que apparece ;

(Canto VI, Est. XCIII.)

(This is indeed, the land that thou hadst sought,
This is true India which doth now appear.)

Soffrer aqui não pode o Gama mais,
De ledo em ver, que a terra se conhece :
Os giolhos no chão, as mãos ao ceo,
A mercê grande a Deos agradeceo.

As graças a Deos dava e razão tinha
Que não sómente a terra lhe mostrava,
Que com tanto temor buscando vinha
Por quem tanto trabalho exp'rimentava,
Da morte, que no mar apparelhava
Mas via-se livrado tão asinha
O vento duro, fervido e medonho,
Como quem despertou de horrendo sonho.

Por meio destes horridos perigos,
Destes trabalhos graves e temores,
Alcançam os que são de fama amigos
As honras immortaes e graos maiores.

(Canto VI, Est. XCIII-XCV.)

No more the Gama could compose his mind
For joy to see that Inde is known and near ;
With knees on deck and hands to Heaven upraised
The God who gave such gift of Grace he praised ;

Praise to his God he gave, and rightly gave,
for he not only to that Bourne was brought
wherefore such perils he and his did brave
wherefore with toil and moil so sore he fought ;
but more, because so barely 'scaped the grave
when raging Ocean death for him had wrought
by the dure fervid winds' terrific might,
he was like one who wakes from dream of fright.

Amid such fierce extremes of Fear and Pain,
Such grievous labours, perils lacking name,
whose fair Honour waveth aye shall gain,
Man's true nobility, immortal Fame.

(Translation by Richard F. Burton.)

The poet then describes the western peninsula of India—the shores of Malabar and Calicut :

> " Esta provincia, cujo porto agora
> Tomado tendes, Malabar se chama ;
> Do culto antiguo os idolos adora,
> Que cá por estas partes se derrama ;
> De diversos Reis é, mas d'hum só fôra
> N'outro tempo, segundo a antiga fama ;
> Sarama Perimal foi derradeiro
> Rei, que este Reino teve unido e inteiro."
>
> (Canto VII, Est. XXXII.)

> (This Province, in whose Port your ships have tane
> refuge, the Malabar by name is known ;
> its antique rite adoreth idols vain,
> idol-religion being broadest sown ;
> of divers kings it is ; but 'twas the Reign,
> as olden legend saith, of only one,
> hight the last King was Sarama Perimal,
> who 'neath one sceptre held the Kingdoms all.)
>
> (Burton's translation).

This description shows how thoroughly conversant the poet was with the geography and history of India where he had passed so many years.

The river Ganges is described in several places, but the sacred property which it possesses in the eyes of the Hindus, is particularly mentioned in Canto X, Est. CXXI :

> " Ganges, no qual os seus habitadores
> Morrem banhados, tendo por certeza,
> Que, inda que sejam grandes peccadores,
> Esta agua sancta os lava, e dá pureza."

> (Ganges whose aecolents bathe, and bathing die,
> and die in lively faith withal secure,
> whatever sins upon their spirits be,
> the Holy waters lave them sinless pure.)
>
> (Burton's translation.)

and again in Canto VII, Est. XX :

" .... que a esperança
Tem de sua salvação nas resonantes
Aguas do Gange .... "

(Whose trust from their stain of guilt to save,
Is fondly placed in Ganges' holy wave.
If to the stream the breathless corpse be given,
They deem the spirit wings her way to heaven.)

(Mickle's translation.)

And even Ceylon with her legends is spoken of in Stanza CXXXVI of Canto X :

" Olha em Ceilão, que o monte se alevanta
Tanto, que as nuvens passa, ou a vista engana ;
Os naturaes o tem por cousa santa,
Pola pedra onde está a pégada humana. "

(In Ceylon, lo, how high yon mountain's brows !
The sailing clouds its middle height enclose.
Holy the hill is deem'd, the hallow'd tread
Of sainted footsteps marks its rocky head.)

(Translation by Mickle.)

Camões was an observant student of the various peoples of India whom he met ; he acquainted himself with the history of the different states, as for instance, Calicut, which was then a separate kingdom of independent status, governed by the Zamorin :

" Porém, como a esta terra então viessem
De lá do seio Arabico outras gentes ;
Que o culto Mahometico trouxessem,
—no qual me instituirão meus parentes,
Succedeo que pregando convertessem
O Perimal ; de sabias e eloquentes,
Fazem-lhe a lei tomar com fervor tanto

Que presuppôs nella morrer santo.
Ñaos arma, e nellas mette curioso
Mercadoria, que offereça, rica
Pera hir nellas a ser religioso
Onde o propheta jaz que a lei publica :
Antes que parta, o Reino poderoso
Co'os seus reparte, porque não lhe fica
Herdeiro proprio : faz os mais acceitos,
Ricos de pobres, livres de sujeitos.
A hum Cochim, e a outro Cananor,
A qual Chale, a qual a ilha da Pimenta,
A qual Coulão, a qual dá Cranganor,
E os mais, a quem o mais serve e contenta.
Hum só moço, a quem tinha muito amor,
Despois que tudo deu, se lhe apresenta :
Pera este Calecut sómente fica,
Cidade já por trato nobre e rica.
Esta lhe dá co'o titulo excellente
De Emperador, que sobre os outros mande.
Isto feito, se parte dilligente
Pera onde em sancta vida acabe e ande.
E daqui fica o nome de potente
Samorim, mais que todos digno e grande,
Ao moço e descendentes, donde vem
Este que agora o imperio manda e tem."

(Canto VII, Est. XXXIII, XXXIV, XXXV, XXXVI.)

(But as this region there and then was sought
by other races from the Arab Bight,
who Mahometic worship with them brought ;—
the same my parents planted in my sprite,—
it hapt their wisdom and their prayers so wrought
upon the Perimal ; and lit such light
that to the Faith convert with fervour high,
he only hoped a Saint in it to die.

He mans his ships and loads with merchandise,
and many an offering curious, rare and rich,
and there religious life to lead he hies
where lies our Prophet who our Law did preach
but e'er abandoned home, his Satrapies,
that lacked lawful heir, he parts to each
and all he loved : Hence his intimates he
from want made wealthy, and from serfdom free.

To this Cochim, to that falls Cananor,
One hath Chalé, another the Isle Piment,
a third Coulam, a fourth takes Cranganor,
the rest is theirs with whom he rests content.
Only one youth, for whom warm love he bore,
when all was parted, did himself present:
nothing save Calecut for him remained,
which, by her traffick, wealth and rank had gained.

On him the title paramount he bestows
of Emperor, with sway o'er every state;
and, made this partage, there he diligent goes
where, after Santon-life, he met his fate:
thus, 'twas the name of Samorim arose,—
of all this region proudest potentate,—
borne by the Youth, and by his heirs from whom
this who now wields imperial power is come.)

(Burton's translation.)

The description of the customs which Camões observed in India, is found in Canto VII, Est. XXXVII:

"A lei da gente toda, rica e pobre,
De fabulas composta se imagina:
Andam nús, e sómente hum panno cobre
As partes, que a cubrir natura ensina.
Dous modos há de gente, porque a nobre
Naires chamados são e a menos dina
Poleas tem por nome, a quem obriga
A lei não misturar a casta antiga."

(The Law that holds the people high and low,
is fraught with false phantastic tales long past:
They go unclothed, but a wrap they throw
for decent purposes round the loins and waist:
Two modes of men are known, the nobles know
the name of Nayres, who call the lower caste
Poleas, whom their haughty laws contain
from intermingling with the higher strain.)

(Burton's translation.)

Their laws of castes are referred to in the following lines:

"Pera os Naires é certo grande vicio
Destes serem tocados, de tal sorte,
Que quando algum se toca, por ventura,
Com cerimonias mil se alimpa e apura.
Desta sorte o Judaico povo antigo
Não tocava na gente de Samaria.
Mais estranhezas inda das que digo
Nesta terra vereis de usança vária :
Os Naires sós são dandos ao perigo
Das armas ; sós defendem da contraria
Banda o seu Rei, trazendo sempre usada
Na esquerda a adraga, e na direita a espada."

(Canto VII, Est. XXXVIII & XXXIX.)

(Vile were the stain, and deep the foul disgrace
Should other tribes touch one of noble race ;
A thousand rites, and washings o'er and o'er
Can scarce his tainted purity restore.
Poleas the lab'ring lower clans are nam'd,
By the proud Nayres the noble rank is claim'd ;
The toils of culture, and of art they scorn,
The warrior's plumes their haughty brows adorn,
The shining falchion brandished in the right ;
Their left arm wields the target in the fight,
Of danger scornful, ever arm'd they stand
Around the king, a stern barbarian band.)

(Translation by Mickle.)

Camões observed with great interest the religious customs of the various Indian races :

" alguns os idolos adoram,
Alguns os animaes, que entre elles moram."

(Some as from Heav'n, receive the Koran's lore,
Some the dread monsters of the wild adore ;
Some bend to wood and stone the prostrate head,
And rear unhallow'd altars to the dead.)

Canto VII, Est. XVII (Mickle.)

and he gives a vivid description of the Brahmins, in Canto VII, Est. XL :

" Brahmenes são os seus religiosos
Nome antigo e de grande preeminencia ;
Observam os preceitos, tão famosos
D'hum que primeiro pôs nome a sciencia :
Não matam cousa viva, e temerosos,
Das carnes tem grandissima abstinencia ;"

(Whate'er in India holds the sacred name
Of piety or lore, the Brahmins claim ;
In wildest rituals, vain and painful, lost,
Brahma, their founder, as a god they boast.
To crown their meal no meanest life expires,
Pulse, fruit, and herbs alone their board requires.)

(Translation by Mickle.)

But he was imbued with the same Christian spirit as his compatriots, and he expresses his deep religious conviction that the conversion of the people was of even more importance than the founding of the Empire :

" Deos por certo vos trás, porque pretende
Algum serviço seu, por vos obrado ;
Por isso só vos guia e vos defende
Dos imigos, do mar, do vento irado."

(Canto VII, Est. XXXI.)

(God, God hath brought you : he hath (sure) some grand
And special business for you to do.
For this alone he leads you by the strong hand,
Through foes, seas, storms and with a heavenly clue.)

(Translation by Richard Fanshawe.)

His lament on the alleged martyrdom of St. Thomas at Meliapor, (1) is one of the most beautiful passages in the Portuguese language :

---

(1) Mylapore was afterwards created into the diocese of St. Thomé, by Pope Paul IV in 1606.

Chorarão-te, Thomé, o Gange e o Indo ;
Chorou-te toda a terra que pizaste ;
Mais te chorão as almas, que vestindo
Se hião da sancta Fé, que lhe ensinaste ;
Mas os Anjos de Ceo, cantando e rindo,
Te recebem na gloria, que ganhaste.
Pedimos-te que a Deus ajuda peças,
Com que os teus Lusitanos favoreças".

(Canto X, Est. CXVIII.)

(Wept Gange and Indus, true Thomé ! thy fate,
wept thee whatever lands thy foot had trod ;
yet weep thee more the souls in blissful state
thou lead'st to don the robes of Holy Rood.
But Angels waiting at the Paradise-gate
Meet thee with smiling faces, hymning God.
We pray thee, pray that still vouchsafe thy Lord
Unto thy Lusians His good aid afford.)

(Translation by Burton.)

Besides habits, customs and religion, Camões has given us a glowing picture of the court life of the Zamorin :

"Assi fallando entravão já na sala,
Onde aquelle potente Imperador
N'huma camilha jaz, que não se iguala
De outra alguma no preço e no lavor.
No recostado gesto se assinala
Hum venerando e prospero senhor ;
Hum panno de oiro cinge, e na cabeça
De preciosas gemmas se adereça.
Bem junto delle hum velho reverente,
Co's giolhos no chão, de quando em quando
Lhe dava a verde folha da herva ardente,
Que a seu costume estava ruminando,
Hum Brahmene, pessoa preeminente,
Pera o Gama vem com passo brando,
Pera que ao grande Principe o apresente,
Que diante lhe acena que se assente.
Sentado o Gama junto ao rico leito,
Os seus mais afastados, prompto em vista
Estava o Samorim no trajo e geito
Da gente, nunca de antes d'elle vista."

(Canto VII, Est. LVII-LIX.)

(The chiefs approach the regal hall of grace,
The tap'stried walls with gold were pictur'd o'er ;
And flow'ry velvet spread the marble floor.
In all the grandeur of the Indian State,
High on a blazing couch, the Monarch sate,
With starry gems the purple curtains shin'd,
And ruby flowers and golden foliage twin'd
Around the silver pillars : high o'er head
The golden canopy its radiance shed ;
Of cloth of gold the sov'reign's mantle shone,
And his high turban flam'd with precious stone,
Sublime and awful was his sapient mien,
Lordly his posture, and his brow serene.
A hoary sire, submiss on bended knee,
(Low bow'd his head), in India's luxury,
A leaf, all fragrance to the glowing taste [1];
Before the king each little while replaced.
The Patriarch Brahmin (soft and slow he rose),
Advancing now, to lordly Gama bows,
And leads him to the throne ; in silent state
The monarch's nod assigns the Captain's seat ;
The Lusian train in humbler distance stand ;
Silent, the monarch eyes the foreign band
With awful mien.)

(Translation by Mickle.)

Thus, the great epic poem, "a work full of great beauties" to quote Voltaire and Faguet, was a mine of information about India and Indian affairs for the Portuguese of the time. "The name of Camões", says Schlegel, "enshrines the collective glories of his country. No bard of ancient or modern times was ever so intensely national, since the days of Homer, so honoured and beloved by his countrymen." Portugal at her zenith was fortunate in having a poet to perpetuate the glories which passed away shortly after ; for the poem, one of the world's masterpieces, will live for ever and thus the memory of Portugal's greatness can never

(1) This refers to the habit of chewing the 'Pan' leaf with beetel nut.

pass away. It will also serve as an interesting link for all the ages to come, between Portugal and the romantic eastern lands over which she held sway for almost a century.

Venerated today as a sacred book by the Portuguese, "The Lusiadas" not only inspires them but is also a means of interchange of aspirations amongst the people who still speak the language of Camões in various parts of the world. Woodberry says, in his 'Inspiration of Poetry', "The Lusiadas is the principal monument of Portugal and the chief national bond that binds her children in one." It was a fitting end to a brave undertaking, when the two aviators, Gago Coutinho and Sacadura Cabral, who were wrecked in the aerial crossing of the Atlantic, presented to their Portuguese brothers in Brazil, the only book which they saved—'The Lusiadas' of Luiz de Camões.

Jeronimo Corte-Real.

Among other poets of this period who have written about India, there is Jeronimo Corte-Real, 1532-1588. He was the admiral of a fleet in the seas of India where he fought about 1571, returning a short time after to Lisbon where we know he was in 1574.

He wrote "Successo do Segundo Cerco de Diu, estando Dom Joham Mascarenhas por capitão da fortaleza. Anno de 1546." (Success of the Second Siege of Diu, with Joham Mascarenhas as Captain of the fortress. Year of 1546). It consists of twenty-one cantos. It was printed in Lisbon in 1574. There is only one copy of this edition, which exists in the Bibliotheca Nacional of Lisbon.

In the opinion of critics, this poem has value on account of the profusion and beauty of its similes, which are almost always striking and original; and on account of its pen pictures which reveal in the poet a decided gift for poetry of a descriptive kind. He also wrote :—

— "Naufragio e lastimoso successo da perdição de

Manoel de Sousa de Sepulveda and D. Lianor de Sá, sua mulher e filhos, vindo da India para este Reyno na nao chamada o Galião grande S. João que se perdeo no Cabo da Boa Esperança, na terra do Natal. E a peregrinação q. tiverão rodeando terras de cafres mais de 300 legoas té sua morte"—1594, Lisboa.

"The Shipwreck and the sad loss of Manoel de Sousa de Sepulveda and D. Lianor de Sá, his wife and children, coming from India to this kingdom in the large Galley called S. João which was lost off the Cape of Good Hope, in Natal. Also the journey which they had made, in passing around more than 300 leagues of lands of Kaffirs until their death." 1594, Lisbon. A copy of this edition is in the Biblioteca Nacional, Lisbon.

This poem is composed of seventeen cantos. The death of D. Lianor and the bitter grief of her husband are delineated with a master hand. There is a translation of "Naufragio de Sepulveda" in French by Ortaire Fournier, Paris, 1844. Camões has treated of the same subject in his Lusiadas, in Canto V., Est. XLVI, XLVII, and XLVIII.

Corte-Real, nobleman and soldier, has much value as a poet and a painter of Indian scenes, yet he cannot rank with Camões. He never had to pass through the trials of the less fortunate but more brilliant poet, for his life was always spent in pleasant surroundings, in the company of admiring friends.

Francisco de Andrade.

The last poet of this epoch to write on Indian subjects was Francisco de Andrade, ?–1614, who was Chief Librarian of the Torre do Tombo and Chief Chronicler of the Kingdom of Phillip II in 1599. He wrote, besides the "Chronicas de Dom João III", referred to on page 107 under 'Historians'.

"O primeiro cerco que os Turcos puzerão ha fortaleza de Diu nas partes da India, defendido pollos Portugueses".

(The first Siege which the Turks made to the Fortress of Diu in India, defended by the Portuguese.) Coimbra 1589.

It is a poem divided into twenty cantos, well written in an elegant style. It contains a vivid description of the manner in which Sultan Bahadur Shah of Cambay met his death and this work is considered by critics to be among the best poems of the second class. There is only one copy of it which is in the Biblioteca Nacional, Lisbon.

Gil Vicente.

A dramatist and play-wright of the period who showed Indian influence in one of his plays, is Gil Vicente, 1470 ?–1540 ?. He had quite early in life a place at Court. His poetic talent developed soon and when he recited his "Monologo da Visitação" in Spanish to the Queen and her relations, she was so pleased with it that she asked him to repeat it for the following Christmas festivities which encouraged him to write "Pastoril Castelhano". For more than thirty years he continued to write plays at the Court of Dom Manoel and of Dom João III where he was a noble figure, declaiming against all that was base in the ruling classes of the kingdom.

The work of Gil Vicente is most comprehensive for it is composed of forty-four pieces which portray the true picture of his times, his play entitled "Auto da Mofina Mendes" being the most celebrated from the Indian point of view. This play is composed of two parts; it was written to celebrate Christmas and was played before the King D. João III, in 1534.

Mofina Mendes, the principal figure in this play, was the keeper of the cattle of Payo Vaz for over thirty years but she cared little about looking after the cattle and was more interested in the conversation of the shepherds. When Payo Vaz asked her for an account of his cattle, Mofina Mendes answered that he should pay the wages he owed her, and as for the cattle she did not know where they were; that seven of the cows had died and three of the oxen; that the calves had been decimated by the wolves; that the goats were wandering about, some in the grove and others jumping about among the rocks; that the kids had been carried off by the foxes; that the goats were leprous and the dogs dead. Payo Vaz judged by this that it was best to dismiss the shepherdess, Mofina Mendes, and in payment of what he owed her gave her a pot of oil. Mofina Mendes, putting the pot of oil on her head, said that she was going to the Fair of Trancoso to sell the oil, and with the money she would get, she would buy ducks' eggs which she would set and bring out ducks. These when sold would bring more than a million reis and thus she would be able to marry a rich and honourable man. On the day of the marriage she would come out richly dressed to meet her fiancé and sing a song :

Vou-me a feira de Trancoso
Logo, nome de Jesu,
e farei dinheiro grosso,
Do que este azeite render
Comprarei ovos de pata,
que he a cousa mais barata
Qu'eu de la posso trazer
E estes ovos chocarão ;
cada ovo dará hum pato
e cada pato hum tostão
que passará de um milhão
e meio, a vender barato.
Casarei rica e honrada
Por estes ovos de pata ;
e o dia que for casada
Sahirei ataviada
Com hum brial d'escarlata,
e diante o desposado
que me estará namorando,
virei de dentro bailando.

assi deste arte bailando
esta cantiga cantando.

(I am going to the fair at Trancoso
After that, name of Jesu,
I shall make much money
And from what the oil will yield
I shall buy ducks eggs,
Which is the cheapest thing
That I can bring
And these eggs will be set
Each egg will produce a duck.
And each duck a "tostão"
Which will become a million
And a half, even if sold cheaply.
I shall marry rich and honoured
Through those ducks' eggs.
And the day I am married
I shall come out arrayed
In a scarlet shawl.
And before the bridegroom
Who will be making love to me
I shall come from inside (the house) dancing

Thus, dancing this way
And singing this song.)

Carried away by these thoughts she let the pot of oil fall on the floor; the pot broke and the oil ran out, thus dispersing in a moment all the dreams of riches and fortune she had woven.

Mofina Mendes then left Payo Vaz and the other shepherds who were present and went away singing a song which said that she was jilted by fortune, and she requested the shepherds not to be angry with her, because human pleasures are dissipated in the same way as the dreams of prosperity conceived at the bottom of a pot of oil, were shattered :

" Por mais que a dita m'engeite,
pastores, não me deis guerra;
que todo o humano deleite,
como o meu pote d'azeite,
ha de dar consigo em terra."

(No matter how good fortune deserts me
Shepherds, don't quarrel with me;
For all human pleasures,
Like my pot of oil,
Will end, as it did, in the ground.)

It should be noted that the dialogue of Payo Vaz with Mofina Mendes has no relation to the principal subject of the play and so it appears to have been inserted only to capture the attention of the hearers and to inculcate a moral lesson.

The erudite orientalist, Vasconcelos d'Abreu, in an interesting critical study has traced the influence of an Indian romance in 'Mofina Mendes'. The most important source of oriental romance in the European novels of the Middle Ages, seems to have been the Indian "Panchatantra" which was translated by an Iranian doctor called Barzoi, by the order of the King Khosru Anushirvan (531-579), into Pehlvi, which at that time was the literary language of Iran.

The original Sanscrit text of the Panchatantra and its Pehlvi translation are lost, but two ancient notable translations, have been preserved—one in Syriac and the other in Arabic.

The Syriac translation was made about the year 570 A. D., and bears the title "Kalilag e Damnag". The Arabic translation was written in the 8th. century by Abdalah ibn Almoçaffa, an Iranian who was converted to Islam, and who died about 760, A. D. His work is called "Kalilah e Dimnah". The Arabic version has exceptional importance because it exercised great influence on the literature of the peoples of Europe during the middle ages. From it, a Hebrew translation was written in 1250 and another in Castillian about 1261. From the Hebrew version, in 1270, a translation was made into Latin by João de Capua, which was called "Directorium Humanae Vitae", printed for the first time in 1480. Then D. João Manuel (1282–1348), the father of Queen D. Constança, (wife of D. Pedro I of Portugal), imitated the book "Kalilah e Dimnah", in the work which he composed in Castillian entitled "Livro de Patronio ou Conde Lucanor", which was printed in 1860.

In the "Boletim da Classe de Letras da Academia de Lisboa," Vol. XIV, 1921, the great Portuguese Orientalist, Francisco Maria Esteves Pereira, published an interesting memorial entitled "Mofina Mendes de Gil Vicente", in which he points out the sources which inspired the Portuguese writer.

" The most ancient form of the fable" says Esteves Pereira, " with which one connects the conversation of Mofina Mendes, is Story VII (Katha) of Book V of the Panchatantra. (1) In the Sanscrit text, the hero of

---

(1) The Panchatantra is a collection of ancient Hindu tales, dated 1199 A. D. called Panchakhyanaka, of the Jaina Monk Purvabhadra, critically edited in the original Sanskrit by Dr. Johannes Hertel, Cambridge, Mass., published by Harvard University. 1908, p. 276.

the fable is a Brahmin, called Svabhava Kripana, which corresponds exactly to the word 'Mofina' in the expression 'Mofina Mendes' used by Gil Vicente to designate the keeper of the cattle of Payo Vaz".

However, this similarity cannot be considered as a direct influence of the Sanscrit text of the Panchatantra, for this work was known in Europe only after its first impression in 1845. The works through which we may presume that Gil Vicente became acquainted with the Indian tale, and was able to sketch Mofina Mendes to us, could not be other than the two versions of the "Livro de Kalilah e Dimnah",—the "Directorium Humanæ Vitæ", by João de Capua, and "Livro de Patronio ou Conde Lucanor" by D. João Manuel; but it is more than likely that it was the last one.

Speaking of the influence which India exercised over Gil Vicente, the Conde de Ficalho says: "Gil Vicente, in his charming dramatic writings, which are like an album of Portuguese profiles drawn from nature with extraordinary vividness, has portrayed the soldier of India." He says this referring to another interesting play entitled "Auto da India". Gil Vicente does not give a name to the principal character in this play but calls him simply "the husband" thus allocating to him all the vagueness of a general type. The hero goes to India, leaving in Lisbon his wife, who in fidelity, does not appear to resemble Penelope. At the end of three years, he returns and recounts the hardships of his journey:—

> "Fomos na volta do mar,
> Quasi, quasi a quartelar:
> A nossa Garça voava,
> Que o mar s'espedaçava.
> Fomos ao rio da Meca,
> Pelejamos e roubamos,
> E muito risco passamos,
> A vela e arvore secca."

(We went at the turn of the tide
Almost, almost at the watch.
Our Garça flew so quickly
That the sea was broken up into foam.
We went to the river of Meca,
We fought and we pillaged,
And we ran much risk
With sails flying, and furled.)

It is exactly the professional language of the sailor, not forgetting the characteristic trace of the battle and sack, "Pelejamos e roubamos" (We fought and pillaged). His wife puts him the typical question:

"However, have you returned rich?" and he answers her rather ambiguously:

"Se não fora o capitão,
Eu trouxera o meu quinhão,
Hum milhão vos certifico,
Callae-vos que vos vereis
que louçam haveis de sahir."

(If it had not been for the captain,
I would have brought my portion,
A million, I assure you.
Be quiet and you will see
How elegantly you will turn out.)

Jorge Ferreira de Vasconcelos.

Another great writer, who could not escape from the influence of India on the people of Portugal, was Jorge Ferreira de Vasconcelos, who was the author of "Eufrosina", written probably in 1527. It was the first of his productions and was received with great enthusiasm by all his contemporaries. It really shows great dramatic talent. Our distinguished writer, Aubrey F. C. Bell, reprinted it in Lisbon in 1919. Referring to Vasconcelos' work, Conde de Ficalho says: "In the comedy 'Eufrosina' of Jorge Ferreira, the Indian man does not actually appear but Silvia de Sousa receives from her brother who is in Goa, a long letter, which is read on the stage. The letter is remarkably well written and with such naturalness that it seems authentic. The brother of Silvia recounts the troubles of his journey, refers with a sneer to Indian girls, promises her to make a fortune to support her and bring her honour, and in the end sends her news for her to give to his acquaintances—to a supposed aunt, Briolanja Soares, he sends the message that her son went to the Maldive Islands, where he made money; to an imaginary Constança Dornellas, he says that her husband had left for China and sold at great profit in Malacca the merchandise that he took with him. The entire letter is very valuable, and very much more significant than if it were a *bona-fide* letter, for it presupposes hundreds of similar letters, whose existence authorised the artist—and Jorge Ferreira was a real artist—to introduce it as a feature of the epoch in a comedy of manners and customs."

Simão Machado. (Father Boaventura)

Simão Machado, a Franciscan monk, was perhaps the most illustrious pupil of Gil Vicente. We do not know the date of his birth or death, but we do know that he lived in 1532. He is well-known by his comedies, "Cêrco de Diu", (Siege of Diu), Parts I & II, Lisbon, 1631, and "Pastora Alfea" where in the delineation of character he shows himself even superior to his master. José Maria da Costa, speaking of Simão Machado in his "Ensaio Biographico e Critico", 1850-1856, Lisbon, Tome VI, p. 153, says: "Simão Machado was a genius eminently dramatic, equal to Gil Vicente in the ease of his dialogue."

Prose writers of the 16th. century.

With the opening of the way to India and the consequent maritime discoveries, a large number of writers sprang up, many of whom were eye-witnesses of the scenes they described and their works are faithful pictures of the time.

Duarte Barbosa.

Duarte Barbosa, ?—1521, was the author of the first book written about India by a Portuguese. We do not know the exact date of his birth, but we know that he was born in Lisbon in the latter part of the fifteenth century. His father was Diogo Barbosa, Knight of the Order of Santiago in the service of Don Alvaro de Bragança, who had gone to India in the year 1501 with João de Nova's fleet. The son followed in his father's footsteps in his Indian career; we do not know when he went to India, nor the date of his return, but we know that he was a scribe in the factory of Cannanore, and by his book, that he must have spent a considerable time in India as he shows a thorough knowledge of those parts of which he writes.

About 1510, he began his "Livro". It is an account of the countries bordering on the Indian Ocean and their inhabitants. Volume I includes the coast of East Africa, Arabia, Persia and Western India as far as the Kingdom of Vijayanagar. The second volume describes the coasts of Malabar, Eastern India, Further India, China and the Indian Archipelago. This work, the notice of which was published in the "Collecção de Noticia para a Historia e Geografia das Nações Ultramarinas", Part II, p. 231, resembles the second part of the anonymous Chronicle of Guzerate (1) in that it is particularly rich in information about the geography of the country and the customs, (2), language and religions of its peoples.

He gives an interesting description of the kingdom of Guzerate in which he tells us about the Baneanes. He refers to their passion for preserving life in much

---

(1) The "Discripção das Costas da Asia" fols. 42 to 98. Fols. 42 to 47 missing. (*Ms. Bibliotheca Nacional, Lisbon*).

(2) "Journal of the Royal Asiatic Society" October 1923. pp. 640–641, article by R. C. Temple.

the same terms as Father João de Lucena uses in his "Vida de Padre Francisco Xavier", (p. 95). At the time Barbosa wrote, the Portuguese had discovered that the Hindus were not Christians as they had thought but still Barbosa seemed to suspect some connection between them as he describes the Hindu Trimurti as the Trinity and shows that the Hindus wished to worship in the Portuguese churches. In his information about Muslim marriages and divorce, he is inaccurate. He agrees with the anonymous Chronicle of Guzerate in his description of Sultan Mahmud. He describes the city of Andava, (Ahmedabad) which after the sack by Humayun in 1535, recovered its dignity as capital of Guzerate.

In his description of Diu, he tells how Malinquas (Malik Ayyaz) the Governor of Cambay, got possession of Diu. This story is confirmed by Barros. The sea fight off Diu in 1508 between Francisco de Almeida and Mir Hosain, Captain-in-Chief of the Egyptians and Guzeratis where the latter was defeated, is graphically depicted.

The trade of Diu and Surat with the India and African coastal towns is described. The account given by Barros of the raid in 1530 in Surat and Reiner (Rander) agrees with that of Barbosa. According to Barbosa, the women of Reiner were not in purdah. Surat was governed by Melocoxim (Melique Gupi of Barros and of the "Chronica de Guzerate"). Barbosa says that the king of Cambay ordered Melique Gupi, who was a great friend of the Portuguese, to be killed on account of evil reports heard against him.

He describes the towns of Chaul, Cintacora (Sadashiv Gad) Dabul and Goa; he tells of the taking of Goa by Afonso D'Albuquerque. Damião de Goes in his "Chronica de D. Manuel", confirms his statement about the strictness with regard to immigration into Goa.

In his description of Vijayanagar (Narsyngua) he gives the history of Bisnaga and tells us of the peoples and customs. Therein is contained the earliest known description of the hook-swinging ceremony and a very accurate account of Brahmin Sati, as well as that of the Lingayats, who had the burial instead of the burning of widows.

Besides geographical and historical details about Dely (Delhi) we find a good account of North Indian Jogis.

He tells us about the kingdom of Malabar, the extent of Muslim influence and the language, religion and customs of its inhabitants. He describes the eighteen castes and the trades in the kingdom of Cannanor.

Cochim (Cochin) and the island of Ceilam (Ceylon) are treated of. He says that two languages were spoken there.

In speaking of Mailapur, he refers to the legend of St. Thomas.

He gives a clear description of the kingdom of Bengal and its relations with the Portuguese. He speaks of its fertility, and refers to its trade in sugar, slaves and eunuchs.

Duarte Barbosa did not mean his book to be a chronicle or history, as he himself says, but it is valuable because he had first-hand knowledge of the places and events described.

Some observations of Barbosa show that he understood well certain facts which were difficult of comprehension. Thus, he says that along the coast of Malabar only one language was spoken which was called Malayalam, and he knew that in other parts of the coast of Coromandel, they spoke a different language from this one, though resembling it, but differing from it as Portuguese differs from Castillian. This observation on the existence of Malayalam and its relations with Tamil is perfectly correct and denotes how much attention he paid to linguistic questions usually disparaged. It is merely one example among many.

We have in English a translation of this book by Stanley and Longworth Dames, London, 1918, Vols.2.

Another author of note who left the world some interesting studies on India, is Gaspar Correa, 1495-1561.

Gaspar Correa.

We do not know anything of his parentage or birthplace; we know only that he left Portugal for India when he was about seventeen in 1512, to serve as a soldier, returning to Portugal after some years in 1529. He made a second voyage to India and there amidst the complications of military duties and the cares of public service, he found time and means to write a most interesting and detailed history of India and its conquests, which embraced a period of fifty-three years, from the time of the discovery of the route to India by sea till the governorship of Jorge Cabral. He made long and exhaustive journeys to the different parts of the dominions about which he was writing, in order to gain first-hand information and to verify for himself the correctness of the facts, localities, and all that he considered indispensable for his work. Though it was written in the rude style of a soldier who had not frequented a University, it bore the hall-mark of truth and impartiality. The main portion of the work describing the period from 1512 till 1550, has all the advantages of contemporary history written by the pen of an intelligent writer. It is a gossipy account founded on a record compiled by a priest, named João Figueira, who accompanied Vasco da Gama. The work is illustrated with paintings and photographs of the Viceroys taken from the pen and ink sketches made by Correa himself. In 1561 he occupied himself in re-writing and perfecting his work but death overtook him before he was able to give it the last few touches. (1)

---

(1) Aubrey Bell says: "Possibly he had not time to include the fourth Lenda in this revision, and this might imply that the

After remaining unpublished for more than three centuries the Royal Academy of Sciences, which already before 1790 had intended to publish this work at its own expense, resolved in 1858 to realize this desire and so began "The Collection of Unpublished Records from the History of the Conquest of the Portuguese in Africa, Asia and America", using for this end, a part of the subsidy which the Portuguese Government had conferred and which was destined originally for the continuation of "The Elementary Picture of the Diplomatic Relations, &c....." the work entrusted to the late Viscount of Santarem.

Gaspar Correa's great work, "Lendas da India" (Stories of India), 4 Vols. 4.°, contains an account of the doings of Vasco da Gama, Pedro Alvares Cabral, João de Nova, Francisco de Albuquerque, Vicente Sodré, Duarte Pacheco, Lopo Soares, Manuel Telles, D. Francisco d'Almeida and other governors till the governorship of Jorge Cabral, 1550. It was published in four volumes by order of the Class of Moral and Political Sciences and Belles Lettres of the Portuguese Academy of Sciences, Lisbon, 1864. These four volumes are :

"Lendas da India."

Vol. I. Lenda de treze annos, desde o primeiro descobrimento da India até o anno de 1510. Parte 1, Lisboa, 1858. Parte 2, 1859. (Story of thirteen years from the first discovery of India till the year 1510, Part I, Lisbon, 1858). It contains XXX-492 pages, and Part II, 1859, pages 493-1013, the last three containing "Errata".

Vol. II. Lenda de dezesepte annos acabados no anno de 1526, Parte 1, 1860. Parte 2, 1861.
(Story of 17 years ending the year 1526). Part I,

---

date of his assassination was in or soon after 1563."—Aubrey Bell —"Gaspar Correa"—Hispanic Notes—p. 58.

1860, pages 1 to 482, Part II, 1861, pages 489-595, with one page of "Errata".

This volume has also lithographic engravings, with pictures of the Viceroys and Governors and views of some cities and fortresses, etc.

Vol. III. Lenda do que se passou no espaço de dezesepte annos que finda em 1537. Parte 1, 1862. Parte 2, 1869.

(Story of what happened in the space of 17 years, ending the year 1537).

Part I, 1862, pages 1-438. Part II, 1863, pages 439-908 and one page of "Errata", with seven engravings.

Vol. IV. Em que se comprehendem os feitos dos annos de 1538 a 1550. Parte 1, 1864. Parte 2, 1866.

(Containing the deeds of the years of 1538-1550). Part I 1864, Pages, 1-472, Part II, 1866, pages 473-757 together with 98 pages of Indices of the historical and geographical names and one page of "Errata"; it contains also 6 engravings.

In English a book exists which is called "The Three Voyages of Vasco da Gama and his Viceroyalty, from the Lendas of India of Gaspar Correa, who accompanied him". It was translated from the Portuguese with notes and an Introduction by the Hon'ble Henry E. J. Stanley, in 1869.

In the opinion of A. Herculano and Castelo de Paiva, Gaspar Correa's "Lendas" are superior in their subject matter to the "Decadas" of Barros or the "History" of Castanheda. "In the arrangement of his scenes, vivacity of colour", says Bulhão Pato, "and picturesque setting he is superior to the other Portuguese historians of the Orient".

Fernão Lopes de Castanheda.

Among the chroniclers of the Portuguese Empire in India a prominent place must be assigned to Fernão Lopes de Castanheda, ?-1559, of Santarem who accompanied his father in 1528 to Goa. We do not know how long he remained in

India. Diogo de Couto tells us that he was there almost ten years, or till about 1538, the year in which he finished his Book VIII. During the time he was in India, he was making investigations both by examining all records and by making zealous enquiries from the captains and noblemen whom he met, in order to write a faithful account of the discoveries and conquests of the Portuguese in India. In this laudable enterprise he spent all his wealth and he was forced for want of money and health to return to Portugal, where he accepted a position in the University of Coimbra as Beadle in the Faculty of Arts, Corrector of Proofs for the University, and Librarian. He had little time left to polish his work and imitate the ancient classic models, for he became tired and ill with continued research and night work and the reading of many papers that he had brought from India. He died on the 23rd. of March 1529 and was buried in the Church of S. Pedro in Coimbra.

His history entitled "Historia do descobrimento e conquista da India pelos Portuguezes" (History of the discovery and conquest of India by the Portuguese), consists of ten books which contain all the wonderful deeds of the Portuguese in Ethiopia, Arabia, Persia and India between the Ganges and beyond, and in China and in the Moluccas. It covers a space of fifty years from the time when Vasco da Gama, Conde de Vidigueira and Admiral of the Indian Seas, discovered the Indies, till the death of Dom João de Castro, Governor and Viceroy of India.

The history was twice only given in complete form to the Press, the first time in 1551-1561, and the second time in 1833. The first book was printed twice, once in the lifetime of the author in 1554 and the second time in 1797.

There is no doubt that Fernão Lopes wrote ten books and that the last two were ready for the press in 1561. The second edition stated that the "History" continues till the death of João de Castro. But in spite of these declarations, copies of the books IX and X are today not to be found. It is quite possible that one day they may re-appear, just as the thirty-one chapters of Book IX have come to light now, being published by Father Wessels. ([1]) Diogo de Coutc gives an explanation of the disappearance, in Chapter I of his fourth Decada, where he says that some noblemen who took part in the siege of Diu and who felt their honour touched by his truthful description of the events, asked the King, Dom João III, to have Book X destroyed. Couto did not think that the order for stopping the publication of the "History" could have been given by Dom João III who died in 1557, for the last book of the history of which we know anything is dated 1561. It must therefore have happened in the Regency of Dom Sebastião and took place after the death of Castanheda.

The first book of the "History" appeared in 1551 and was known all over Europe, and three years afterwards, translations in French and Spanish appeared, as well as one in Italian. At the end of the first book there are the following words: "This First Book of the History of India was printed in the very loyal and noble city of Coimbra by João de Barreira, King's Printer, in the same University".

The elegance of his style is subordinate to the sincerity of his narrative. Though Castanheda does not possess the majesty of the style or the erudition of João de Barros, he must be regarded as a greater authority as he had first-hand knowledge of what he wrote. Having a personal acquaintance with the language, manners and customs of the peoples of India, he gave vivid pictures and faithful descriptions of the countries

(1) Aubrey Bell—Hispanic Notes. Gaspar Correia, p. 58.

he visited. Like other famous authors and poets of his time, he was a soldier as well as a writer, and was able to describe the battles and methods employed in warfare with scientific accuracy of facts as well as with the gifted pen of a natural historian.

More impartial than Barros, he points out the errors and even the crimes of his countrymen and disapproves of the wrongs done to India. The work of Castanheda is supposed to be that from which Luis de Camões derived the historical material about India for his "Lusiadas". (1)

Teixeira de Aragão in "Vasco da Gama" and in "Vidigueira" refers in 1898 to the historian in the following terms: "Without possessing the eloquence of Barros, he employed the best twenty years of his life in writing the history of the discoveries, working hard to justify and verify his facts as much in India as in Portugal."

João de Barros 1496-1570.

João de Barros, 1496-1570, was the first State chronicler to write about India. His choice expressions and his pure style have made his writings classic: he has justly been called the Portuguese Livy. He belonged both to the Court of Dom Manuel and of Dom João III. The former recognising his talent, though he was only twenty years old at the time, requested him to write the History of India which duty he afterwards so ably performed in his four "Decadas da Asia", though

---

(1) See "Een en dertig hoofstukken uit het verloren gegane Livro IX van Lopes de Castanheda's Historia do Descobrimento e Conquista da India pelos Portuguezes (31 Chapters from the last Book IX of the "History of the Discovery and Conquest of India by the Portuguese" by Lopes de Castanheda.) Text in Portuguese, notes in Dutch, edited by Father C. Wessels, *in Bijdragen tot de Taal-Land-en Volkenkunde van Nederlandsch India*, No. 498, Vol. 85, pp. 1-65, with 3 plates.

the death of the King postponed the writing for some years. Although he never went to India, he had special facilities for the study of India, for in 1525 he became Treasurer of the House of India, Mina and Ceuta, in Lisbon, where he served till 1528. In spite of the various official appointments which he received from time to time he never desisted from his literary work, his days being given up to his official duties and his nights to his books. About 1540, the King accepted his offer to write about India, but before the first Decada was published, he gave to the world some of his minor works.

In 1552, Barros printed his first "Decada da Asia" (1) under the title of :

> "Da Asia de Joam de Barros, Dos feitos que os Portuguezes fizeram no descobrimento e conquista dos mares e terras do Oriente". Lisboa 1552.
>
> (Asia by Joam de Barros. Of the deeds which the Portuguese did in the discovery of the seas and lands of the Orient. Lisbon 1552.)

The second Decada was published in 1553, under the title of :

> "Segunda Decada da Asia de Joam de Barros. Dos feitos que os Portuguezes fizeram no descobrimento e conquista dos mares e terras do Oriente". Lisboa 1553.
>
> (The second Decada of Joam de Barros. Of the deeds which the Portuguese did in the discovery and conquest of the seas and lands of the Orient. Lisbon 1553.)

The third Decada was published in 1563. It was known as :

> "Terceira Decada de Joam de Barros. Dos feitos que os Portuguezes fizeram no descobrimento e conquista dos

(1) There are copies of the first and second "Decadas" published 1552 & 1553 in the Bibliotheca Nacional of Lisbon.

> mares e terras do Oriente. Lisboa 1563.
> (The third Decada of Joam de Barros. Of the deeds which the Portuguese did in the discovery and conquest of the seas and lands of the Orient. Lisbon 1563.)

There is a copy of this edition of the third Decada in the Bibliotheca Nacional of Lisbon.

The fourth Decada was not published till 1615. It was called :

> Quarta Decada da Asia de Joam de Barros. Dedicada a el Rei D. Filippe II Nosso Senhor. Reformada, accrescentada e illustrada com notas e taboas geographicas por João Baptista Lavanha. Madrid 1615.
> (The fourth Decada of Asia of Joam de Barros. Dedicated to the King D. Filippe II Our Lord. Revised, added to and illustrated with notes and geographical tables by João Baptista Lavanha. Madrid 1615.)

Decadas I, II and III were published for the second time in Lisbon in 1628. Ultimately all four Decadas were reprinted in Lisbon in eight volumes in 1777 and 1778.

The "Decadas" comprise the history of the first four decades of the Portuguese rule in India.

The first Decada tells us how the Portuguese kingdom was formed, and how the Portuguese set out to make discoveries. The discovery of Africa was due mainly to the enterprise of the Infante Dom Henrique, who sent out expeditions for exploration. Dom Henrique continued making discoveries, while Dom Affonso took charge of the kingdom.

During the reign of Dom João, and his son, Dom Affonso, Guinea, the Congo territory and the Cape of Good Hope were discovered, an expedition was fitted out to find the route to India, and missionaries were sent to the Congo. About the same time Christopher Columbus discovered the New World.

The memorable voyage of discovery of Vasco da Gama is described when, after reaching Moçambique and Melinde, he arrived at Malabar, and from there returned to Portugal.

The discovery of Brazil by Pedro Alvares Cabral is also described in this Decada. Details of Vasco da Gama's second voyage to India in 1502 as Admiral, and his difficulties with the Zamorin of Calicut are also given. Here begins a description of the wars which were waged between the various Indian potentates and the Portuguese; the different cities of the west coast of India, as well as the various kings and princes with whom the Portuguese came into contact through trade or conquest, are described.

The Decada closes in 1505, with a picture of the kingdom of Sofala, its gold mines, its people, and the relations established between this kingdom and Portugal. (1505—1515).

The second Decada deals with the early history of the Portuguese in India under Portuguese Governors, the voyage of Tristão de Cunha and Affonso de Albuquerque on their way to India, and the wars which were carried on by Albuquerque and the Viceroy, Dom Francisco de Almeida.

Here we read also of Albuquerque's work in Calicut; the history of Goa is dealt with, and Albuquerque's capture of Goa with the help of Antonio de Noronha is described. A detailed account is given of Albuquerque's many victories over Yusuf Adil Shah and his captains; the various voyages of Albuquerque in the eastern seas, and the several expeditions against the King of Cambay and Adil Shah are described, until Albuquerque's return, in 1515, to Goa, where he died.

The third Decada opens with the troubles at Goa on account of Ismail Adil Shah. It also treats of the various expeditions sent out by
1516-1526 King Dom Manuel to Ceylon, the Maldive Islands, Bengal, Siam and China. The Kingdom of Ethiopia, whose King was

Prester John, is described, as also the wars with Adil Shah which continued.

The happenings in India, when the King of Cochin was at war with the Zamorin of Calicut, are dealt with; and we are told how Burhan Nizam Shah gave permission for the erection of a Fortress at Chaul, and of the continuation of the troubles with Adil Shah and the Moors.

This Decada ends with a description of the work of one of the Governors (Dom Henrique) in India, till his death in the fortress of Cannanore.

Decada IV (1526—1539) begins with a narration of the usual trouble which the Governor had with Calicut, and the quarrels amongst the succeeding Governors. The taking of the city of Diu in the time of the Governor Nuno de Cunha is described.

It also tells us how, in the meanwhile, the Portuguese captains were busy on the west coast, and this is followed by a description of the kingdom of Gujerat, its history, and the flight of Prince Bahadur Khan from his father, the return of Bahadur Khan after his father's death, the story of his own rule, and his plans to capture Diu.

There is a historical description of the Moghuls, the causes which brought them to India and their relations with Bahadur Shah, of the reasons which made Bahadur Shah give up Diu to the Portuguese and how he repented his action.

The wars between the various princes of the Deccan, after the death of King Mahomed Shah and the siege of Golconda by Ibrahim Adil Shah (1) are described, and mention is also made of the combination of the forces of Asad Khan with those of Ibrahim

(1) Fernão Mendes Pinto in his "Peregrinação" makes a slight reference to Adil Shah in 1535.

Adil Shah, to drive out the Portuguese from Goa.

It is also shown how the King of Calicut, seeing that the Portuguese at this time were harassed on all sides, took advantage of this and attacked the Portuguese but was defeated.

It mentions the details of a conspiracy of the King of Cambay to retake Diu, and contains a description of the Kingdom of Bengal, the customs of its people and its history.

The Decada ends with the attempt made by Sulaiman, Emperor of the Turks, to overthrow the Portuguese in India, and tells us how his ships came to Diu, where Antonio de Silveira was in the fortress which was badly damaged and how the Portuguese suffered great loss, until the siege was raised and a treaty signed. At this time Dom Garcia de Noronha arrived in India, where he insulted Nuno de Cunha who left for Portugal, dying on the way in 1539.

The general style and subject matter may be judged from the following selection which incidentally is also an admirable specimen of his method and manner as a historian :—

> (The King of Cannanore, when he saw Dom João de Nova return in such a few days with the ships which, as he said, were as loaded with victory as with spices, also wished to celebrate it at once and ended by giving him all the cargo which he wanted ; then in order to please him still more he sent to tell him that he should not mind that he had made little impression on the Zamorin ; for according to the news he had received, in that battle 417 people had been killed, on account of which all Calicut was plunged in mourning.
>
> João de Nova, having been despatched from the coast of India with so many victories and the good luck which God had given him, proceeded on his way to Portugal ; and even during this journey another good fortune befell him beyond the Cape of Good Hope. For God showed him a very small island to which he gave the name of St. Helena in which he took in water (for his ship), though from India till that place he had already twice done so;

once in Melinde and the second time at Moçambique.

It appears that God had created that island in that place, in order to give life to all who came from India ; because from the time it was found until to-day, every one tries to take it, as it has the best water on the whole route ...... So much is this the case that ships arriving there consider themselves saved and to have arrived successfully at the end of their journey owing to the great straits in which they are before arriving and on account of the refreshment which they find there, as we shall see further on, when we give the reason for this.

Leaving that place, João de Nova arrived at the Kingdom of Portugal on the 11th. of September, 1502, where the King received him with great honour owing to his successes in fighting and his prudence in the business which he had concluded.) (1)

---

(1) "El-rei de Cannanor, quando viu João da Nova em tão poucos dias tornar com as naus, como elle dizia tão carregadas de vitorias ccmo de especiarias, tambem o quis festejar com bom despacho, acabando de lhe dar toda a carga que havia mester. E ainda para o mais contentar, mandou-lhe dizer que não cuidasse que tinha feito pouco dano ao Samorim : pois segundo tinha nova, naquela peleja lhe matara por conta quatrocentas e dezassete pessoas, por causa das quais todo Calecute era posto em pranto....

Despedido João da Nova da costa da India com tantas vitorias e boas venturas que lhe Deus deu, fez sua viagem caminho deste Reino ; e ainda neste caminho, passado o Cabo de Boa Esperança, teve outra boa fortuna : que lhe deparou Deus uma ilha mui pequena, a que ele pôs nome " Santa Helena " em que fez sua aguada, posto que da India até ali tinha feito duas : uma em Melinde, outra em Moçambique.

A qual ilha parece que a criou Deus naquele lugar para dar vida a quantos homens veem da India ; porque, depois que foi achada até hoje, todos trabalham de a tomar, por terem a melhor aguada de toda esta carreira—ao menos a mais necessária que se toma, quando veem da India. E tanto, que as naus que ali veem ter se hão por salvas e navegadas pela necessidade que elas trazem, pelo muito refresco que nela acham, como diante veremos, dando razão de quem foi causa disso.

(João de Barros—Decada I, Book V, Chapter X.)

In speaking of the first Decada, Mendes dos Remédios says :—

"The first of them, published one year before the departure of Camões for India, 1553, inspired, in the opinion of many writers, the conception of the Lusiadas. For this reason, if for no other, they deserve to be registered with affection in the memory of all Portuguese. But the Asia of Barros is, apart from the purity and elegance of its language, an excellent repository of ethnographical information about India. The deeds of the Portuguese had on the other hand, a true singer and apologist in João de Barros. He might even be accused of having erred on the side of partiality, but as Sismondi wrote: 'One is able sometimes to learn the truth better from partial writers of their country's deeds, than from those who do not have any feeling; at least the former have something real,—sentiment.' " ([1])

Manuel Severim de Faria writes :—

"Everyone knows and sees that João de Barros conceived the chronicle of the Portuguese voyages and conquests as a civic duty and that he executed it as an epic poem in prose. Should such a conception contain the criticisms of the meanness and villainy which formed the reverse of the medal which he struck in commemoration of the events and facts whose sum total constitutes

---

([1]) "A primeira delas, aparecida um ano antes da partida de Camões para a India (1553) provocou, na opinião de muitos escritores, a concepção dos Lusiadas. Só por isso mereciam elas ser registadas com amor na memória de todos os portugueses. Mas a Asia de Barros é, aparte a pureza e louçania da linguagem, um repositório excelente de notícias etnográficas da India. Os feitos dos portugueses tiveram, por outro lado, em João de Barros um verdadeiro cantor e apologista. Pode talvez ser acusado por êsto lado, mas, como escreveu Sismondi, 'chega-se mais vezes a conhecer a verdade pelos escritores parciais da sua pátria, do que por aqueles que nada sentem ; pelo menos os primeiros teem uma cousa verdadeira—o sentimento' ".

(Mendes dos Remédios—"História da Literatura Portuguesa", page 170).

one of the greatest collective marvels in the world?" (1)

He reveals himself in his Decadas to be a clear, far-sighted, political economist, at a time when Political Science was in its infancy. He showed, long before Adam Smith, some familiarity with the subject and expressed new ideas about the future of Asiatic commerce.

João de Barros, according to the opinion of Monsenhor Dalgado (2) from his place in the "Casa da India" in Lisbon, knew much more of the Orient and in particular of India, especially with respect to its geography and ancient history, than many renowned travellers, ancient or modern.

"João de Barros and Diogo de Couto were true orientalists", says Sousa Viterbo. "They are the true precursors of the modern orientalists and investigators. Many times they drink from the original sources, other times they have recourse to interpreters. They have a thirst for knowledge which is all the more admirable, when we realise how few were the materials on which they could lay their hands." (3)

Manuel Severim de Faria says about him: "In order to write truthfully, João de Barros had the most truthful accounts that he could get hold of for this

---

(1) "Tôda a gente sabe e vê que João de Barros concebeu a crónica das navegações e conquistas portuguesas como dever de civismo, e que a executou como poema épico em prosa. Cabiam então numa concepção destas as críticas das misérias e torpezas que formavam o reverso da medalha que êle cunhou, para celebrar acontecimentos e factos cujo conjunto constitui uma das maiores maravilhas colectivas do mundo? ..."

(Antologia—João de Barros. Introduction to Decada I, page LXXI, and volume 9, and Indice of the Decadas).

(2) Glossário Luso-Asiático, Vol. I, Introdução.

(3) Sousa Viterbo, "Orientalismo em Portugal no século XVI"—(Boletim da Sociedade de Geographia de Lisboa, Vol. 12, p. 317-330, 1893.)

purpose; for having to treat of three things—the deeds of the Portuguese, information about the kings and nations of the Orient, and the true geographical situation of their provinces,—all the papers which dealt with Portuguese history, were given over to him, those of the Royal Armies as well as the accounts and letters of the Viceroys which were comprehensive, as they dealt with everything which belonged to their rule." (1)

As a writer on India João de Barros is most valuable. He has given us graphic descriptions of personages like Ibrahim Adil Shah and his minister, Asad Khan, and he speaks of the relations of the Portuguese with other States in India. Regarding information about the kings of the Orient and their peoples, he obtained documents to verify all his statements. He was not content with letters only, but sent for the chronicles of those kingdoms written in their respective languages, as we see in the First Decada, Book IX, Chapter III, in which he relates information about the Malabaris taken from one of their religious books and from their history. He had also with him the chronicles of the Kings of Gujerat, Vijianagar and the Deccan.

In his Decada IV, Book X, Chapter 21, Barros says that the papers which were given to him relating to the Governor, Nuno de Cunha, alone filled two large boxes.

João de Barros made use of Lopo de Sousa Coutinho's History of the First Siege of Diu, published in Coimbra, 1556. Coutinho was an eye-witness of the siege in 1538.

Barros says: "With reference to the entrance of the Mahomedans in Gujerat, according to the

---

(1) Life of João de Barros by Manuel Severim de Faria. Lisbon, 1778, P. xxxii.

writers of the Kingdom of Gujerat, they themselves in their histories disagree ....but in this narration of ours we shall follow the more useful opinion of the writers of the same Kingdom of Gujerat." (Decada IV, Book V). Further on he says: "The Persian Chronicles, from which we take some things about their Kings for this our history..........."

The geographical news and the customs of the Moghuls, which he gives, were also drawn from Persian documents. (1)

With respect to the Deccan, he says: "About the coming of the Muslims by force of arms into India, there is a great difference of opinion amongst the Hindus, especially with regard to the time, because the Muslims of the Gujerat kingdom write it in one way, those of the Deccan kingdom in another, and chronicles of the Hindu Kings of Bisnaga (2) follow another way, but all agree on this that the conqueror became

---

(1) Decada IV, Chapter I.

(2) "Chronica dos Reis de Bisnaga". A manuscript of the 18th. century published by David Lopes, Lisbon, 1897.

"The Chronicle which we now publish" says the erudite Professor David Lopes, "is a precious document for the history of Bisnaga. There does not exist, in any language that we know of, any thing which can compare with it, whether with respect to the actual historical facts, or whether as regards the description of the country, (especially of the Capital) products, customs, &c."

This manuscript contains two parts. The part which goes up to page 80, seems to be by Fernão Nunes, and that from page 80 to page 123, by Domingo Paes. The first must have been written about 1535. The second part is still more ancient and must have been compiled about 1525.

Both the Chronicles, of which the originals exist in the National Library of Paris, were sent from Goa probably to the celebrated historian, Barros.

These Chronicles were translated into English by Robert Sewell, and make a part of his interesting book "The Forgotten Empire."

king of the Delhi Kingdom. And because we have heard all these chronicles and they were interpreted to us, we follow in this account that record which now the Mussalmans have, who ruled the Deccan Kingdom to which we referred, because it agrees as regards time fairly well with the general chronicle of the Persians, the "Tarikh" of which we made mention in the beginning, and which with other volumes of Persian history and cosmography of those parts, we listened to." (1)

João de Barros was not only well-versed in classic literature and knew by heart his Ptolemy but he had also studied Arabic and Persian manuscripts; he knew about the accounts engraved in gold by the Hindus and even bought a Chinese slave to interpret for him some Chinese geographical documents which fell into his hands." (2)

Towards the end of 1567, he retired from his official work in connection with India. He lived till the 20th. October, 1570, and was interred in the Hermitage of St. António in Leiria.

Diogo do Couto
1542-1616

Diogo do Couto continued the account so ably begun by João de Barros. Born in Lisbon in 1542, he received a good classical education; but owing to the death of the Infante D. Luiz in whose service his father was, and the subsequent death of his father, Couto was constrained to give up his university course and take up arms, like most of the noblemen of that time, for which purpose he went to India at the age of fourteen. There he acquired the personal experiences which João de Barros did not have. He

(1) Decada II, Book V, Chapter 2.
(2) Conde de Ficalho's "Garcia da Orta e Seu Tempo", page 204.

served eight years as a soldier in India and showed by his signal bravery that neither a classical education nor an inclination for a literary life is an impediment to a military career. He discharged his military duties so well that he was recalled to Portugal some ten years later to receive the reward for his services. He then left the Army and returned to Goa where, as a peaceful civilian, he continued his classical studies which had been interrupted in his youth by his military service.

Couto was the personal friend of Camões who consulted him very often and took his advice with regard to several places in his poem. He once accompanied Camões on his return to Lisbon in 1570. He describes his meeting with that poverty-stricken "Prince of the Poets of his time" in his Decada VIII, Chapter 28, as follows:

> "Vinham os matalotes e camaradas Heitor da Silveira, o Drago, Fernão da Gra, e eu; e o dia que vimos a roca de Cintra, faleceo Heitor da Silveira, por vir já muito mal; e as náos chegaram em fim de Maio, ou já em Junho. Em Moçambique achamos aquelle Principe dos Poetas de seu tempo, meu matalote e amigo Luiz de Camões, tão pobre, que comia de amigos, e para se embarcar para o Reyno logo ajuntamos os amigos toda a roupa que houve mister, e não faltou quem lhe desse de comer, e aquelle inverno que esteve em Moçambique, acabou de aperfeiçoar os seus Lusiadas para os imprimir, e foi escrevendo muito em hum Livro que hia fazendo, que intitulava "Parnaso de Luiz de Camões", livro de muita erudição, doutrina e filosofia, o qual lhe furtaram e nunca pude saber no Reyno delle, por muito que o inquiri, e foi furto notavel; e em Portugal morreo êste excellente Poeta em pura pobreza."

> (Then came sailors and comrades, Heitor de Silveira, the Drago, Fernão da Gra, and myself, and the day we saw the rock of Cintra, Heitor de Silveira died, for he was returning already very ill; and the ships arrived in the end of May or the beginning of June. In Moçambique we found "that prince of the poets of his time", my fellow passenger and friend, Luiz de Camões, so poor that he had to be supported by his friends, and in order that he might embark for the kingdom (Portugal), his friends gathered together all the clothing that was necessary for

him. And there were not lacking those who gave him food. And that winter when he was in Moçambique, he had just completed the finishing touches to his Lusiadas in order to print it, and he was writing much in a book which he was making, which was entitled "The Parnassus of Luiz de Camões"—a book of great erudition, instruction and philosophy, and which was stolen from him. And I could never hear of it in Portugal, in spite of my many enquiries, and it was a notable theft; and in Portugal this excellent poet died in abject poverty.)

After the coronation of the King D. Felippe II in 1581, he appointed Diogo de Couto to continue the Decadas of João de Barros as Chief Chronicler of the Kingdom. On the 25th. February, 1595, he founded the Archives in Goa, and he was nominated the first Keeper which gave him facilities for writing and becoming acquainted with original documents and original sources. He was indefatigable in his research and Manoel Severim de Faria says of him: "By his courtesy and kindness, he made himself well-known in India and loved by all the famous men, nobles and investigators, even the pagan princes of those countries." (1)

Diogo de Couto's history is the best source for the history of the second half of the sixteenth century.

Diogo do Couto's great work, "As Decadas da Asia: Dos Feitos que os Portuguezes Fizeram na Conquista e Descobrimento das Terras e Mares do Oriente." (The Decadas of Asia: Being the Deeds that the Portuguese did in the Conquest and Discovery of the Lands and Seas of the Orient), consists of nine Decadas and ninety books—a number which few Portuguese chroniclers have ever reached. He intended to continue the work of João de Barros, whose Decada IV,

---

(1) "Vida de Diogo de Couto", by Manoel Severim de Faria, page IX.

deals with the period ending with the death of Nuno de Cunha in 1539, but as this Decada had not appeared when Couto commenced his history, he began from the period twelve years earlier and continued the account till 1600, and thus the fourth Decada of Barros and of Couto form a duplicate of the twelve years under the governorship of Lopes Vaz de Sampaio and Nuno de Cunha. Diogo de Couto's work was perfectly original, as João de Barros' work had remained in manuscript form in the possession of his widow, and was published, for the first time, in 1615, many years after the Fourth Decada of Diogo de Couto. The Tenth Decada was written first in order that the work should begin with the day when the King was crowned. (1) Then followed the Fourth, Fifth, Sixth, Seventh, Eleventh and Twelfth Decadas.

Decadas VIII and IX were finished in 1614, when he was already seventy-two years old. These precious volumes were stolen from him by some one who, knowing their value, wished to reap the benefit of them after his death. (2) But the copy of the following extract from Diogo de Couto's letter to the King about this theft, shows how nobly and courageously the old man met this blow and averted its consequences :

" But God, Our Lord, Author of all good, Who did not consent to such a manifest robbery, wished that some fragments and memoirs should remain; which together with what I remembered of the things which I saw which these two Decadas contain, the time of Dom Antão de Noronha (3), of Dom Luiz de Ataide, (4)

---

(1) "Vida do Diogo de Couto" by Manoel Severim de Faria, page x-xi.

(2) Decadas VIII and IX were dedicated to the King, Felippe II, 28th. January 1616. According to Innocencio da Silva, these Decadas were stolen before this date.

(3)—1564-1568.

(4)—1568-1571.

of Dom António de Noronha, (1) of Dom António Nunes Barreto (2) and the second governorship of Conde Dom Luiz de Ataide (3) when I fought in this State, were recorded in most of the things which I found remaining with me. God our Lord permitted me to be led in such a way that I again began to compile these two Decadas after the manner of an epilogue in which I have a resumé of the most notable and substantial events which happened, and thus I repaired the loss caused by the theft which they made me, as best I could. And when in some future time, these books will appear, immediately they will be recognised thus by my style as well as by the subject matter." (4)

Decada IV has as its title :

> "Decada Quarta da Asia. Dos feitos que os Portuguezes fizeram na conquista e descobrimento das terras e mares do Oriente, quando governaram a India, Lopo Vaz de Sampaio e parte de Nuno da Cunha. Lisboa." Por Pedro Craesbeck, 1602 fol.

> (Decada IV of Asia. Of the deeds accomplished by the Portuguese in the conquest and discovery of the lands and seas of the Orient, during the governorship of Lopo Vaz de Sampaio and part of the rule of Nuno da Cunha. Lisbon.) By Pedro Craesbeck, 1602 fol.

The first Governor, Lopo Vaz de Sampaio, (1526-1529), occupied himself with the various States lying adjacent to the Portuguese territory in India, viz. Cambay, Cochin and Cannanore. He also laid the foundation for the kingdom of Malacca and had several

---

(1) — 1571-1573.
(2) — 1573-1577.
(3) — 1578-1581.
(4) Decada VIII, Lisboa, 1786.—Letter to the King D. Filippe II, in Tomo V, Parte I, 21558, B. N. L.—Goa, 28th. January, 1616.

encounters with the Portuguese rivals, the Turks, by whom he was defeated, partly owing to the disputes among the Portuguese captains. The next Governor, Nuno da Cunha, (1529-1538), followed the programme laid down by his predecessor: he strengthened the Portuguese possessions in India by wars and alliances with the adjacent kingdoms, he consolidated the power of the Portuguese in Malacca, and, on the whole, secured a stronger footing for his nation in the East.

Decada V is called :

> "Decada Quinta da Asia. Dos feitos que os Portuguezes fizeram na conquista e descobrimento das terras e mares do Oriente em quanto governaram a India Nuno da Cunha, D. Garcia de Noronha, D. Estevam da Gama, e Martim Afonso de Sousa. Lisboa." Por Pedro Craesbeck, 1612 fol.

> (Decada V of Asia. Of the deeds accomplished by the Portuguese in the conquest and discovery of the lands and seas of the Orient, while Nuno da Cunha, D. Garcia de Noronha, D. Estevam da Gama and Martim Afonso de Sousa governed India. Lisbon.) By Pedro Craesbeck, 1612 fol.

In Decada V, Part I, there is a curious bit of information about the voyage which a pilot, Diogo Botelho, made to Portugal in a small ship, causing wonder and admiration amongst the most daring mariners of his time.

The second part of this Decada is a treatise on the principal religious systems of India, written with such detail, clearness and precision that no writer on India of our time, would disdain to acknowledge the work as his own (1). In Chapters III, & IV, Book VI, Decada V, Diogo de Couto gives a description of the beliefs, rites and ceremonies of all the Hindus who lived

---

(1) "Vida de Diogo de Couto", by Manoel Severim de Faria.

between the Indus and the Ganges. He tells us about the books which the theologians used to teach in their schools. He also discusses the differences between the castes, &c. He wrote this description being in the place itself and in close contact with Hindu theologians. (1) In one place, the chronicler says:

> "............ e a mim me aconteceu (sendo Viso Rey da India D. Antão de Noronha) ir de Goa para Chaul por terra na força do inverno com dous ou tres companheiros, e quando achavamos lugares de Bragmanes, não nos queriamos agazalhar em outros, sem embargo de nos não darem a comer senão o que eles comiam e do grande resguardo, e cerimonia com que nos communicavam, porque nos agazalhavam em varandas, que tem na face dos aposentos, e faziam o comer dentro em suas casas à sua vontade, e quando o traziam o punham no chão, afastado de nós dez ou doze passos, e tornavam-se a recolher, e nós o iamos buscar. Depois de comermos, tornavamos os pratos a seu lugar, que eles vinham arrecadar e traziam vasos cheios de água, que deitavam por cima primeiro que os tocassem; e depois que nos iamos faziam grandes purificações, lavando-se com muitas cerimónias e embostando as varandas, como se fôramos feridos de algum mal contagioso."

> "And to me it happened, (the Viceroy of India being Dom Antão de Noronha), that I went from Goa to Chaul by land in the depth of winter with two or three companions and when we came to the places of the Brahmins, we did not want to stay in any other place, even if we had to eat only what they had to eat themselves, and they had great caution and ceremony in the way in which they had communication with us, for they placed us in verandahs which were facing the private rooms, and they cooked the food inside in their houses as they liked, and when they brought it, they put it on the floor, advancing with nervous jerks ten or twelve paces and then drawing back, and then we would go to get the food. After having eaten we would put the plates back in the same place and

(1) Diogo de Couto "Decada" V, Book VI, chapters III & IV.

they would come to remove them and would bring pots full of water, which they would throw over them before touching them. And after when we would go away, they would make great purifications, washing themselves with great ceremonies and plastering the verandahs with cow-dung as though we were suffering from some contagious disease. (1)

Speaking of the castes, the same chronicler says :

" As to the castes, the greatest impediment to the conversion of the Hindus is the superstition that they keep themselves separate in their castes without being touched, or having communication or mixing with others, as superiors with inferiors, those of one rite with those of another. And they are so fixed in this, that many of them have arrived at the extremity of life, (near death), only on account of not touching the food or anything belonging to another person, through the fear of losing caste and becoming polluted."

Speaking of marriages, he says :

" These Hindus arrange their marriages at a certain time of the year with great ceremonies, their feasts lasting for the space of fifteen days or more, in which they give great banquets ; and when the bride goes to her husband's house it is with great ceremonies and on no account may she speak to her husband nor they (the husbands) speak to their wives before their parents, nor can they name one another before them, nor eat together, which they observe so strictly that even after some of them become Christians, they keep up these customs with their wives ; but this state of things lasts only till they have had children." (2)

He tells us in his Decada V (and this was con firmed in the past century by Caldwell), (3) about

---

(1) Diogo de Couto, Decada V, Book VI, chap. IV. p. 41-42.

(2) Diogo de Couto, Decada V, Book VI, p. 46-47.

(3) Reverend Robert Caldwell, author of " A Comparative Grammar of the Dravidian and South Indian' Family of Languages", 2nd. edition, London, 1875.

the work of the "venerable" pariah, Valuvar, who composed one thousand three hundred and thirty poetic and religious aphorisms, contained in a book called 'Kural', and he tells us the subjects with which they deal. There is no translation of this book into Portuguese, but the Reverend G. U. Pope, forty years ago, made a translation of it into English, and, since then, another and better translation has been made by V. V. S. Aiyar.

According to Dalgado, Diogo de Couto was the first orientalist to identify the Christian legend of "Barlaam and Josaphat" with that of Buddha, an honour now claimed by others. (1)

> A este nome tem dedicado os Gentios por toda a India grandes e soberbos Pagodes, vendo-nos esta historia, estivemos cuidando a teriam os antigos Gentios destas partes em suas escrituras conhecimento do santo Josaphat, que foi convertido por Barlão, que em sua lenda temos ser filho de um grande Rey da India, e que tivera a mesma criação, e todos os mais termos que temos contado da vida deste Budão. E como a historia de Josaphat havia de ficar escrita pelos naturaes, (que nada lhes fica por escrever , parece que por tempos lhe vieram acrescentar muitas fabulas, como eles teem na vida de Budão, que nos deixamos, porque nem em dois Capitulos as concluiremos da maneira que as elles tem.
>
> E porque nos vem a proposito o que nos disse hum homem muito antigo das terras de Salsete em Baçaim do santo Josaphat, nos pareceu bem trazê-la. Andando-nos

---

(1) "Vida de Diogo de Couto, Chronista do Estado da India e Guardamor da Torre do Tombo della", by Manoel Severim de Faria.

See Dalgado, Glossário Luso-Asiático, Vol. I. Introdução XVI.

See also IX Edition, Encyclopaedia Britannica, pp.—375 & 376. It recognises Diogo de Couto as the first historian to identify the legend. Confirmed afterwards in July 1859 by M. Laboulaye, in 1860 by Dr. Liebricht and in 1870 by Prof. Muller.

nesta Ilha de Salsete vendo aquele raro, e admirável Pagode (que chamam do Canará) fabricado em uma ferra, e talhadas em uma só pedra muitas salas, e uma delas tamanha como a grande dos paços da Ribeira de Lisboa, e mais de trezentas cameras pela terra assima quasi em caracol, cada uma com sua cisterna a porta, na mesma pedra viva, da mais fria e excelente agua, que se pode desejar, e nas portas da sala grande, formosissimas figuras de vulto tamanhas como gigantes, de obra tão subtil, e prima, que nem em prata se podiam esculpir melhor ; com outras muitas grandezas, que deixamos por não ser comprido.

E perguntando a este homem velho, que dissemos, por esta obra, e o que lhe parecia por quem fora feita, nos disse que sem duvida aquela obra se fizera por mandado do pai do Sto. Josaphat, para o recolher e crear nela, como diz a sua lenda. E como nos temos dela, que fora filho de um grande Rey da India, bem pode ser, como já dissemos que fosse este o Budão, de que elles cantam tantas maravilhas. "

(To this name have the Gentios dedicated large and imposing pagodas all over India. Hearing the story we wondered if the ancient quafirs had in any part of their scriptures shown a knowledge of St. Josaphat who was converted by Barlaam, which in the legend we have, is said to be the son of a great King of India, and which story had the same origin as all the rest which we have retailed of the life of this Buddha. And as the story must have been written by the natives (who left nothing unwritten), it seems that in times back many fables came to be added, as they have done in the life of Buddha, which we rejected because our story does not end in the way theirs does.

And because we remember that a very old man of the island of Salsette in Baçaim told us about St. Josaphat, it seemed good to us to translate it. Walking about in this island of Salsette we saw this rare and wonderful pagoda (which they call of Canará), built on a mountain and many rooms hewn out of one stone only and one of them of a size as large as the palace of the Ribeira of Lisbon, with some 300 rooms from the ground upwards almost in spiral, each one with its cistern at the door, in the same bright stone, with as excellent cold water as one could wish for, and at the doors of the large room most beautiful figures of gigantic size, of work so subtle and fine that not even in silver would it be possible to sculpture it better ; with many other beauties which we do not attempt to describe for want of space.

Asking the old man, of whom we spoke, by whom did he think this work was done, he told us that without doubt it was done at the order of the father of St. Josaphat in order to shelter him, as the legend says. And as we have in our story that he was the son of a great King of India, it can well be, as we already said, that this was the Buddha of whom they recount so many marvellous tales.) ([1])

Decada VI : (1545-1551).

" Decada Sexta da Asia. Dos feitos que os Portuguezes fizeram na conquista e descobrimento das terras e mares do Oriente, em quanto governaram a India D. João de Castro, Garcia de Sá, Jorge Cabral e D. Affonso de Noronha."

Por Pedro Craesbeck, 1614. "

(Decada VI of Asia : Of the deeds accomplished by the Portuguese in the conquest and discovery of the lands and seas of the Orient, while D. João de Castro, Garcia de Sá, Jorge Cabral and D. Affonso de Noronha governed India). Printed by Pedro Craesbeck, 1614.

It deals with the work of three Governors of Goa. During the first half of the 16th. century they spent most of their time fighting against the Turks, the Arabs and the various Indian Princes. The first Governor, Dom João de Castro, (1545-1548), was very capable and was victorious in his struggles with the Arabs and with Ibrahim Adil Shah. During his rule, Diu was taken by the Portuguese. The second Governor, Garcia de Sá, (1548-1549), was threatened with grave dangers from the Turks and the Indian Princes. He was succeeded by Jorge Cabral (1549-1550), as Governor, who carried on incessant wars with the different Indian Rulers. This Decada also tells of the advent in 1542 and the preaching of St. Francis Xavier and later about

---

([1]) Lendas de Barlaam e Josaphat. Decada V, VI. 2. pp-16-17.

the King of Ceylon, who pretended to be a convert.

Decada VII : (1551-1564).

" Decada Septima da Asia. Dos feitos que os Portuguezes fizeram na conquista e descobrimento das terras e mares do Oriente, em quanto governaram a India D. Pedro Mascarenhas, Francisco Barreto, D. Constantino de Bragança, o Conde de Redondo, D. Francisco Coutinho, e João Mendonça."

Por Pedro Craesbeck, 1616.

(Decada VII of Asia : Of the deeds accomplished by the Portuguese in the conquest and discovery of the lands and seas of the Orient, while D. Pedro Mascarenhas, Francisco Barreto, Constantino de Bragança, the Conde de Redondo, D. Francisco Coutinho and João de Mendonça governed India.)

Printed by Pedro Craesbeck, 1616.

It describes the relations between Portugal and Abyssinia, Ethiopia and India, and the influence of Christianity on these territories. The cathedral of St. Catherine of Goa was made a seat of an Archbishop and the churches of St. Cruz of Cochin and of " Our Lady of Assumption " of Malacca, were made into Bishoprics. The Viceroys of this period were Dom Pedro Mascarenhas (1554-1555), Constantino de Bragança and D. Francisco Coutinho. Besides the wars with the Turks, there were wars with the Mussalmans of Ceylon, Malabar and Pegu. But from all these encounters the Portuguese returned successful, and their fleet was ever busy with the Turks.

Decada VIII : (1564-1571).

" Decada Oitava da Asia. Dos feitos que os Portuguezes fizeram na conquista e descobrimento das terras e mares do Oriente, em quanto governaram a India D. Antão de Noronha e D. Luiz de Ataide."

(Decada VIII of Asia : Of the deeds accomplished by

the Portuguese in the conquest and discovery of the lands and seas of the Orient, while D. Antão de Noronha and D. Luiz de Ataide governed India.

This Decada, printed in 1673, treats, among other things, of the league of the Mohammadan Princes of the Deccan against the kingdom of Vijayanagar (1565), and also the doings of the Portuguese in connection with Ceylon, Pegu and Cochin in the war of Cannanore during the Viceroyalty of Dom Antão de Noronha, (1564-1568). It also describes the events of the war of Bijapur with Goa during the time of the Viceroy, Dom Luiz de Ataíde (1568-1571), and the steps taken by the Portuguese against Ali Adil Shah.

Decada IX : (1571-1581).

" Decada IX de Asia. Dos feitos que os Portuguezes fizeram na conquista e descobrimento das terras e mares do Oriente, emquanto a India governaram D. Antonio de Noronha, Francisco Barreto, e Antonio Moniz Barreto."

(Decada IX of Asia. Of the deeds accomplished by the Portuguese in the conquest and discovery of the lands and seas of the Orient, while D. Antonio de Noronha, Francisco Barreto, and Antonio Moniz Barreto governed India.)

In Decada IX, we find that the King of Portugal had divided his eastern possessions into three Governorships ; Dom Antonio de Noronha (1571-1573) was elected Viceroy of the portion from Cape Guardafu till Ceylon ; Francisco Barreto (1573-1577) was made Governor from Cape Correntes till Cape Guardafu, and Antonio Moniz Barreto (1577-1578) was Governor from Pegu to China. This Decada deals with the events of the rule of these Governors and their relations with Ibrahim Adil Shah II and with Malacca.

Decada X : (1518-1588).

" Decada Decima da Asia. Dos feitos que os Portuguezes fizeram na conquista e descobrimento das terras e mares do Oriente, emquanto na India governaram Fernão Telles, D. Francisco de Mascarenhas e D. Duarte de Menezes."

(Decada X of Asia. Of the deeds accomplished by the Portuguese in the conquest and discovery of the lands and seas of the Orient, while Fernão Telles, D. Francisco de Mascarenhas and D. Duarte de Menezes governed India.)

Decada X deals with the period of Fernão Telles' Viceroyalty up to the succession of Manuel de Sousa Coutinho. This period is most interesting for it gives copious accounts of the relations between the Turks and the Persians. At the beginning of this period there were troubles with Daman, Diu and Malacca, and towards the end we see the growing power of the Rajah of Ceylon who became the enemy of the Portuguese and made alliances with the neighbouring powers. The Viceroys of this period all recognized Philip as King and made the people of the countries, over which they ruled, take an oath of allegiance to him.

Decada XI : (1588-1595).

"Decada Undecima da Asia. Dos feitos que os Portuguezes fizeram na conquista e descobrimento das terras e mares do Oriente, emquanto governaram Manuel de Sousa Coutinho e Mathias de Albuquerque."

(Decada XI of Asia. Of the deeds accomplished by the Portuguese in the conquest and discovery of the lands and seas of the Orient, while Manuel de Sousa and Mathias de Albuquerque governed India.)

During the period embraced by Decada XI, the Portuguese under Manuel de Sousa Coutinho were contending with the Mussalman powers of the Deccan. They were busy exploring the coasts of Africa; at the same time war was carried on against the Sinhalese and the King of Melinde and in India the Zamorin and the Malabaris had to be held in check.

Decada XII: (1595-1601).

"Decada Duodecima da Asia. Dos feitos que os Portuguezes fizeram na conquista e descobrimento das terras e mares do Oriente."

(Decada XII of Asia. Of the deeds accomplished by the Portuguese in the conquest and discovery of the lands and seas of the Orient.)

Decada XII deals with the period between 1596 and 1601. Diogo de Couto was unable to complete his work as death intervened. This Decada describes the political condition of the Gangetic basin, as well as the relations of the Portuguese with Pegu, China and even Japan. The Portuguese were still having trouble with Ceylon and the many battles fought are described. During this time the Dutch fleets began to visit India and the Dutch occupied Bengal and the East Indies.

In his "Life of Diogo de Couto", Manoel Severim de Faria says:

"The style which Diogo de Couto maintained throughout his Decadas, is very clear and plain but sententious, as of one who judges the actions of each person and shows the causes of the adverse or prosperous events which the Portuguese experienced in those parts. At the same time, he compares favourably with others as far as the truth, which is the soul of history, of what he wrote is concerned; for wherever he treated of the customs of those peoples and remote provinces and of their exact geography, he had the distinct advantage over many of knowing them personally, as one can clearly see in his Decadas in which he points out the errors that were made in these matters by those who wrote before him (1) about things pertaining to the East."

The last edition of all the Decadas was published

---

(1) "O estilo, que nestas Décadas guardou Diogo de Couto he muito claro, e chão, mas cheio de sentenças, e com que julga as acções de cada hum, e mostra as causas dos successos adversos, e prosperos, que naquellas partes tiveram os Portugueses. Porem, ainda que nesta parte pode ser com outros comparado na verdade

in Lisbon in 1778 to 1788 in fourteen volumes.

Besides the Decadas, Diogo de Couto wrote:

(1) Falla, que fez em nome da Camara de Goa ....—... a André Furtado de Mendonça, em dia do Espirito Sancto de 1609, Lisboa, 1610 fol.

(Discourse which in the name of the Municipal Council of Goa, André Furtado de Mendonça made on the Day of Pentecost—Lisbon, 1610.)

(2) Vida de D. Paulo de Lima Pereira, Capitão Mor das Armadas do Estado da India, Lisboa, 1765. 427 pp.

(Life of D. Paulo de Lima Pereira, Captain-General of the State of India. Lisbon, 1765. 427 pp.)

(3) Observações sobre as principaes causas da decadencia dos Portuguezes na Asia. Escriptas em forma de dialogo, com o titulo de Soldado Pratico. Lisboa 1790.

(Observations on the principal causes of the decadence of the Portuguese in Asia, written in the form of a dialogue with the title of "Practical Soldier". Lisbon 1790.)

Moved by his zeal for the public good, he wrote this book, in which he treated of the abuses and evils, which, during his time, were introduced into the Government of India.

Diogo de Couto died in Goa at the age of seventy-four on the 10th December, 1616.

Alvaro Velho.

Among the numerous writers who have chronicled the fascinating story of the discovery of this land of romance by the hero of Portugal, is Alvaro Velho, who was one of those to accompany Vasco da Gama in his first voyage of discovery to India. We know

---

do que escreve, que he a alma da historia, no que trata dos Principes do Oriente, nos costumes daquelles povos, e remotas Provincias, na situação da sua verdadeira Geografia, levou a muitos conhecida vantagem; como se pode claramente ver das suas Decadas, nas quaes se mostram os erros, que nestas materias tiveram os que antes delle escreveram as cousas do Oriente".

(Vida de Diogo de Couto, by Manoel Severim de Faria.)

nothing else about his personality, but he is believed to be the author of :

> "Roteiro da Viagem, que, em descobrimento da India, fez Dom Vasco da Gama pelo Cabo da Boa Esperança, em 1497."
>
> (Log-book of the voyage which Vasco da Gama made during the discovery of India by way of the Cape of Good Hope in 1497).

It was published for the first time by Diogo Kopke and Doctor Antonio de Costa Paiva, Oporto, 1838—three hundred and forty years after the work was written. It has a picture of Vasco da Gama, a letter about the voyage and a facsimile of the manuscript from which the edition was printed. It is preceded by an erudite Introduction by the editors in which they give their arguments why Alvaro Velho is to be considered the author of this work. In this book, just as any modern traveller would do, he gives us most interesting information about the drugs and the trading commodities of the Orient, and the book is a vocabulary of the language of Calicut. The said "Roteiro" was translated into French by Arthur Moreleto.

Dom Afonso de Albuquerque.

Dom Afonso de Albuquerque, known as the "Great" on account of his heroic deeds which called forth the admiration of Europe and the astonishment and terror of Asia was born in the year 1453, about six leagues from Lisbon, in the town of Lhandra.

He was the second son of Gonçalo de Albuquerque and Dona Leonor de Menezes, a daughter of Conde Atouguia. He was educated in the palace of King Dom Afonso V. He took part in many successful engagements, both in Europe and in Africa, which was the auspicious prelude to his victories in Asia, where he went on the 5th. of April 1503.

There is scarcely any part of the coast of the Orient

which did not feel his power. Twice he was victorious in Goa, the second conquest weakening the power of the proud Adil Shah of Bijapur so much that for a long time he lamented the loss of the place which was destined to become the capital of the Portuguese Empire in India. Albuquerque died on the 16th. of December 1515, when he was sixty-three years of age.

During his government he wrote many letters which reveal a most complete comprehension of the political state of India. They were published by the "Academia das Sciencias" of Lisbon under the direction of R. A. de Bulhão Pato, Lisbon, 1884. Among these, the most interesting are the following :

1. Two answers which he sent to two letters from Cogeatar.
2. An answer to a letter from Lourenço de Brito, Captain of Cannanore.
3. Information sent by Father Luiz da Ordem Seráfica to the King of Narsinga (Vizianagar), in which he tells what happened in the conquest of Calicut.
4. Letter written to Sheik Ismael.
5. Instruction given to Ruy Gomes for Sheikh Ismael.
6. Letter to the King of Ormuz.
7. Letter written to Timoja Aguazil Mor, Captain of the people of Goa and Lord of the lands of Cintacora.
8. Letter to Adil Shah, when he (Albuquerque) conquered Goa.
9. Orders which he gave to Antonio de Miranda de Azevedo, with a present for the King of Siam.
10. Letter to Sheikh Ismael. Informs him that he has done all honour to his Ambassador. He sends him Fernão Gomes de Lemos to give him information which he desires with respect to the Portuguese. Gives him an account of the taking of Ormuz, where he hopes to return. He explains to him the advantage of an alliance against the Sultan about which it would be convenient to send messengers to the King of Portugal.
11. Letter of Sheikh Ismael (Adil Shah) to the King Dom Manuel, informing him of the visit of his Ambassador to Afonso de Albuquerque to assure peace and the best

friendly relations between him and the King Dom Manuel of Portugal. (1)

12. An extract from a letter of Pero Vaz d'Orta to the King Dom Manuel praising Afonso de Albuquerque, giving various bits of information relating to Moçambique, and informing him that he was going in search of the country of Prester John. March 4th. 1507. (2)

13. Order of the Viceroy Dom Francisco de Almeida that Lourenço de Brito, Captain of the Fortress of St. Angelo of Cannanor should keep Alfonso de Albuquerque prisoner and incommunicable in the tower of the fortress. September 9th. 1509.

14. Letter to the King. Intimates his intention to take Goa; shows the advantage which will result from this deed for the holding of India secure. Cannanor, October 17th., 1510.

15. Letter to the King: He says he sent the letter about taking Goa the same evening; continues to narrate what he did and what he is doing for the expulsion of Turks. He gives an account of the message which he sent to the King of Vijayanagar, of the securities given to the inconsequent heathen officials who remained in the city and of those concessions to the Portuguese who had married captive Arabs. Goa, December 22nd., 1510.

19 Letter to the King. Gives an account of having found in ruin the fleet which he left in India when he went to Malacca; of the malpractices of the Vicar of Goa who was going back to Portugal; about other disorders in Goa; he dwells on the necessity of holding India fast. Cochin, April 1st., 1512.

17. Letter to the King in which he tells how he set free the Ambassador of Prester John from Chaul where he was captive; and of the reception of the same Ambassador in Goa. Message to Sabaio, etc.

18. Letter to the King states that already dying, he has accomplished his mission leaving India secure. He asks for favour for his son. In this last letter, Albuquerque says:

---

(1) "Tipografia" da Academia Real das Sciencias, Lisboa, 1884, Tomo II.

(2) "Tipografia" da Academia das Sciencias, Lisboa, 1884, Tomo III.

I do not write to your Majesty with my own hand, because now dying, I am unable to do it. I feel already the agony and hiccough of death. Senhor, I leave a son to continue my memory. To him I leave all my possessions which are few; but I leave him the duty of continuing to serve my own and his King as I did, which is much. Things pertaining to India will themselves speak for him and for me. I leave India with its principal States taken, and in your power without having anything else to worry about except guarding them and closing very well the gate of the Strait. It was this that Your Majesty gave me to do. I, Senhor, always counselled you and still to-day I do the same that you secure your hold on India in order that you may realise from it the revenues and take from it its expenses. I ask Your Majesty that, by your kindness, you will remember. all this and that you will make my son great and that you will show him all your satisfaction with my work. I put his future in the hands of Your Majesty and of Her Majesty. To you I look that you will make my deeds appear great since I die while in your service, and for the pension, to which I am entitled and which Your Majesty knows I gained for the most part, I ask that it may be given to my son and he will for me kiss Your Royal hands.

At Sea, December 6th., 1515.

This letter defines the proud, noble, warlike and affectionate character of the great Portuguese hero who was called Afonso de Albuquerque.

Dom Afonso de Albuquerque.

Dom Afonso de Albuquerque, 1500-1580, better known as Bras de Albuquerque, the natural son of the great Afonso de Albuquerque, was born in a villa on the margin of the river Tagus.

The first edition of his great work was published in 1557, with the title:

"Os Commentarios de Afonso de Albuquerque Capitão geral e governador da India collegidos por seu filho Afonso d'Albuquerque das proprias Cartas que elle escrevia ao muito poderoso Rey Dom Manuel o Primeiro. deste nome em cujo tempo governou a India. Vam se partidos em quatro partes, segundo os tempos de seus trabalhos."

(Commentary of Afonso de Albuquerque, Captain General and Governor in India, collected by his son, Afonso d'Albuquerque, from the actual letters which he wrote to the very powerful King, Dom Manuel, the first of that name, in whose reign he was Governor of India. The letters are divided into four parts according to the time of his work.)

The Commentaries are dedicated to Dom Sebastião. Two reasons the author gives for printing the work: to remind the King of the obligation to the descendants of the man who gave important service to his great grandfather, and the slight attention paid by the historians of India to the work of his good father. These are the exact words of Afonso de Albuquerque's son: "Two reasons principally among others obliged me greatly to compile this history of the great deeds of Afonso d'Albuquerque, Captain General and Governor of India, to which he put the name Commentaries, collected from the actual originals, which he in the midst of his work, wrote to the King Dom Manuel, Your Majesty's great-grandfather."

The second edition was published in Lisbon in 1576, the third was published in Coinbra in 1923. The fourth edition was prefaced and revised by Antonio Baião, the learned Director of the Torre do Tombo.

The attentive reader of the Commentaries could clear up many points of history, for, besides coming to know the life of Albuquerque, he would find important elements for the history of Bijapur, Vijianagar, Calicut, Cochim.

The description of the conquest and reconquest of Goa by Albuquerque with the aid of Timoja is brilliant. (1)

---

(1) See Heras "Aravidu Dynasty of the Vijianagar Empire", page 57.

The Commentaries are highly praised by João de Barros in his "Decadas da India", Book X, Chapter VIII.

Another writer says of him: "He has shown such a love for the truth, such moderation and tact in referring to the enemies of his father, so much modesty in his details of the action of that hero, that one can say that the portrait which he has drawn, far from being exaggerated, underrates the original". (1)

Dom João de Castro.

Dom João de Castro, (1500-1548), the fourth Viceroy of India and tenth Governor who ruled for two years and nine months, died in Goa on the 5th. of June 1548. He wrote :—

"Primeiro Roteiro da costa da India desde Goa até Dio: Narrando a Viagem que fez o Vice-Rei Dom Garcia de Noronha em socorro desta ultima cidade 1538-1539. Por Dom João de Castro, Governador e Vice-Rei, que depois foi, da India. Segundo Ms. Autographo Publicado por Diogo Kopke, Porto 1843."

(The first log-book of the coast of India, from Goa to Diu, narrating the voyage which the Viceroy Dom Garcia de Noronha made in aid of Diu, 1538-1539. By Dom João de Castro who was afterwards Governor and Viceroy of India. According to autographed manuscripts published by Diogo Kopke, Porto, 1843.)

It has 284 pages, and a preface which is explanatory and descriptive of the subject treated, an index and a facsimile of João de Castro.

---

(1) "Il y montra un grand amour de la verité, une grande moderation beaucoup de menagement pour la personne des ennemis de son père, et tant de modestie dans le détail des actions de ce Heros, qu'on peut dire que le portrait qu'il en ait bien loin d'être outre, est beaucoup au dessous de son originel.—(P. Lasitan, Histoire des découverts et conquêtes des Portuguais. Vol. I.).

The "Roteiro" was dedicated to the Infante Dom Luiz. It refers to the voyage of the fleet which Garcia de Noronha commanded when he was taking help to India. Dom João de Castro accompanied the fleet as Captain of the ship "Grifa". They left Belem on the 6th. of April, arriving at Goa on the 11th. of September 1538.

To this log-book, Dom João de Castro added some notes relating to the second voyage which he made to India in the year 1545. Of this "Roteiro" there exist two copies, one incomplete and both not too reliable, in the Library of Evora, whose Librarian, Dr. Joaquim Heliodoro da Cunha Rivara wrote about them in Nos. 67 and 68 of the "Panorama".

> "Facsimile do manuscripto original". Ao serenissimo e iminentissimo principi ifamte dom Lois;
>
> Como eu muitas bezes cuidase em que modo poderia servir Vosa Alteza nesta arte de cosmografia em que ao presente amdo emborilhado, temdo sabido que por imbemções de nosos istrumentos não se podia já achar cousa algũa que ẽ presemça de Vosa Alteza parecese nova, e ali vemdo o pouco proveito que se tira dos argumentos sotis forjados comtra os tristes pilotos e marinheiros me fiz noutra volta e prepuz em minha vontade de ocupar apontamento em portos de que os imperitos navegantes podesem tirar algũ fruto e como quer que a todos seja notorio que o pomto principal da navegação e a monografia jaz em favor as alturas das cidades, distancia de lugares, emtradas, de bahias, de portos, de promontorios mostra conhecimento dos tempos que ordem e comcerto tenham entre si os mares, e com isto termos berdadeira emformação do varar das agulhas, parece-me cousa justa e necessaria escrever nesta parte porque como quer que a bahia da cidade de goua seja mais que outra algũa frequemtada e sabida, não me pareceo nececario fazer dela algũa taboa menos dar ovidos e resguardos aos que perdem ocazião de emtrar, sómente quiz fazer mencão de quanta cousa aja no banco o qual sol' das muitas bezes e em limpios discoursos, portamto abemos de saber que nesta bahia semdo por mar o menos fumdo que nela ha he 22 palmos de agoa e o mais 24 e daqui em noutro tempo faz diferença.

To the most serene and most eminent Prince the Infante D. Luiz ;

(Having often thought how I could serve you in the art of Cosmography in which I am at present occupied, and convinced that by means of our instruments we could not find anything which would be new for your Highness and knowing the weakness of the arguments set up against the unfortunate pilots and sailors, I resolved to undertake a new voyage by sea and from it to gather notes from which the less experienced sailors could derive some benefit. All know that in navigation matters, the principal points are these: the height of the cities, the distances of places, the entrances, bays, ports and promontories, the knowledge of the seasons, the order and the unison of the seas between them, and all this constitutes real information to regulate the variations of the compass, a motive for which I have found it just and necessary to write on those points, and as the bay of Goa is more than any other frequented and known, it seems to me to be useless to write about it (or to make a table respecting it) but only to make description of its bank. In summer, the greatest tide rises to 24 hands and the least to 22, being however different in the other seasons.)

A letter of Dom João de Castro to Dom João III dated 16th. December 1546, is in the Biblioteca of Ajuda. (1) This letter consists of forty-five pages together with a "Relação" (Account) which came with this letter from people who lived in India at that time. The "Relação" is contained in pages forty-six to sixty-seven. It gives an account of the work going on in the State of India, particularly about the rebuilding of the fortress of Diu. (2)

Jacinto Freyre de Andrade, who has quoted some letters of Dom João de Castro, in writing about him, said : "In the hours when he was free from the cares of war he wrote, treating copiously of all the coast which

(1) Cod. 52—vii—No. 33.
(2) 52-63 MSS, 33 Fol. 112.

lies between Goa and Diu, outlining the lowlands, the level around the sea, in which are the cities which form the ports ; the monsoons, the condition of the seas, the strength of the currents, the force of the rivers, all with such detailed and correct geography, that this work alone would make him well-known, if he were not already wellknown through his military successes."

Dom João de Castro also wrote :

1. "Carta escrita de Dio ao Senado de Goa em 23 de Novembro de 1546."

   (A letter written from Diu on the 23rd. November 1546, to the Municipality in Goa); It has also been printed in Jacinto Freyre de Andrades work.

2. " Relação de que passou no sítio de Dio."

   (Memoirs of what happened in the place of Diu.)

3. " Carta a Aleixo de Sousa Chichorro, Vedor da Fazenda da India."

   (Letter to Aleixo de Sousa Chichorro, etc.)

4. " Roteiro da Viagem da India até o Estreito de Sues."

   (Log-book of the voyage from India to the Strait of Suez). This last work has been highly praised.

Born in India probably at the beginning of the 16th. century, Antonio Galvão, ?-1557, was nominated Governor of the Moluccas where he discharged his duties with exemplary honesty and justice.

Antonio Galvão.

He was respected and liked so much by the people that he was actually offered the throne of Ternat, a small island belonging to the archipelago of the Moluccas. He went back to Portugal and tried to find some employment there. During the following seventeen years, he depended on the charity of his friends, during which time he was occupied in writing his work which is now published entitled :

Tratado que compôs o nobre e notavel Capitão Antonio Galvão dos diversos e desvayrados caminhos, por onde nos tempos passados a pimenta e especearia veyo da India as nossas partes e assim de todos os descobrimentos antigos e modernos que são feitos até a era de mil e quinhentos e cincoenta com os nomes particulares das pessoas que os fizeram e em que tempos e as suas alturas—Biblioteca Nacional, Lisboa.

(A dissertation which the noble and notable Captain Antonio Galvão wrote about the different and various ways by which in past times the pepper and spices came from India to our parts and also of all the discoveries, ancient and modern, which were made in the era of 1550, with the particular names of the persons who made them in those times and at those stages. (1)

Galvão died in a hospital in Lisbon on the 11th. of March 1557. His friend, Sousa Tavares, to whom he left his manuscripts, published by the King's Printer, Joham da Barreira, on the 15th. December, 1563, this curious work which is a valuable contribution to the literature of the sixteenth century, and copies of which the writer found in the Bibliotheca Nacional of Lisbon.

Father João de Lucena.

Father João de Lucena, 1549-1608, a Jesuit priest who was born in the town of Trancoso, has left us:

"Historia da vida de Padre Francisco de Xavier, e do que fizerão na India os mais Religiosos da companhia de Jesu."
Composta pelo Padre Joam de Lucena da mesma companhia, Portugues natural da villa de Trancoso. Impresso por Pedro Craesbeck em Lisboa. Anno de Senhor 1600.

("History of the life of Father Francisco de Xavier, and what the other priests of the Company of Jesus did in India."
Composed by Father Joam de Lucena of the same Company, a Portuguese native of the town of Trancoso. Printed by Pedro Craesbeck, Lisbon, 1600.)

---

(1) Lisbon—1563-80. Printed in Lisbon in 1731. Translated into English for the Hakluyt Society in 1862. 242 pages.

The book was translated into Italian, printed in Rome in 1613 and in Spanish at Seville, in 1619. It is one of the best Portuguese classics. There is a fine copy of the 1600 edition in the Bibliotheca Nacional, Lisbon.

The work consists of ten books and nine hundred and eight pages. It deals with the places and peoples with whom Francisco Xavier came in contact during his mission in the East. His description of the India of his time and the people, is most interesting. He gives a graphic picture of the customs of the people and of the Hindu religion in Chapters XI and XII of Book II. The Italian traveller, Pietro della Valle, who was at Goa, refers to that description in his "Viaggi". (1)

Speaking of the people of India, he writes :

> "Outros andam continuamente visitando as praças onde os Mouros caçadores lhes vam vender os passaros, que elles não deixam de comprar por nenhum preço, sómente pera que lançando os logo a voar, os tornem a por em sua liberdade. Da mesma maneira tem currais deputados pera o gasalhado, e cura de toda a sorte de alimarias, que por doẽtes, ou velhas seu donos deitam almargem. E logo, porque se conheça bem o autor desta sua misericordia, se encontrarem un homem ao desemparo ou o virem lançado por terra pisar dos que passam, nem o ajudaram, a alevantar, nem poram sómente os olhos nelle."

(Others go about continually visiting the market places, where the Arabs go to sell birds, and they buy them at any price asked, just in order to set them at liberty, (2) In the same way they have places set apart for animals, and cure all those which through illness or old age have been turned out by their owners; and then in order to know well the

(1) Pietro della Valle "Viaggi", 3 vols, Venice 1681.
This book is translated into English by Edward Grey for the Hakluyt Society, in 2 vols.

(2)—Compare page iii "The Book of Duarte Barbosa," Translation-Hakluyt Society, 1918, about the Kingdom of Guzerate, the description of the "Baneanes".

persons who show this mercy towards animals, it is necessary to say that if they saw a man dying by the roadside without help, or saw him fallen on the ground under the feet of passers-by, they would not help him to get up, nor even look in his direction.)

In another part, he says:

"Das cousas do ceo, e eternas ha entre elles muy pouca, ou nenhũa noticia, nas temporais, e da terra sam espertos, e tam entendidos, que nam dam ventagem nas futilezas dos tratos, e contratos aos mercadores de Europa." p. 94.

(About things pertaining to Heaven and eternal things, they have among them little or no accounts; in the temporal and earthly matters, they are clever and so well-versed, that the merchants of Europe do not get the advantage over them through the cunning of their deals and contracts.")

We may judge from this that Lucena, like other Portuguese writers of this period, was not acquainted with the vast Sanskrit religious literature and based his knowledge merely on what he had learned from indirect sources about India.

The book also contains many references to D. João de Castro, about the victories he won over the King Mahmud III, of Guzerate, of the aid he sent to Dom Joam Mascarenhas, Captain of Diu, (p. 376) about his courtesy and goodness, how he was given the title of Viceroy and a vivid description of his death. (p. 394).

Antonio de Castilho.

Antonio de Castilho, Knight of the Order of Aviz, and some say Commander of Mora, became the Chief Librarian of the Royal Archives of the Torre do Tombo. He wrote:

"Commentario do Cerco de Goa e Chaul, no anno de MDLXX, Viso-Rey Dom Luiz de Ataíde. Escripto por Antonio de Castilho, guarda mor da Torre do Tombo por mandado d'ElRey Nosso Senhor e agora novamente reimpresso por Lucas da Sylva de Aguiar. Lisboa Occidental, na officina Joaquiniana da Musica. M.DCC.XXXVI.

(Commentary on the Siege of Goa and Chaul in the year 1570 in the time of the Viceroy, Dom Luiz de Ataide written by Antonio de Castilho, Keeper of the Torre do Tombo, by order of the King our Lord and now again reprinted by Lucas da Sylva de Aguiar. Lisbon Occidental, in the Office of Joaquiniana da Musica. 1736.)

It was printed in Lisbon in 1573 and again in 1736. This second impression is rare, for to-day there is only one copy of it in the National Library of Lisbon. The work consists of two books of sixteen pages each. The style and subject matter may be judged by the following extracts :

" Não ficou muitos dias na praya por vingar o sangue de D. Fernando, e de seus companheiros porque Antonio Cabral andava ao mesmo tempo no rio de Chapora, com quatro sustas darmada tolhia os mantimentos, que da terra firme acodião ao campo dos Mouros, e a entrada delles em Bardez : teve aviso de algumas destas, como avante pelo rio acima estavão navios de carga, e se fazião almadias, galvetas, e outras embarcaçoẽns que o Hidalcão esperava para o passo de Goa : determinou tomar terra nesta parte, e saindo nella com cincoenta soldados, poz o fogo as aldeias, e embarcaçoẽns, e meteo a fio da espada toda a gente, que se poz em defeza, com tão bravo destroço, q. não ficou em toda esta ribeira mais que o rasteo da sua vitoria."

(He did not stay many days on the shore to revenge the blood of Dom Fernando and his companions, because Antonio Cabral was at the same time sailing in the river Chapora with four ships of the fleet. He intercepted the supplies going from the land to help the Moorish camp, and their entrance into Bardez ; he was warned that there were cargo ships in front up the river and that they were making narrow boats, sloops and other ships for which Adil Shah waited, to march to Goa ; he determined to take the land in this part and advancing from it with 50 soldiers set fire to the villages and ships and put to the sword all the people who defended themselves, with such wild destruction that on the whole of this coast nothing remained but the trail of his victory.)

"Depois ella succedeo outra dos paroas Malabares, que a furto das vigias darmada entrarão no rio de noite, ao longo da terra, em favor do Nisamaluco; e aprazada da sua parte, e da nossa a batalha, fizerão azas dos remos, viradas as proas contra Chaul de cima; espantados do primeiro varejo, ensinarão ao Nisamaluco que perdia o tempo e a esperança; mas elle não esfriava o primeiro fervor. Mandou acestar derredor da Cidade trinta e duas peças dartilheria, e barião por todas as partes em roda, sem amainar de dia, nem de noite a tormenta. Trabalhado Chaul de furia tão brava não ficava outro reparo a gente de guerra, salvo os entulhos daquellas tranqueiras, onde alguns tiros por industria dos Mouros tambem cahião a fio direito. Começou o espanto enfraquecer muitos dos nossos, que vião a profia do cerco, mortes, estragos, incendios, ruinas em todas as partes; e no meyo destes trabalhos o Capitão-Mor esforçava com o rosto de fora, e com palavras alegres as gentes, acodindo a reforçar tranqueiras, segurar repairos, entreter os soldados que queriam fazer mais saidas, do que soffria a falta das muniçoens e a grandeza de tantos perigos."

(After that it happened that other Malabar warships in favour of Nizam-ul-Mulk entered the river at night stealthily avoiding the vigilance of the fleet; and as the battle was delayed both on their part and on ours, they lent wings to their oars, the prows turned against Chaul from up the river; astonished at the first censure, they led Nizam-ul-Mulk to believe that he was losing time and hope but his early enthusiasm did not grow cold. He sent to be placed behind the city 32 pieces of artillery and bombarded around on all sides without ceasing the torment day or night. Chaul was moved by a fury so wild that no other defence remained to the warriors except the mounds of earth of those parapets against some shots which by the efforts of the Moors also had fallen in direct line. Many of our people began to be weakened by the fear of those things which come in the train of a siege, deaths, despoliation, fires, ruins on all sides; the Chief Captain with his face looking outwards and with words of encouragement urged the people on, helping to reinforce trenches and strengthen parapets, holding back the soldiers who desired to make fresh attacks, and who were suffering from the lack of ammunition and the greatness of so many dangers.)

Another celebrated traveller who left behind the story of his wanderings, is Antonio Tenrreyro, a native of Coimbra. The date of his birth is not known; in his early youth he was in India where he not only distinguished himself in his military career, but was ordered to accompany Balthazar Pessoa when the latter was sent as Ambassador to Persia by Dom Duarte de Meneses, Governor of India, in September 1523. This journey gave him the opportunity of becoming acquainted with the countries through which he passed, and as he made himself proficient in Turkish and Persian, another more difficult task was given to him by the Captain of Ormuz. He was sent overland as messenger to Dom João III to inform him that Nuno de Cunha was in Melinde and that the Rumes did not come to India. After a long and adventurous journey, he arrived safely in Portugal in May 1529. King João III received him with great demonstration of joy and affection, praising the valour which he had shown in braving such a perilous journey.

Antonio Tenrreyro.

He wrote a description of it entitled:

> "Itinerario de Antonio Tenrreyro Cavaleiro da Ordem de Christo em que se contem como da India veyo por terra a estes reynos de Portugal. Coimbra, 1560 (Journey of Antonio Terreyro, Knight of the Order of Christ, which he did by land from India to Portugal. Coimbra, 1560.)

A great exponent of Indian Botany was Garcia da Orta, a Doctor in Medicine of the University of Alcala and Salamanca, who was a Professor of Philosophy in the University of Lisbon. The dates of his birth and death are not known, but it is calculated that he died somewhere about 1570. We know, however, that in 1534 he embarked for India with the fleet, the Admiral of which was Martim Affonso de Sousa.

Garcia da Orta.

In the large city of Goa, he lived for nearly thirty years, and, as with a physician's privilege, he visited the Durbars of the Viceroys, the reception rooms of the hospitals and the houses of the poor and the rich alike, he commanded profound esteem and respect and won the confidence not only of the Viceroys but even of the Indian Princes.

He wrote a book which was printed in Goa in 1563, with the title of :

" Colloquios dos simplices e drogas."

(Conversations about herbs and drugs.)

It was at once translated into the principal European languages and a translation of it exists even in English. The chief topic of the book is not medicine, for he deals with many men and matters of his time. In his 'Colloquio' of Ber (Colloquios, 3iv. and following), Garcia da Orta gives detailed information in these sketches about the Kings of India and their titles, which are relatively the most exact which are given to us by Portuguese writers of the sixteenth century. It is from these that results in a great part the knowledge which they had at the time in Europe about those Princes and States, through the resumé made in Latin by Carlo D'Ecluze. (1)

After Martim Affonso de Sousa, the person of whom Garcia da Orta speaks in his book with the greatest respect and apparent affection, is undoubtedly his friend, Nizamaluco, Burhan Nizam Shah. (2) We learn from the 'Colloquios' that he visited him many times, that he passed in his Court long sessions, and that he was treated there with special consideration.

---

(1) Cf. Conde de Ficalhó's "Garcia da Orta e o Seu Tempo", page 222.

(2) 1508-1553, of Ahmednagar.

He used to teach Portuguese to the heir presumptive to the throne. In the journey that he made to meet Nizam Shah and while travelling in his company, he had the opportunity of visiting the principal cities of his state. He tells us that he visited Ahmédnagar, Daulatabad and Chakan. At the Court he was able to observe closely the habits and the daily life of the Asiatics and had occasion to meet and have discussions with the Doctors of Persia, Arabia and of India itself. It was there, as he tells us clearly, that he learned the nature of certain drugs and their names in the various languages then spoken in India.

Garcia da Orta was a true man of science, an antecedent of the old Geoffroy, of the zealous Guibourt, of the humble Dr. Pereira, of the investigator Daniel Hanbury, and of the learned Dr. Flückiger.

In his book "Garcia da Orta e Seu Tempo", Conde de Ficalho says : " In his medical doctrines as in his methods of treatment, Garcia da Orta is always sincere, simple and relatively rational". He also says : "Garcia da Orta describes with great detail Asiatic cholera—noting the serious type of dry cholera, recognizing the necessity of not losing a moment in fighting the attack, prescribing and external treatment, followed today by all the clinics in a general way and prescribing an internal treatment in which he mixes an opiate. All this is simple, rational, well-observed, expounded with clearness sufficient to establish on a secure base the medical reputation of our compatriot."

"Os Colloquios" contains many new things worthy of mention : " haud pauca nova aut memorabilia continet," as a learned writer on Botany, called Sprengel, said in an appreciation of the book, in his " Historia Rei Herbariae, I, 380 ".

This is what Dr. Flückiger wrote in a study on Indian Drugs : " The Colloquios are, above all, notable for their fund of information and for their circumstantial description. No one ever described Indian drugs more carefully, or gathered about them information more valuable than did Garcia da Orta. In spite of his defects which, for the greater part, one should attribute to his time, the 'Colloquios' will occupy a place of honour in the history of Indian drugs."

Francisco de Andrade.

Francisco de Andrade, already mentioned amongst the Poets, was more historian than poet. He wrote:

> "Cronica do Muyto Alto e Muyto Poderoso Rey Destes Reynos de Portugal, Dom João o III deste nome Dirigida H. A. C. R. M; D'Elrey Dom Filippe o III, Composta por Francisco de Andrade do seu Conselho, e seu Cronista Mor. Part I".
>
> (Chronicle of the very high and very powerful King of the Kingdom of Portugal, Dom João III of his name, &c. Compiled by Francisco D'Andrade, the Chief Chronicler of Dom Filippe III, Part I.) In four parts and four volumes, Coimbra, 1796.)

This book besides treating of the Portuguese History in India during the reign of Dom João III, throws new light on the struggles between Ibrahim Adil Shah and Meale Khan, adding to the information given by Ferishta. The author relates facts in a truthful manner. "Thus", he says, "in things relating to India, I followed some copious and widespread facts which came to my hand and which seemed to me more believable than others which I could have, because they were written by an honourable man who said of himself that he came to India a few days after it was discovered, and that he undertook the work of writing the things which happened during the whole course of his life which covered sufficient time and which, moreover, he had seen with his own eyes, because he was present at the time of their happenings; and about those which did not see, he took such accurate information, that he could write as truthfully as if he had seen them; and for this work he did not expect, nor wish to have, any praise or reward, except to write the truths of his history, pure and clean and divested of all respective particulars which could cause some writers, either to embellish poor works which one could not, in full faith rely on, or to praise and overlaud some good works more than they deserve."

Besides this, he wrote the following book :

> "Vida e feitos de Dom Vasco da Gama, descubridor da India, e dos mais Fidalgos daquella familia, que militarão na India."
>
> (Life and deeds of Vasco da Gama, the discoverer o India, and of the other nobles of that family who fought in India.)

This work was written at the instance of Dom Francisco da Gama, Conde de Vidigueira. ([1]) He took the more detailed facts from "Lendas da India" (History of India), written by Gaspar Correa.

Damião de Goes, 1501-1574, Chief Librarian of the Torre do Tombo and Chief Chronicler of the Kingdom,

Damião de Goes.

was born in the town of Alemquer, about 1501. He was a highly cultured man, erudite and artistic, having travelled much in Europe. In 1533, he was nominated Treasurer of the House of India, but he did not accept the place.

João de Barros was assigned the duty of writing the Chronicles of Dom Manuel but he could not for certain reasons do so, and therefore Damião de Goes was given the task. Damião de Goes wrote about the period 1507-1521, till the death of Dom Manuel. He took much about Dom Manuel from the work of Barros in

---

([1]) Dom Francisco da Gama, Conde de Vidigueira, the 16th. Viceroy, governed Portuguese India till 1600.

"Decadas de Asia", which were at that time already published. His book was called :

"Chronica d'El Rei Dom Manuel". [1]

(Chronicle of the King Dom Manuel).

The Chronicle was printed for the first time in 1556-1557.

The first part of the Chronicle of Dom Manuel contains a narrative of the great events of the Portuguese of the fifteenth century, and of the first years of the sixteenth. In it the deeds in Africa and the wonderful Asiatic voyages are spoken of. One finds therein the names of Vasco da Gama, Pedro Alvares Cabral, Duarte Pacheco, Afonso de Albuquerque and Tristão de Cunha.

The second part speaks of the work of Dom Francisco de Almeida in India.

In the third part, we read about Diogo de Lopes de Sequeira and Afonso de Albuquerque in Goa, and about the execution of the vast political and economic plan of Albuquerque.

In the fourth part is described the episode of the fight of the elephants with rhinoceroses, animals which had been sent them from India. The "Overseas" predominates in the whole Chronicle.

In Volume II chapter 42, about belief, doctrine, ceremonies and customs of the Kanarese, Brahmans, Nairs and about the geographical position of Malabar and of the City of Calicut, he bases his remarks almost entirely on Duarte Barbosa. Damião de Goes says: "They (the Brahmins) are for the greater part men gifted in Philosophy and Mathematics, which

---

(1) Bibliotheca de Clássicos Portugueses, Vol. L. IX.
See Barcelona Encyclopidae for list of works of Damião de Goes.

sciences were very ancient in India, because, when Alexander arrived in India, these sciences were known and had been so long in existence that no one knows when they began."

" Speaking of Timoja, a native of Onor and a pirate, Damião de Goes says that it was through his advice that Vasco da Gama turned towards Angediva. (1) The efforts of the Mahomedans to expel the Portuguese, are spoken of, they, for this end, constructing more ships in the port of Goa. He says that Timoja informed Albuquerque who immediately destroyed the fleet and took Goa. The tolerance of Adil Shah, a Shiah, towards Hindus, who in Goa occupied high positions, is mentioned.

The book of Damião de Goes also throws light on the civil administration of the first Adil Shah. Thus in Chapter III, he tells us that every person who entered Goa was registered as an immigrant with all the marks of one. "About this island, the Çabaio and his son took great care and not a man entered it unless he was registered with his identification marks, the place from where he came, and the name of his parents. For this they had officials in Panjim, Agacim, Benestarim, Gondalim, and Duagasim, which are only a short distance from where one enters the island." (2) He refers to the docks where they built the ships of Goa, (3) and he also refers to Conçalim. Damião de Goes, in Chapter VI, treats of " some things in the districts of Narsinga, the power of the King and the order of his household." The description which the chronicler

---

(1) Damião Goes, Vol. II, Chap. 43, p. 15.

(2) Chronica d'El-Rei D. Manuel, Third part, Chap. III, Page 99.

(3) Chronica d'El-Rei D. Manuel, Third part, Chap. IV. Page 102.

makes of the city of Vijianagar is interesting. "There everything is majestic, grand ......"

The Chronicle was so faithfully, impartially and well written, that some critics place him at the head of the classic writers following João de Barros.

Besides these authors whose works on India are of the utmost historical and literary value, there is a large number of minor writers, such as Lopo de Sousa Coutinho, Fabiam da Mota, Diogo Botelho Pereira, Luiz de Barros d'Silva and Belchior Nunes Barreto, who have written on subjects in connection with India.

Lopo de Sousa Coutinho.

Lopo de Sousa Coutinho was born between 1514 and 1515. He was eighteen years old when he went to India leaving for that place in 1532 or 1533. He distinguished himself greatly by his bravery in the siege of Diu in 1538, and published his book called:

> "Livro primeiro do cerco de Diu, que os Turcos puzeram a fortaleza de Diu."
>
> (First book of the Siege of Diu, which the Turks made to the Fortress of Diu.) Coimbra, 1556.

In proof of his being a man of great knowledge and austere truthfulness, it is enough to say that João de Barros accepted and made use of what he wrote.

Father Gastão.

Father Gastão was a Member of the Order of Preachers (Pregadores), and also of the Congregation of Oriental India, where he served for many years principally in the Factory of Cruz. He wrote a letter to commemorate the heroic deed of Duarte Pacheco Pereira, which he performed against the King of Calicut, defeating his formidable fleets which were sent against the State. He also wrote:

"Tratado da Guerra entre os Reyos de Cochim e Calicut. (1)

(Treatise on the war between the King of Cochin and Calicut.)

This work is mentioned in Decada II, Book VII, Chapter VIII, of Barros, who says :

"a qual guerra durou seis meses a neste tempo entre o Çamorij e el Rey de Cochij ouve cartas, recados e outras meudezas segundo ɔ q. escreueo frey Gastão hum religioso que estaua na feitoria com os nossos em hũ tractado que fez da guerra entre estes dous Reys : de que sómente tomamos o necessario com outra maes informação porq. em todo o discurso desta Asia maes trabalhamos no substancial da historia q. no ampliar as meudezas que enfadão y não deleitão."

(That war lasted six months and in this time, between the Zamorim and the King of Cochin, there passed letters, messages and other documents, containing detailed information according to which Father Gastão, a monk who was in the Factory with our people, wrote a treatise about the war between the two kings: from which we took only the necessary portions together with other information because in all the discourse about this part of Asia, we cared more for the actual historical facts, than for increasing the insignificant details which beautify the work without making it clear.)

This work is also mentioned by John Franco Bar reto in a manuscript contained in the Biblioteca Nac ional, Lisbon, and also by Father Pedro Monteiro, Cla ustri Dominicani , Vol. III, page 224.

---

(1) This book is lost. We searched in Lisbon in all the libraries for a trace of this treatise of which Barros speaks and which is mentioned in the Bibliotheca Lusitana of Barbosa. It is the opinion of research workers in Lisbon that the said manuscript must have disappeared with many others in the earthquake of 1755.

Father Fernando de Santa Maria was born in Villa Viçosa. He belonged to the Sacred Institute of the Order of Preachers (Pregadores), and took the degree of Bachelor of Theology. He became a member of the Mission in India, and was so enthusiastic in making converts in the Kingdom of Cambay and the island of Solor, that he became Prior of the Convent of Goa, and the Vicar-General of the Congregation of India, which place he held with exemplary dignity and prudence. He died in September 1586, being 70 years of age. He wrote :

Father Fernando de Santa Maria. 1516-1586.

> " Historia do Cerco de Goa, governando a India Dom Luiz de Athayde." (1568-1571)
>
> (History of the siege of Goa during the governorship of Dom Luiz de Atayde in India.)

Belchior de Moraes was a native of Tavira in the kingdom of Algarve. He was most experienced in nautical affairs owing to the number of times he had filled the office of pilot during his long career in India. In order to facilitate the work of pilots, he wrote :

Belchior de Moraes.

> " Roteiro de Portugal para a India, e da India para Portugal em a náo de Santo Antonio Nebry des 3 de Agosto de 1576."
>
> (Log-book of the journey from Portugal to India and from India to Portugal in the ship St. Antonio Nebry, 3rd. August 1576).

Fabiam da Motta was born in Bombarral near Lisbon. He was a noble by birth being the son of the poet Henrique de Motta who figures in the Cancioneiro of Garcia de Rezende. [1] He left for the East with the Viceroy, Dom Garcia de Noronha, in India,

Fabiam da Motta.

---

[1] Nobiliario de Rangel Macedo. Collecção Pombalina, 387, fls. 388.

in the year 1538. During his long stay of twenty years in India, holding the office of the Commissioner of Customs in Goa and filling various military posts where he gained immortal glory, he wrote :

> " Historia da India em que se relatão as acçoens de Vice-Rey Dom Garcia de Noronha, até o governo de Francisco Barreto. 1558. "

> (History of India in which is related the actions of the Viceroy Dom Garcia de Noronha till the time of the Governor Francisco Barreto. 1558.)

Diogo Botelho Pereira.

Diogo Botelho Pereira was born in India. He was the son of Antonio Real, who was Captain of Cochin, at the time when Francisco de Almeida was Governor. (1505-1509). As a boy he showed great ability especially for Science, and applied himself with great diligence to Mathematics, Geography, and the study of all nautical things in which he became expert. For some time he was a distinguished soldier in India, and, wishing the reward for his service, went to Portugal, where the King, Dom João III, made him a noble of his household. But, as he refused the Captaincy of Chaul, he offended the King who sent him degraded to India with the fleet which left Portugal in 1524, according to Castanheda's " Historia da India ", Book VIII, Chapter 14, or, according to Diogo de Couto's Decada V, Book II, Chapter 5, and Francisco de Andrade's "Chronica de Dom João III ", Part II, Chapter 13, in the Armada in which Vasco da Gama left.

As soon as Diogo Botelho Pereira arrived in India, he tried to find some way of proving his fidelity, as he had been falsely accused in the eyes of the Sovereign. Knowing the great joy that the King Dom João III would have with the certainty of the establishing of the fortress of Diu by the Governor, Nuno da Cunha, because it was a key to the entrance to the Kingdom of

Cambay, he (Diogo Botelho Pereira) determined to be the bearer of the happy news and, in order to effect this, he built in Cochin a small boat with sails and oars, thirty-two spans in length, twelve in width and six in height, and, embarking in it accompanied by five Portuguese and some of his slaves, left Dabul on the 1st. of November 1535 without saying where he was going till they were out on the high seas, when he declared his intention of going to Lisbon.

Botelho Pereira doubled the Cape of Good Hope on the 20th. of January 1536. No words can describe the dangers to which he was exposed on the journey, which, besides being so prolonged, threatened to have a tragic end, owing to the vessel being so small. It was many times covered by waves and very nearly overturned. Ultimately he was deserted by his companions who, tormented with hunger and thirst, resolved to kill him and, in the tumult which followed, he received a wound on his head. He was hoarse for many days in consequence of having to shout to keep the men quiet, and he had to guide the bark by gestures until he recovered his voice.

Triumphant over the dangers of the sea and the infidelity of his companions, he arrived in Lisbon in May 1536, and, knowing that the King was at Almeirim, went in his pinnace up the Tagus to Salbateria, and appearing before the King, explained that the reason which had moved him to undertake such a dangerous journey was to exonerate himself from the false charge with which his enemies had accused him, the charge that he preferred the service of the King of France to that of Portugal.

He showed the fortress drawn with his own hands, built by Nuno da Cunha in Diu, and recounted the terms of peace which had been drawn up by Sultan Bahadur King of Cambay. This news so pleased the King that he rewarded him with the Captaincy of St.

Thomé. He then went to Cannanore.

Diogo Botelho Pereira wrote "Carta de Marear" in which he described the world as it was at the time of the discovery of the way to India by sea. He presented this book to the King, Dom João III, the first time he returned to Portugal.

He also wrote :

> "Descrição da Forteleza de Diu fundada pelo governador Nuno de Cunha, e Relaçãc das Pazes celebradas com El Rey de Cambaya Sultão Bahadur."
>
> (A description of the fortress of Diu founded by the Governor, Nuno de Cunha, and of the terms of peace arranged with the King of Cambay Sultan Bahadur.)

This work is spoken of by Francisco de Andrade in the "Chronicas de Rei João III", in Part III, Chapter 13, as follows: "As he was a skilled engineer (speaking of Diogo Botelho Pereira), he took all the measurements of the fortress, recording the height, width and length of the walls and of the moat, and remembered accurately all the particulars about it, and the number of pieces of artillery which were placed there, and of all the rest that seemed to him necessary for a complete account to the King, if he wished to speak of it; and had at hand the transcription of the conditions on which they made peace, so that there should be nothing left for which he would not be able to give an explanation."

Father Pedro Martins.

Father Pedro Martins was a native of the city of Coimbra and son of Pedro Afonso and Barbara Fernandes. He was admitted to the Company of Jesus when he was fourteen years old on the 25th. of May, 1556. After studying Sciences and Arts, he received the degree of Doctor of Theology on the 16th. of July, 1573. He wrote :

"Relação do naufragio que padeceo nos baixos chamados da India."

(An account of the shipwreck which he suffered in the shoals of India.)

This account serves as a basis for Fr. Pierre du Jarric's "Histoire", part II, Book I, Chapters XI and XII.

Father Francisco Rodrigues.

From the pen of Father Francisco Rodrigues we have the following letters:

1. "Carta escrita de Goa a 12 de Dezembro de 1557 em que refere o estado espiritual de Goa, e a conversão da filha del Rey de Meale."

   (A letter written from Goa on the 12th. December, 1557, in which he refers to the spiritual state of Goa, and the conversion of the daughter of King Meale.) It was translated into Latin with others in Venice in 1559.

2. "Carta ao P. Leão Henriques, Reytor do Collegio de Evora, escrita de Goa a 5 de Dezembro de 1560."

   (A letter to Father Leão Henriques, Rector of the College of Evora, written from Goa on the 15th. of December 1560.) A part of this letter was transcribed by Father Franco.

Father Balthazar Dias was a member of the Sacred Company of Jesus, and one of the great missionaries of the Orient. He left Portugal on the 24th. of March 1553 in the ship "St. Bento". Arriving in the city of Goa he was nominated by Father Belchior Nunes Barreto, Vicar of that Province. He was most successful in his evangelic preaching, his audience being so numerous that it was necessary to preach in tents and fields, because the temples were not big enough for such a large congregation. He wrote:

Father Balthazar Dias.

1. "Carta escrita de Goa de 15 de Dezembro de 1555 ao Santo Ignacio."

   (Letter from Goa on the 15th. December, 1555, to Father St. Ignatius.)

2. "Carta para o P. Belchior Nunes Barreto, em que relata o martyrio de V. P. Affonso de Castro e trinta Christãos em 1558."

(Letter from Father Belchior Nunes Barreto, in which he relates the martyrdom of V. P. Affonso de Castro and thirty Christians in 1558.)

Father Luiz Froes.

Father Luiz Froes was the son of José Affonso de Beja, a noble of the house of Infante D. Luiz (son of the King Dom Manuel) and of his wife Lucrecia Froes Pereira, a brother of Nuno Roiz of Beja, a Father of the Company of Jesus. He was in India many years before going to Japan. He afterwards accompanied some Japanese Princes to Rome. (1) He returned to Japan where he died in 1597.

Amongst a large number of letters, we have :

1. "Carta escrita de Goa 30 de Novembro de 1557." 12 fol.

(Letter written from Goa on the 30th. of November, 1557.). It has been translated into Italian with others.

2. "Primeira carta de Goa do Irmão Luiz Froes sobre a conversão da filha do Rey de Meale de 12 de Dezembro de 1557."

(First letter from Goa by Father Luiz Froes about the conversion of the daughter of the King of Meale, dated 12th. December, 1557.)

3. "Duas cartas escritas de Goa aos Padres do Collegio de Coimbra em Novembro de 1559".

(Two letters written from Goa to the Priests of the College of Coimbra, in November 1559). They were translated into Italian with others at Venice in 1562.

---

(1) Luiz Froes. Rome.

Vide Mobiliario de Rangel Macedo, Collecção Pombalina, 378, flo. 88 and 89. Bibliotheca Nacional, Lisbon.

4. "Carta escrita de Goa ao Padre Geral em primeiro de Dezembro 1560, outra escrita em 8 do dito mez aos Padres de Portugal."

(Letter written from Goa to the Father General on the 1st. of December 1560, and another written on the 8th. of the same month to the Priests in Portugal.)

5. "Segunda carta de Goa do Irmão Luis Froes sobre a conversão da filha do Rey de Meale de 12 Dezembro de 1560."

(Second letter from Goa by Father Luis Froes about the conversion of the King of Meale, dated 12th. December, 1560.) (1)

6. "Carta escrita de Goa a 13 de Dezembro de 1560."

(Letter written from Goa on the 13th. of December 1560). Translated into Latin and printed at Venice in 1562.

7. "Duas cartas escritas de Goa no primeiro de Dezembro de 1561, aos Padres de Portugal."

(Two letters written from Goa on the first of December 1561 to the Priests in Portugal). Translated with others into Italian at Venice in 1561.

---

(1) The first and second letters are the same with only a slight difference of words and dates, as we noted in comparing them both in the Library of the Academia das Ciências and in the Biblioteca of Ajuda. Father Luiz Froes gives us the following information about Meale Khan (the same Meale Khan of Farishta): "Meale is an Arab already advanced in years, prudent and experienced and according to the opinion of the Arabs, a great observer of Islam and well-versed in the Traditions and the Quran."

(Cod. 49. iv. Fol. 506)

See my article "Jesuits in Asia, Letter of Luiz Froes", 1931.

8. "Carta escrita de Goa em 16 Dezembro 1561 aos Padres de Portugal, e em que trata do martyrio do Padre Gonçalo de Silveira."

(Letter written from Goa on the 16th. of December, 1561, to the Priests of Portugal, in which he treats of the martyrdom of the Priest, Gonçalo da Silveira). Translated into Latin in 1588.

The manuscripts were in the Collection of Evora, but now they are to be found in the Biblioteca of the Academia das Ciências, Lisbon.

Father Luiz de Gouvea.

Father Luiz de Gouvea was a member of the Company of Jesus, which esteemed Order he joined in 1552, when he was twenty six years old. He wrote the following letters:

1. "Carta escrita de Coulão a 25 de Fevereiro de 1560 aos Padres de Goa."

(A letter from Coulão written on the 25th. of February 1560, to the Priests of Goa.)

2. "Carta escrita de Coulão em Domingo de Palmas de dito ano aos mesmos Padres."

(A letter written from Coulão on Palm Sunday of the same year to the same Priests.)

3. "Carta escrita de Coulão a 19 de Mayo de dito anno."

(A letter written from Coulão on the 19th. of May of the same year.)

4. "Carta escrita de Cochim para o Provincial no anno de 1561; aos Irmãos da Companhia."

(A letter written from Cochin for the Provincial in the year 1561, to the Brothers of the Company.)

5. "Carta escrita em 8 de Janeiro 1563 aos Padres de Portugal"

(A letter written on the 8th. of January 1563 to the Priests of Portugal.)

6. "Carta escrita a 12 de Janeiro de 1564, aos Padres de Casa de S. Roque de Lisboa."

(A letter written on the 12th. of January 1564, to the Priests of Casa de S. Roque of Lisbon).

João Nunes Barreto.

The letters of João Nunes Barreto, who was a native of Oporto, are interesting from the Indian standpoint. He wrote:

1. "Carta escrita de Goa em o primeiro de Dezembro de 1556 a El Rey, Dom João III."

(Letter written from Goa on the 1st. of December 1556 to the King, Dom João III). It is very long and the original is kept in the Archives of Casa Professa of St. Roque in Lisbon.

2. "Carta escrita de Goa ao Padre Luiz Gonsalves de Camara a 6 de Novembro de 1556."

(Letter written from Goa to the Priest Luiz Gonsalves de Camara on the 6th. of November 1556.)

Father Ayres Brandam.

Another writer of letters on Indian subjects was Father Ayres Brandam. We do not know his birthplace. He was admitted to the Company of Jesus in Goa in the year 1552, when he was twenty-three years old. He wrote:

"Carta de Goa, escrita em 23 de Dezembro de 1554 aos Irmãos da Companhia de Jesus, em que narra a morte de S. Francisco Xavier, e como o seu corpo fora recebido em Goa."

(Letter from Goa dated the 23rd. December 1554 to the Brothers of the Company of Jesus, in which he narrates the death of St. Francis Xavier, and how his body was received in Goa.) It was printed with others, which the Archbishop, Dom Theotonio de Bragança, published in 1598.

Fr. Jorge Caldeyra.

Father Jorge Caldeyra, a Jesuit who joined the priesthood in Goa on the 4th. of November 1559, wrote:—

1. "Carta escrita de Goa a 11 de Dezembro de 1564."
(Letter from Goa dated the 11th. of December 1564).

2. " Carta escrita de Goa a 6 de Dezembro 1565. "
(Letter from Goa dated the 6th. of December 1565.)

Father Gaspar Villela

Father Gaspar Villela was born in the town of Aviz in Traz-os-Montes. He was educated in the Convent of Ordem Militar de S. Bento, and joined the Company of Jesus, and with Father Belchior Nunes Barreto left for India in 1551, as a missionary. In 1554, he went to Japan where he made many converts and there he built three churches. In 1571, he returned to Goa. He had learned the Japanese language in which he not only used to preach but also to write. He wrote, besides others, the following letters which contain new references on Indian History :

1. " Carta escrita de Cochim a 24 de Abril 1554 aos Irmãos do Collegio de Coimbra. " (1)
(Letter written from Cochin daded the 24th. April 1554 to the Brothers of the College in Coimbra.)

2. " Carta escrita de Cochim a 4 de Fevereiro de 1571 aos Padres da Companhia de Portugal. " Evora, 1598. (2)
(Letter written from Cochin dated the 4th. of February 1571 to the Fathers of the Company in Portugal.)

3. " Carta escrita de Cochim a 4 de Fevereiro de 1571 para hum Irmão da Companhia. " Evora, 1598. (3)
(Letter written from Cochin dated the 4th. of February 1571 to a Brother of the Company.)

---

(1) It was published in the book "Cartas do Japão", Vol. I, printed in Evora by Manoel da Lyra, 1598. A manuscript copy exists in " Cartas do Japão " in the Academia das Sciencias of Lisbon. (fls. 260 and 261). Translated into Latin by Father Manoel da Costa.

(2) We saw a copy of this letter in the Biblioteca of Ajuda (Portugal).

(3) A copy of this letter is found in the Biblioteca of Ajuda.

4. " Carta escrita de Goa a 6 de Outubro de 1571 aos Padres do Convento de Aviz em Portugal. " Evora, 1598.

(Letter written from Goa dated the 6th. of October 1571, to the Fathers of the Convent of Aviz in Portugal.)

5. " Carta de Goa a 20 de Outubro de 1571. " Evora, 1598.

(Letter from Goa dated the 20th. of October 1571." (1)

Fr. Amador Rebello.

Also worthy of mention are :

" Alguns capitulos tirados das cartas que vieram este anno de 1588 dos Padres da Companhia de Jesus ". Lisboa, 1588.

(Some chapters taken from letters which came this year of 1588 from the Fathers of the Company of Jesus). Lisbon, 1588.

and

" Compendio de algumas cartas que este anno de 1597 vieram dos Padres da Companhia de Jesus que residem na India ...... 1598, Lisboa ",

(Compendium of some letters which came this year, 1597, from the Fathers of the Company of Jesus, who live in India ...... 1598, Lisbon),

which were written by Father Amador Rebello.

Chrónica de Guzerate.

While in Lisbon, we saw a most interesting manuscript called :

" Chronica Geral dos Sucessos do Reyno de Guzerate a que chamão Cambay."

(General Chronicle of the Events of the Kingdom of Guzerate which is called Cambay.)

Ms. No. 299, F. G. 1 Vol. in 4° of 98 folios, Biblioteca Nacional, Lisbon.

The Chronicle consists of 41 folios and is the first part of the manuscript which also contains the :

---

(1) There is a copy in the Biblioteca of Ajuda and also in the Biblioteca Nacional, Lisbon. (Secção dos Reservados. cod. 586.)

" Descrição Geral de Todas as Costas, Reinos, e Ilhas da India ".

(General Description of all the Coasts, Kingdoms and Islands of India.) 42-98 folios, with folios 42-47 missing.

There was also a third part called " Chronica Troyana ", (Chronicle of Troy), but this has been separated from the volume.

The " Chronica de Guzerate " was written in 1535, (1) by an anonymous author.

The Chronicle opens by speaking of events which were taking place in the kingdom of Guzerat after the death of Sultan Modafar. The narrative continues till the date, 17th. November 1535, when Sultan Bahadur, hard pressed by the Moghul King, withdrew to the fortress of Diu, to await help from the Portuguese in order to prevent his being captured, together with his wives and mother.

The details are now generally known through the article by Sir Denisson Ross, published in the Cambridge History of India, Volume III, Chapter XIII, which is based on the said Chronicle.

In the Historical Archive of Nova Goa, I examined a curious manuscript entitled " Tombo de Chaul e Diu ". In it one finds important data for the economic history of Guzerat during the sixteenth century, supplementing in part the information which the " Chronica de Guzerate " gives.

Tombo de Chaul e Diu.

The " Tombo " of the fortress of Diu was written by Simão Botelho. It consists of 50 folios and was

---

(1) Cf. " .... omde agora esta aos xbij de Nouembro de 1535 annos." (.................. where he is now on 17th. November 1535).

(" Chronica de Guzerate ".)

compiled in 1592. The following is the summary of its contents:

> Contracts made with the Kings of Cambay. Goanese customs duties. Declarations about the Customs of Diu and its claims. Customs of Gogola. Income from Indigo. Income from the fisheries, etc.

It begins: " In a very ancient book, the 'Tombo', compiled by the Revenue Commissioner, Simão Botelho, are set forth the contracts noted before on the margin."

CHAPTER II.

The Gongoric School, 1580-1706.

The period of the Renaissance, as is well-known in the history of literature, was followed by a rapid decline. All over Europe the same decadence was noticeable. In England, the school of Euphuism sprang up, evincing bad taste and extravagance in language and the choice of literary subjects. France had its school of Preciosity which was imported from Italy where Marino, 1569-1625, became the head of a galaxy of stars known as the Marinistas. He corrupted the Italian literary taste by his abuse of antithesis and hyperbole. In Spain, Luis de Gongora, 1516-1627, wrote in a lyrical and narrative style full of obscure and ridiculous metaphors and he gave the name to the Gongoric school which included the writers in Spain of his time.

Political and literary decadence.

As Portugal was part of the Peninsula and in such close proximity to Spain, it naturally suffered from the Spanish literary influence; but, besides this, there was another more potent cause for the decline of Portuguese literature in the accession of the Spanish kings to the Portuguese throne. The kingdom of Portugal which had become independent of Castillian power under Afonso Henriques, now succumbed to Spanish domination and the great oriental Portuguese empire which had already shown symptoms of decline, began to break up. The Spanish rulers had not that interest in preserving the eastern empire intact, which the true Portuguese sovereigns had felt. Political errors were causing permanent wars and the territory recently added to the eastern dominions was neither organized nor properly consolidated. The governors, who had been sent out, cared only to exploit the country and return home enriched by their spoils.

Such was the political state of India at the time of the accession of the Spanish kings. During their rule, their influence in Portugal was so powerful that many Portuguese writers began to write in Spanish, so much so that even on India there are books written by Portuguese authors in the Spanish tongue. (1) But though Portuguese literature was rapidly sinking to a low level, a few works written in India about that country maintained a higher standard. The influence of the Jesuit Fathers also, who had come to India in 1542 and spread the treasures of their learning and their schools all over the different parts of the Portuguese

---

(1) As for example the works of Father Sebastião Manrique Maya, a native of Oporto, who wrote :

"Itinerario de las Missoens de la India Oriental com una summaria relacion del grande, y opulento Imperio del Emperador, Xauxiahan Corrombo, Gran Mogol y de outros Reys infiels, en cuyos Reinos assisten los Religiosos de S. Augustin."

(Itinerary of the Missions of Oriental India, with a summary of the relations with the great and opulent Mogul Emperor, Shah Jehan, and other kings in whose kingdom the monks of St. Augustine lived.) Published in Rome at the instance of Guillelmo Halle in 1653.

Another writer worthy of mention is Manuel de Faria e Sousa, (1590-1649). His work concerning India is entitled : "Asia Portugueza". It was translated into English and published under the title of "Portuguese Asia" : or the History of the discovery and conquests of India by the Portuguese", by Captain J. Stevens. London, 1694 and 1695 in 3 volumes.

possessions, helped to maintain the high literary standard. These indefatigable priests had introduced the art of printing into Goa in 1556, the first work which was published being "Conclusiones Philosophicas" (Philosophical Conclusions), followed by the Catechism written by the great Francisco Xavier. At the same time the first verses of Camões were given to be printed in the same press.

Not only the Fathers of the Company of Jesus, but all missionaries, though of various nationalities, wrote in Portuguese, which was the most widely known European language in India at the time, a phenomenon very easily explained. Some time after the arrival of the Portuguese in India, their tongue modified and simplified, became the *lingua franca*, the common means of communication between the Europeans and other nationalities, and between the people themselves speaking different languages. (1) And this explains why Manucci, the renowned Italian traveller, wrote a part of his Memoirs in Portuguese, which is contained in his "Storia do Mogor", and which was afterwards translated by Irvine. (2) In 1663, a Portuguese priest

---

(1) See Dalgado's "Glossario", p. 17.

(2) Manucci knew Portuguese to the point of writing in this language a part of the "Storia do Mogor" (History of the Moghuls), entitled "Guerra de Golconda e Visapour com varios successos até a era do 1700". 3 vols. (War of Golconda and Bijapur with various events till the era 1700).

Portugueses e Maratas, Vol. II, Sambhaji, by Professor Pissurlencar.—Bragança & Co., Nova Goa, p. 53, Note 3.

From the Berlin Codex of Manucci, Introduction, Vol. I, p. XXXII one learns that the wars of Golconda and Bijapur form the second volume of his "Storia do Mogor".

I had the pleasure of examining the 1715 edition of Father François Catrou's work "Histoire générale de l'Empire du Mogol depuis sa fondation jusqu'à present sur les mémoires Portugais de M. Manouchi, Venitien". Manucci ascribes the change from

asked some French missionaries who intended to go from Surat to China, "But after leaving Surat, in what language will you have to explain yourselves?" The reply was, "In the Portuguese language which is the common language; because they neither know nor learn French. Latin and French are equally unknown to the people of the country." (1)

Influence of the Jesuits on the literature about India.

The Jesuits spent much time and energy in studying the various languages (2) of the country with the object of being able the more easily to conduct their religious propaganda. They devoted themselves to these studies with such zeal, that Father Stephens, an English priest who was in Salsete and Goa for thirty years, was the author of the first grammar of the modern languages of India and also the writer of a brilliant poem popularly known as the Christian Purana, (3) published in 1640, Goa, in Marathi with a mixture of Concani words.

Portuguese into French or vice-versa to the necessity of using a language understood by his amanuensis of the moment.

(1) See P. Manuel Godinho's "Relação do Novo Caminho que fez por terra e mar, vindo da India para Portugal", 2a. ed., Lisboa, 1842, p. 45.

(2) See C. Rivara's "Ensaio Historico da Lingua Concani", Nova Goa, 1858, p. 792.

(3) Father Thomas Stephens (the first Englishman in India) was born at Bulstan in the diocese of Salisbury, about the year 1549. He left Lisbon in April 1579 and arrived at Goa in October of the same year. He acquired a complete mastery of Sanskrit and the local vernaculars—Marathi and Concani—and composed several works in the vernaculars and in Portuguese for the benefit of missionaries and converts. Of his compositions, there remain to us only the Concani Catechism of the Christian Doctrine, a Grammar in Portuguese of the Concani language, which was the first Grammar of an Indian language by a European, and the great Puran. ("The Indian Caste, Konkani, or Goan Castes", by J. A. Saldanha, B.A., L.L.B.).

Through their religious and political missions, the Jesuits came in contact with the courts of various Indian states so that the information which they received and circulated had great importance. Regarding the importance of the works of the Jesuit Fathers, Vincent Smith says: "The Fathers were highly educated men, trained for accurate observation and scholarly writing". (1)

The opinion of Vincent Smith is corroborated by the works of Father Hosten, Father Heras and others. Though it is true that some of the Jesuits wrote in Latin, many, however, wrote in Portuguese.

One cannot expect to find in this period of decadence, works on India of the same value as those of the brilliant period which preceded it, whether on account of the general decline in literature or whether for the reason that the subject of the discoveries had already been dealt with exhaustively and the impressions awakened in the minds of the people had ceased to stimulate them. Withal, there are many writers who have left works of much importance when regarded in the light of sources for the writing of the history of India.

There were apparently no lyric poets of note who wrote about India during this period. There were many epic poets but they are immeasurably distant from the adorable Camões and the greater number of them have been forgotten. At this time Camões was widely read and appreciated and during the Spanish domination, the 'Lusiadas' was reprinted no less than thirty-six times.

Epic poets.

---

(1) Vincent Smith, "Akbar the Great Mogul: 1542-1605" Oxford, 1919. p. 7.

Francisco de Sá de Meneses, of Oporto, ?-1664, was the author of "Malacca Conquistada", the hero of which is Afonso de Albuquerque and the scene of action the oriental metropolis which gives its name to the poem. Garrett praises this work very highly but there are also those who say that it is the worst of the Portuguese epic poems. The hero of the poem, as well as the secondary personages, is well delineated, and the poem contains a few descriptions of the manners and customs of Oriental people. But its value from a historical point of view is unfortunately insignificant because it is full of gross inaccuracies of facts, exaggerations and high flown metaphors which demonstrate only too well the pernicious influence of the time.

Francisco de Sá de Meneses.

There was, however, no lack of historians in this epoch, a few of them especially in the beginning of the period, being worthy successors of men like João de Barros and Damião de Goes.

Historians and Travellers.

The chroniclers of the preceding century were audacious travellers who spared no pains to verify their statements. But the majority of the historians of the seventeenth century were priests, who, apart in the serenity and solitude of their cells, wrote coldly and dispassionately in elegantly turned phrases, of facts of which they had no first-hand knowledge; and thus their work was characterised by a lack of simplicity, life and colour.

Of the historians who belonged to the beginning of the period, Bocarro is the most important, for his Decada XIII is a continuation of the Decadas of João de Barros and Diogo de Couto. The dates of his birth or death are not known, but he was known to be still living in 1635. He was the Chief Librarian of the Royal Archives, and Chronicler General of India, in

Antonio Bocarro.

which office he was not only the successor of Diogo de Couto in investigating and examining documents, but also in the style in which he wrote and continued the " Decadas of India."

Decada XIII of the History of India was written by him and published under the direction of Rodrigo José de Lima Felner, Lisbon, 1876. The work of Antonio Bocarro to which he gave the name of Decada I, narrates the events which took place in the Portuguese State of India during the five years of the viceroyalty of Dom Jeronymo de Azevedo from 1612 to 1617. and does not link up, as the author wished, with the Decadas of Diogo de Couto.

Between the Chronicles of these two writers there is an interval of twelve years during which time the governors, Ayres de Saldanha, D. Martin Affonso de Castro, Dom Frei Aleixo de Menezes, André Furtado de Mendonça and Ruy Lourenço de Tavora ruled in turn.

In order to fill up this gap, the Academia das Sciencias, Lisbon, determined to publish a part of the "Documentos remettidos da India", or " Livros das Monções", with a view to amplify and confirm what Bocarro had written about Dom Jeronymo Azevedo. These documents were printed in three volumes with the title of " Documentos remettidos da India " under the direction of R. A. de Bulhão Pato—Volume I, Lisbon 1880, Volume II, 1884, and Volume III ,1885,—documents which were kept in the National Archives of the Torre de Tombo of Lisbon and form a part of the first nine books of the sixty-two existing there. This collection comprises original documents and authentic copies. (1)

---

(1) We know with respect to these books, that they were sent from the Secretariat of the General Portuguese Government of India to Lisbon with other books and papers of different

"The title of Decada XIII does not appear to us", says Bulhão Pato, "to be given by Bocarro, who called his work in the first volume, Decada I, and, in the second volume, Decada II. Besides this, the date of the dedicatory letter of the second volume is 1635. Decada XII of Diogo de Couto was published for the first time in 1645.

That Antonio Bocarro was a most conscientious writer is clearly seen from the way in which he reveals to us the difficulties which he could not overcome for want of necessary documents, and the evidence of important facts by eye-witnesses, who were no longer alive.

He is always impartial and severe in his appreciation of men and things. He neither hides the wickedness inherent in the principal personages of his time, nor conceals the state of decadence to which the Portuguese power had fallen in India.

Bocarro describes in his works scenes enacted twenty years before his time. In this Decada XIII is lightly sketched a person who has the most lively interest for us. It is an Englishman—called Shirley, which Bocarro writes as Sarley—an intelligent, clever and audacious man who, sent to Spain by the Shah of Persia (1603), now is represented as ambassador, now as merchant. After being for some years in Madrid, he disappears suddenly from the Court, leaves for England and reveals to his government the reason why he went to Spain. (1)

---

corporations, according to the Royal order dated the 10th. February 1774. On the 21st. April 1777, the boxes containing these volumes were sent from the Secretariat of India to Portugal. On examining the respective books with relation to the dates one can see that, besides those of the years complete from 1605 to 1651, there are some detached documents which date up till the year 1699. (Vide T. Aragão's "Descripção das Moedas". Vol. III.)

(1) "E assy mandou na era de 1603 a Hespanha a Sua

In his Decada there are valuable records for the history of the first struggles of the English with the Portuguese for the sovereignty of the Indian seas, and also we find given reasons why the English were

---

Magestade, por embaixador com as suas primeiras pretençoes, um dom Roberto Sarley, de Nação ingles, que tinha assistido muitos annos com elle ; homem de notavel astucia e invenção quasi n'isto conforme a natureza do mesmo Xá. Este, depois de assistir em Madrid alguns annos, tractado e respeitado como embaixador de um rei tão poderoso, desappareceu da corte, e se foi a Inglaterra sua patria, e communicou com o rei d'ella a materia da embaixada que tinha trazido a Hespanha ; parece que por ordem do mesmo Xá, convidando aos ingrezes com o contracto da seda, debaixo de lhe prometterem, como depois de entender, de o ajudarem com as suas naus contra nos, pera tomar a fortaleza de Ormuz. Os ingrezes que depois que começaram a declinar da verdadeira fé catholica romana de Christo Nosso Senhor, não repararam em crime nem abominação contra os catholicos, vieram de mui boa vontade em uma cousa e outra, pela entrada que já começavam ter em Surrate d'onde faziam conta carregar de roupas para a Persia e trazerem d'ella sua seda com aventejados intereses."

(And thus he sent to Spain to His Majesty, in the era of 1603, as ambassador with first credentials, one Roberto Sarley, of English nationality who had worked for many years with him, a man of notable astuteness, and inventive genius, in this respect resembling the Shah himself. After working at Madrid for some years, treated and respected as ambassador of a king so powerful, he disappeared from court and went to England his native land, where he informed the King of England of the nature of the mission which had taken him to Spain. It seems that it must have been by order of the Shah of Persia that he invited the English to help him with their ships against us, under promise of a contract of silk, as afterwards became apparent, to take the fortress of Ormuz. The English who, after they commenced to break away from the true Roman Catholic Faith of Christ our Lord, shut their eyes to crimes and offences against the Catholics, entered quite willingly into one thing or the other through the footing which they had already established in Surat where they counted on loading stuff for Persia, and buying from that country its silk with advantageous interests.)

Bocarro, Decada XIII, Vol. I, Chap. VII, p. 32.

expelled from the Court of Jehangir, during whose reign they had come for the first time, and why they lost the protection of the Court of Jehangir, according to the Treaty of Peace of the 7th June 1615. (1)

Antonio Bocarro knew about the Treaty of Peace which had been made between Jehangir and the Portuguese, and which exists in the original Persian in the Archives of the Government of Goa. (Livro das Pazes No. 1). (2) The said treaty was translated and published by the Rev. J. Heras in the Proceedings of the Indian Historical Commission, 1927.

Besides Decada XIII, he wrote :

> "Livro das Plantas de todas as Fortalezas, cidades e Povoaçoens do Estado da India Oriental com as descripçoens da altura em que estão, e de tudo que ha nellas, Artilharia, Presidio, gente de Armas, e Vassalos, rendimento, e despeza, fundos, Reys da terra dentro, o poder que tem, e a paz, e guerra, que guardão, e tudo que está debaixo da Coroa de Espanha."
>
> (Book of the Plans of all the Fortresses, Cities and Towns of the State of Oriental India, with a description of their state and of all that was in them : Artillery, Garrison, Men of Arms, Vassals, income, and expenditure, capital, border Princes, of the power they have, the peace they preserve, the war they wage and everything that is under the Crown of Spain).

---

(1) The Portuguese thought they had the right to the seas as discoverers of the way to India. And the English, under Doctor Hawkins, entered the Court of Jehangir and were well received. Jehangir also made war against the Portuguese because, as he had protested and taken the part of the English, the Portuguese seized a ship returning from Mecca laden with treasure, which belonged to the mother of Jehangir. Jehangir shut all the churches and opened war on the Portuguese, expelled them and made a treaty in Goa.

(2) "Capitulos das pazes que se fizeram entre os Vassalos de El-Rey Jahangir e os Portuguezes por Nawab Muqarab Khan e Gonçalo Pinto da Fonseca".

(Biker 1881, p. 189; "O Cronista de Tissuary", Vol. III, p. 269). This document is not known to Vincent Smith.

It was dedicated to His Most Serene Majesty, King Philip IV of Spain and III of Portugal. Bocarro in this book wrote about Shah Jehan and his relations with the Portuguese. He also wrote about the destruction of the Hugli Fortress of India. This most important book, written in 1632, may be found in manuscript in the Library of Evora, only a few chapters of it having been published by Cunha Rivara in "Chronista do Tissuary." A second copy exists in the British Museum.

Jacinto Freire de Andrade

Jacinto Freire de Andrade, 1597-1657, is important amongst the writers on India for his "Vida de D. João de Castro" (Life of Dom João de Castro), the fourth Viceroy of India. In the phrase of Quental: "He is an emphatic historian without philosophy but conscientious and learned". His book is a complete biography in four volumes beginning with a description of the early life and education of Dom João de Castro. It gives the fullest details of his viceroyalty in India and concludes with his death and burial and a minute description of his family. The book contains many shrewd observations on the people of India. Referring to the people of Ibrahim Adil Shah (1535-1558) he says: "Amongst this so barbarous a people men reign oftener by making use of their opportunities than by observing what is right." This book has been translated into English by Sir Peter Wyche.

Antonio Pinto Pereira

Antonio Pinto Pereira, a native of the village of Mogadour, well-versed in the science of Political History, left a work published some years after his death which occurred in 1587. It is entitled:

> "Historia da India, no tempo em que a governou o Viso-rey, D. Luiz de Athayde."
>
> (History of India in the time of its Governor, Luiz de Athayde.) It was printed in Coimbra in 1616.

With the exception of one hundred and sixty-two pages, the second volume of this work was never published in complete form. There is a copy of this book in the Biblioteca Nacional, Lisbon.

Antonio Rodrigues da Costa.

Antonio Rodrigues da Costa, 1656-1732, a Member of the Royal Academy of History, wrote a short historical work on India called:

> " Relação dos sucessos e gloriosas acções militares obradas no Estado da India, ordenadas e dirigidas pelo Vice-Rei e Capitão general d'aquelle Estado Vasco Fernandes Cesar de Menezes." Lisbon, 1716.
>
> (A report of the successes and glorious military deeds in the State of India ordered and directed by the Viceroy and Captain General of that State, who was Vasco Fernandes Cesar de Menezes). Lisbon, 1716.

This report, which Barbosa mentions as having been written in 1715, was reprinted and combined with three others. The second impression consisting of twenty-two pages, is entitled :

> " Relação do progresso das armas Portuguezas no Estado da India, no anno 1713, sendo Vice-Rei e Capitão General do mesmo Estado Vasco Fernandes Cesar de Menezes ".
>
> (An account of the progress of the Portuguese arms in the State of India in the year 1713, Vasco Fernandes Cesar de Menezes being the Viceroy and Captain General of the same State).

Besides this work, he wrote :

"Consulta do Conselho Ultramarino a sua Magestade (King D. João V) no anno de 1732 ". This manuscript was published for the first time in the "Registo Trimensal do Instituto Histórico Geográfico do Brasil", tomo VII, from page 498. It is a curious and most interesting document for the history of the State at that epoch.

Francisco de Pina e de Mello.

Francisco de Pina e de Mello was a noble youth and head of the family of Pina de Aragão, who came to Portugal with the Queen, Saint Isabel. He was born on the 7th. of August 1695, in the town of Montemor on the river Mondego in the province of Beira. He wrote:

"Vida e acçõens do grande Afonso de Albuquerque, Governador da India".

(Life and deeds of the great Afonso de Albuquerque, Governor of India).

Manuel Jacome de Mesquita

Manuel Jacome de Mesquita was a resident of Goa of whose birthplace and personal history we know nothing. He wrote the following work on India:

"Relação do que succedeu na cidade de Goa, e em todas as mais cidades e fortalezas do estado da India, na felice acclamação del-rei D. João IV de Portugal, e no juramento do principe D. Theodosio conforme a Ordem que deu o conde de Aveiras João da Silva Tello e Menezes, Vice-rei e capitão general do mesmo estado."

(An account of what happened in the city of Goa and in all the other cities and fortresses of the State of India during the happy acclamation of King Dom João IV of Portugal and in the taking of the oath of Prince Dom Theodosio in accordance with the order which the Count of Aveiras, João da Silva Tello e Menezes, gave, he being the Viceroy and Captain General of the same State).

It was published in Goa in the Jesuit College of St. Paul in 1643 (1); it contains twenty-five pages and the only copy in existence is in the Library of Evora.

---

* Diccionario Lusitano by Barbosa e Machado gives the date as 1644.

Father Antonio de S. Miguel.

Father Antonio de S. Miguel was a Franciscan monk of the province of Madre-de-Deus in Oriental India. The following work in the Library of Evora, being uncommon, deserves special mention:

" Batalha naval na barra de Goa, ganha pelo capitão Antonio Telles de Menezes." Outubro 1637.

(A naval battle off the coast of Goa, won by Captain Antonio Telles de Menezes.) October 1637.

Salvador de Couto de Sampaio.

On the same subject, Salvador de Couto de Sampaio has left us an account of the war between the Dutch and the Portuguese, 1637-1638, entitled:

" Relação dos successos victoriosos que na barra de Goa houve dos hollandezes Antonio Telles de Menezes, capitão geral do mar da India, nos annos de 1637 e 1638 ".

(Account of the victories which Antonio Telles de Menezes, Captain General of the Indian Sea, had over the Dutch in the Shoals of Goa in the year 1637-1638).

This work was printed in Coimbra by Lourenço Craesbeck in 1649. One copy of it exists in the Royal Library of Ajuda.

Dom Constantino de Sá e Noronha.

Dom Constantino de Sá e Noronha was born in Lisbon in 1586 and was killed in a battle against the Sinhalese in 1630. He was lamented by all on account of his high moral and political virtues about which his son, João Rodrigues de Sá, wrote in his book entitled :

" Rebellion Ceylão, y los Progressos de su Conquista ".

(Rebellion of Ceylon and the progress of its conquest).

Constantino de Sá e Noronha's work on India is entitled :

"Descripção dos Rios, Plantas, Portos do mar, e forma da Fortificação da ilha de Ceilão, enviada a Portugal em o anno de 1624, com as fortalezas excellentemente delineadas".

(A description of the Rivers, Fortresses, Sea-ports and plan of the fortifications of the Island of Ceylon. sent to Portugal in the year 1624, with the fortresses excellently drawn).

Cosmé Lafeta

Cosmé Lafeta was in the Orient for many years, and, gifted with great understanding, wrote in the year 1605:

"Informação do Estado da India."

(Information about the State of India).

This is a manuscript and, according to Barbosa e Machado, is now kept in the Library of H. E. the Marquis of Gouvea.

I found an interesting reference to Lafeta in the book (still a manuscript in the Library at Evora) "Breve Tratado da Victoria de Chaul", L. do Antonio Barbosa, Portuguez, 1635. In this manuscript there are some chapters relating to the Capitão Mor (Chief Captain) Cosmé de Lafeitta.

Father Jacobo Fenicio.

Father Jacobo Fenicio wrote: "O Livro da Seita dos Indios Orientaes", (The Book of the Religious Systems of the East Indies), which was brought to light recently in 1933 by Dr. Jarl Charpentier with an erudite introduction and notes. From this introduction we quote the following:

"Father Jacobo (or Jacome) Fenicio was born at Capua about 1558. In 1580 he entered the Society and already in 1583 set sail for India. When arriving there in 1584 he was stationed at Cochin, was made vicar of St. Andrew in Porca in 1587 and kept on in that position from the years 1594 to 1604 and again in 1619. In the year 1600, he went to the Court at Calicut and must have spent some years there; at least he is reported to have stayed there during the years 1605-06 and 1608-09. At about seventy-five years of age he died at Cochin in 1632." (p. LXXIII).

Fenicio, according to Dr. Charpentier's research, brought his work to an end in 1609 or a very few years after that.

Father Antonio Monserrate.

Father Antonio Monserrate left a "Relação de Equebar" which was a summary which he himself had made from his own work "Mongolicæ Legationis Commentarius" or "The First Jesuit Mission to Akbar". This "Relação de Equebar" (Account of Akbar) has been edited and translated by Father Hosten in The Journal and Proceedings of the Asiatic Society, Bengal, 1912, pp. 185-221, under the title of "Father A. Monserrate's "Account of Akbar", 26th. November, 1582.

Father Pierre du Jarrie made copious extracts from Peruschi's "Informatione del Regno... di Mogor" and Peruchi was the first person to use the document and thus the whole of his Chapter VIII of "Libre IIII, Seconde Partie de l'Histoire des Choses plus memorables advenues dans les Indes Orientales" is based on Monserrate's authority. Cf. Journal of the Asiatic Society of Bengal, p. 188, May, 1912.

P. Manuel Barradas.

P. Manuel Barradas wrote: "Descrição de Ceilão em 1613" which has been translated by D. W. Fergusson in Volume IV of the "Monthly Literary Register". He probably wrote: "Relação de varias novas" being an account of the civil war of Vijianagar found in the Jesuit Archives, slightly different from the story of Barradas by Sewell, "the Forgotten Empire", pp. 221-231. ([1]).

In the Library of Visconde da Esperança is an unpublished manuscript of Manuel Barradas dedicated to His Majesty, with a prefatory letter dated the 1st. December 1618, in which he treats exclusively of Indian Theogony and Cosmogony. It consists of five books. Book I has eight chapters. It speaks of the races of Oriental Indians, principally those of Malabar. Book II consists of fifteen chapters about the laws of the Indians, but with special reference to those of Malabar. Books III and IV treat of the same subject.

Book V has for its subject "The cult of the false gods of the Orientals of Malabar." It treats of the way in which they raise temples and pagodas to their idols; of the Pagoda of Rettora; of the Pagoda of Cape Camorin; of the Pagoda of Trinate and of Ramagen in Cranganor; and about some famous pagodas which the author saw in the north of Portuguese India (in Canara, Baçaim, Malsa, Condontim and Elefanta).

Dr. Charpentier shows that Father Barradas borrowed liberally his information contained in his last work from Fenicio's book.

Captain Barreto de Resende.

"Breve tratado ou epilogo de todos os Visorreys que tem havido no Estado da India, successos que tiverão no tempo de seus governos, armadas de navios e galeoẽs que do reyno de Portugal, forão ao dito Estado, e do que succedeo em particular a alguãs dellas nas viagens que fizerão".

(Brief treatise or epilogue of all the viceroys who have been in the State of India, the successes they had during their governorship, the ships or galleys that went to the said State, and what happened to some of the ships in the journey which they made.)

([1]) Extracts were published in English in the Journal of Indian History by the Rev. H. Heras.

Cf. "The Great Civil War of Vijianagar, 1614-1618", by the Rev. J. Heràs, M. A., pp. 164-188.

20

This book is divided into three parts: the first contains all the pictures of the Viceroys who had been in the State until 1634, with descriptions of their governments; the second part contains the plans of the fortresses which existed from the Cape of Good Hope to the Fortress of Chaul, with a full description of all that there was in each of the said fortresses, their income and expenditure and other things which concerned them; the third part contains all the fortresses from Goa to China, and amongst those are included the fortresses which did not belong to Portugal, but which, because they were on the same coast, were included for the sake of interest.

The book was written in 1635 by Captain Pedro Barreto de Resende, Knight of the Order of São Bento de Avis, who was a native of Pavia. He was Secretary to the Conde de Linhares, Viceroy of India, nominated in 1629 and retired in 1635. Each chapter is preceded by a full length photograph of the Governor who is treated of in the text. The pictures, forty-four in number, are illuminated, the last being that of Dom Miguel de Noronha, Conde de Linhares. This manuscript is to be found in the British Museum, and a copy in the Paris National Library and it is in a perfect state of preservation (1).

This manuscript has no relation with the other one entitled: "Compendio Universal de todos os Viso-Reis" (Universal Compendium of all the Viceroys) which was published in Goa by Ismael Gracias and attributed by him to Father Pinheiro Xavier.

Another writer worthy of mention is Father Antonio de Andrade, who was born in 1581, and was a

---

(1) Collection of Sloane La Figanière, "Catalogue of Portuguese Manuscripts in the British Museum, Lisbon, 1853, p. 162.

Father Antonio de Andrade.

native of the little town of Oleiros in the region of Beira Central, today in the district of Castello Branco. In 1596 he joined the Company of Jesus in Coimbra, and after completing his novitiate and staying for a short time in Portugal, came to India in 1600. He was sent to the Moghul Mission whose headquarters were at Agra. He left Agra on the 30th. March 1624 with the intention of accompanying Jehangir, the Mogul Emperor, who was then on his way to Lahore. On his arrival at Delhi, he met a large number of pilgrims who were on their way to the famous temple of "Badrinath" and wishing to take advantage of the opportunity which was offered him of going as far as the temple and from thence to Tibet, he resolved to travel with the pilgrims.

Antonio de Andrade was the first European who dared to scale the snow-clad slopes of the Himalayas, cross the desert and enter Tibet, where he stayed for twenty-five days. On his return he sent detailed information about his travels to that country:

> "Novo descobrimento do gram Cathayo ou Reinos de Tibet, pelo Padre Antonio de Andrade da Companhia de Jesus, Portuguez, no anno de 1624".
>
> (New discovery of the great Cathay or the Kingdoms of Tibet, by Father Antonio de Andrade of the Company of Jesus, a Portuguese, in the year 1624).

This was followed by another letter on his second journey to Tibet: "Carta do Segundo Anno do Tibet no anno de 1626". (Letter of the second year of Tibet in the year 1626).

Both these letters were published by Francisco Maria Esteves Pereira in his "O Descobrimento do Tibet", Coimbra, 1921. In the Appendix to his book is published another letter in which Antonio de Andrade refers briefly to the events which took place in his second journey from Agra to Chaparangue, addressed probably to the Father Provincial of the Company of Jesus in Goa. This last letter was printed in "Relaçam Geral do estado da Christandade da Ethiopia do que de novo socedeo no descobrimento do Thybet". Lisbon, 1628.

The letters of Father Andrade contain some facts of historical importance with regard to the difficulties that had to be faced in making a journey in India in those days. According to Vincent Smith, kings were constantly travelling from Delhi to Lahore.

Gaspar Ferreira Reymão.

Gaspar Ferreira Reymão was the Head Pilot of the Kingdom of Portugal and a Knight of the Order of St. Iago. Nothing much is known about him except that he wrote :

> "Roteiro da Navegação e Carreira da India, com seus caminhos, signaes, e aguagens, e differenças da agulha, tirado do que escreveu Vicente Rodrigues, e Diogo Afonso, pilotos antigos".
>
> (Log-book of the navigation and tides of India with its ways, signals, watering places and the differences of the compass taken from accounts of Vicente Rodrigues and Diogo Afonso, ancient pilots). Printed in Lisbon 1612.

Antonio Gil Preto.

Antonio Gil Preto was a native of the city of Goa and Chronicler of Portuguese India, concerning which country he wrote :

> "Breve Relação da Viagem que fes para a India no anno de 1672, arribado ao Brasil, e chegada a Goa da Nao Almirante S. Pedro de Rates, morte de Arcebispo D. Fr. Christovão da Sylveira, vida e acçõens do mesmo Arcebispo".
>
> (A brief account of the voyage to India in the year 1672, touching at Brazil and arriving at Goa; of the Admiral Ship St. Pedro de Rates; death of the Archbishop, Dom Friar Christovão da Silveira, and the life and deeds of the same Archbishop).

A Manuscript copy existed in the Library of the Convent of "Our Lady of Grace" belonging to the monks of St. Augustine in Goa.

Fr. Manoel Godinho.

The Jesuit priest, Father Manoel Godinho, has left us:

"Relação do novo Caminho que fez por terra e mar vindo da India para Portugal no anno de 1663, o padre Manoel Godinho de Companhia de Jesus enviado a Magestade del Rey N. S. Dom Afonso VI, Lisboa, 1665".

(An account of the new way which Father Manoel Godinho of the Company of Jesus, took by land and sea on his way from India to Portugal, in the year 1663, which was sent to His Majesty the King, our Lord, Dom Affonso VI, Lisbon, 1665.

The second edition was published in Lisbon in 1842.

Fr. Fernão Guerreiro.

Father Fernão Guerreiro joined the Company of Jesus at Evora, when he was seventeen years old. Having completed his studies he dedicated himself to preaching. He has given us the following works on India: (1)

(1) "Relação annual das cousas que fizerão os Padres da Companhia de Jesus na India e Japão nos annos de 1600 e 1601 e do processo da conversão, e Christandade daquellas partes tirada das cartas geraes, que de la vierão".

(Annual Report of the things done by the Fathers of the Company of Jesus in India and Japan, in the years 1600 and 1601, and about the progress of conversion and Christianity of those parts, taken from the general letters which came from there).

It was published in Lisbon in 1603 and translated into Castilian by the Jesuit priest, Father Antonio Collasso, Procurator of the Province of Portugal in the

---

(1) Father Hosten on different occasions has published portions of these volumes, i. e. such as bore on Bengal under Mughal domination.

Court of Madrid, and printed in Valladolid by Luis Sanches in 1604.

(2) "Relação annual das cousas que fizerão os Padres da Companhia de Jesus, nas partes da India Oriental, e no Brasil, Angola, Cabo Verde, Guiné, nos annos de 1603, e do processo da conversão e christandade daquellas partes tirada das cartas dos mesmos Padres, que de la vierão".

(Annual Report of the things which the Jesuit Fathers did in the various parts of Oriental India and in Brazil, Angola, Cape Verde and of the progress of conversion and Christianity of those parts, taken from the general letters of the same Fathers which came from there).

Published in Lisbon, 1605.

(3) "Relação annual das cousas que fizerão os Padres da Companhia de Jesus, nas partes da India Oriental, e em algumas outras da conquista deste Reyno, nos annos de 1604 e 1605 e do processo da conversão e christandade daquellas partes".

(Annual Report of the things which the Jesuit Fathers did in the various parts of Oriental India and in some other parts conquered by Portugal, in the years 1604 and 1605, and of the progress of conversion and Christianity of those parts.

Published by Pedro Craesbeck in Lisbon, 1607.

(4) "Relação annual das cousas, que fiserão os Padres da Companhia de Jesus nas partes da India Oriental, e em algumas outras da conquista deste Reyno no anno de 1606 e 1607, do processo da conversão, e christandade daquellas partes. Tirada das cartas dos mesmos padres que de la vierão".

(Annual Report of the things which the Jesuit Fathers did in the various parts of Oriental India and other parts of the conquest of the Kingdom in the year 1606 and 1607, and of the progress of conversion and Christianity of those parts. Taken from the letters of the same priests who came from there).

It was published in Lisbon by the same printer in 1609.

Father Antonio de Gouvea, an Augustine priest, Titular Bishop of Cyrene in Africa, Ambassador and Pontifical Legate in Persia, where he went twice in 1602 and again in 1620, was born in the city of Beja and died in Spain in the Villa of Mancanares of Membrilla on the 18th. of August 1628, being about 60 years old. With reference to India, he wrote :

Father Antonio de Gouvea.

> " Jornada do Arcebispo de Goa, Dom Frey Aleixo de Menezes, Primaz da India Oriental, religioso da Ordem de S. Agostinho, quando foi das serras do Malabar, lugares em que moram os antigos christãos de S. Thomé e os tirou de muytos erros e heresias em que estavam. Recopilada de diversos tratados de pessoas de autoridade, que a tudo foram presentes. Da-se noticia de muytas cousas notaveis da India ".

> (A journey of the Archbishop of Goa, D. Friar Aleixo de Menezes, Primate of Oriental India and a monk of the Order of St. Augustine, at the time when he went to the mountains of Malabar where the early Christians of St. Thomé lived. It was collected from several treatises by persons of authority, who were present at everything. It contains the account of many notable events of India).

It was printed by Diogo Gomes Loureiro in Coimbra, 1606.

Father Domingos do Espirito Santo was a native of Lisbon. He joined the Order of St. Augustine in 1601, and the following year left for Goa, where he afterwards studied Philosophy in the College of which he was twice the Rector. He was well-versed in Moral Theology and History, and he received high honours in his Order. He died in Goa in 1628. He produced two works concerning India worthy of mention :

Father Domingos do Espirito Santo.

> (1) " Historia da fundação do Real Convento de Santa Monica de Goa ".

(History of the foundation of the Royal Convent of St. Monica of Goa).

This book, which later in 1699 was published in Lisbon, was used in manuscript form by Father Agostinho da Santa Maria in his book, " Agostinho Descalço."

(2) " Tratado de Contractos " (Treatise on Contracts.)

In the book are found various forms of the contracts made all over India (Manuscript).

Simão Torrezão Coelho.

Simão Torrezão Coelho was a Doctor of Canonical Law and Prior of the Church of St. Martinho of Lisbon. His work on India is called :

" Elogio de Dom João de Castro, vice-rei da India ".

(Eulogy of Dom João de Castro, Viceroy of India.)

This book was published with a commentary by João Pinto Ribeiro in Lisbon, 1643.

Cosme da Guarda.

" Vida e acçoens do famoso e felicissimo Sevagy, da India Oriental, Escripta por Cosme da Guarda, natural de Mormugão, dedicada ao Exmo Sr. Duque Estribeiro-Mor, Lisbon Occidental, 1730 ".

(Life and actions of the famous and most Happy Sivaji, of Oriental India, written by Cosme da Guarda, a native of Mormugão, dedicated to Exmo. Sr. Duque Estribeiro-Mór, Lisboa Occidental, 1730).

The editor Dom Caetano Pacheco de Gouvea says in his dedication to the Duke that the book came into his hands by chance, and that he had no knowledge of Cosme da Guarda, a native of Mormugão, other than one could find out from the first page of the copy from which he produced this edition.

It seems that the name, Cosme da Guarda is an assumed one, as Barbosa expressly declares in his Vol. I of Biblioteca Lusitana, page 600. However, whoever the author may be, he speaks on page 40 of "The King Aurangzeb, the Great Mogul, who had reigned for years and is still reigning today, 28th. of August, 1695." From this allusion one concludes that the work was written in the year 1695, one year before Krishnaji Anant Sabhasad, the first Maratha biographer of Shivaji, finished his chronicle "Sabhasad Bakhar".

"Internal evidence shows", says Dr. Sen in his 'Foreign Biographies, of Shivaji', "that Guarda was an orthodox Roman Catholic. His approval of most of the Indian customs mentioned in his work might very well suggest an Indian origin, but his ignorance of the Hindu law of marriage would strongly contradict such a theory". (p. xvii).

The work is almost entirely a romance, as Professor Jadunath Sircar says (1) of this book, "full of gross inaccuracies of facts, useless digressions, general descriptions, commonplace remarks, and bazar gossip. It tells us nothing new that it is historically true." The book gives us some information, but this is not enough to warrant the statement that it is historically important, as the writer, Mr. Justin E. Abbott claims (2). The work of Cosme da Guarda was recently (1929) translated into English by Dr. Surendranath Sen in his "Foreign Biographies of Shivaji".

---

(1) (a) Professor Jadunath Sarcar's article "Sources of the History of Shivaji", critically examined in the Journal of Bihar and Orissa Research Society, March-June, 1924.

(b) Professor Pissurlencar in his "Sivaji com Sangue Portuguez ?", Nova Goa, 1922, page 39, is of the same opinion, which is based on his studies of the Portuguese sources about the Mahratta monarch, made in the Archives of Goa.

(2) See Journal of the Royal Asiatic Society, 1923, p. 667: "The historic value of an early account of Shivaji

Mosseh Pereira de Paiva.

Mosseh Pereira de Paiva was a Portuguese Jew who appears to have lived in India in the second half of the 17th. century. He wrote a work concerning the Jews of Cochin, entitled:

> "Noticias dos Judeos de Cochim, mandadas por Mosseh Pereira de Paiva".

It was published in Amsterdam in 1678, and is a rare work written in the Portuguese language. There is a copy in the Library of the "Academia das Sciencias", Lisbon. It was newly published with an introduction by Moses Bensabat Amzalak in Lisbon, 1923. Dr. José Leite de Vasconcellos, Professor of the Lisbon University, informed us that he had seen a copy of the "Noticias" in the library of the erudite English lover of books, Mr. E. N. Adler. The learned Kayserling referring to the "Noticias" cites the edition of 5447 (1687) and again a Spanish translation with the following title: "Relation de las Noticias de los Judios de Cochim".

The learned Steinschneider has a most notable article about the Jews of Cochin in his monumental catalogue of the Hebrew books of the Bodleian Library, an article consisting of nearly three columns (pages 2722-24) in which he says that the first information printed about the Jews of Cochin was the "Noticias" of Mosseh Pereira de Paiva.

This author was editor of the Azharot of Elias Adem which was sent from India by Moss Levy Belilio and printed in Amsterdam in 1688 by Phoebus. A year before the same author and printer published a

---

contained in a Portuguese work written in 1695", by Mr. Justin E. Abbott.

small sheet, extremely rare, in Yiddish entitled "Kennis der Jehudim von Kocheir o der Zeitung an Indien", and in 1668 as the second edition "Wahshafhije Rantschaft oder Hindushim aus Fstandia". Both these books were prefaced by Haham de Amsterdam Isaac Haham Aboat.

Language and Poetry.

The contribution to language and poetry in this period is meagre and without importance. We have from the pen of João Franco Barreto:

João Franco Barreto

"Discurso apologetico sobre a visão do Indo e Ganges que o grande Luis de Camões representou em o canto IV dos Lusiadas a el-rei D. Manuel, &c."

(An apologetic discourse upon the vision of the Indus and the Ganges, which the great Luis Camões represented in Canto IV of his 'Lusiadas', as having appeared to the King, Dom Manuel, &c.)

Dom Antonio Alvares da Cunha.

Dom Antonio Alvares da Cunha, 1626-1690 was a Knight of the "Order of Christ", and the keeper of the Torre do Tombo. He was also one of the founders and Secretary of the "Academia de Generosos". He wrote the following letter:

"Carta a João Nunes da Cunha, Conde de S. Vicente... quando foi eleito Vice-Rei da India."

(A letter to João Nunes da Cunha, Count of S. Vicente, when he was elected Viceroy of India.)

This letter was published in Lisbon, by Antonio Craesbeck de Mello, without a date. It is written in triple rhyme, a rare edition of which there is only one copy in Figaniere's collection. This work was reproduced in the second volume of "Fenix Renascida". ([1])

Another writer worthy of mention is Antonio de Valle de Moraes who went to India as a soldier, accompanying the Viceroy, Dom Pedro da Sylva in 1635. He was a poet whose art was cultivated amidst the din of war. He wrote: "Nautica Lusitana" in six cantos, describing his journey from Lisbon to Goa.

Antonio de Valle de Moraes.

With regard to literature on the subject of religion produced during this period, we have to note the works of some writers.

Religion.

Father Agostinho de Santa Maria, an Augustinian monk whose name in the world was Manuel Gomes Freire, was born in the town of Estremoz on the 28th of August 1642. He died at the age of 86, on the 3rd. April 1728, in the Convent of Boa Hora of Lisbon. He was a laborious and most prolific writer which is proved by the many works he composed and published, besides those which remained unedited after his death and were probably lost. He wrote:

Father Agostinho de Santa Maria.

> "Historia da fundação do Real Convento de S. Monica da cidade de Goa...fundado pelo Illus. e Revo. Sr. D. Fr. Aleixo de Menezes, Primaz das Hespanhas e da India...Em, que refere os prodigios que houve em sua erecção, as grandes contradições, trabalhos, e vexações, que depois de fundado

---

([1]) "Collecção intitulada 'A Fenix Renascida' curioso arquivo dos disparates poeticos do periodo Gongorico" (A collection of poetry called "A Fenix Renascida" belonging to the Gongoric period, which contains many curious poems).

Historia Comparativa da Litteratura Portuguesa de J. Barbosa de Bettencourt. Page. 279.

padeceram as religiosas, &c.....Com as vidas das fundadoras e de muitas outras religiosas."

(A History of the foundation of the Royal convent of St. Monica in the city of Goa—founded by the most illustrious and most reverend Lord, Friar Aleixo de Menezes, Primate of Spain and India—in which are related the marvels which happened in its erection, the great contradictions, troubles and vexations suffered after its foundation by the nuns, etc......With the lives of the founders and many other nuns.)

It was printed in Lisbon by Antonio Pedrozo Galram in 1699.

Father Diogo de Sancta Anna.

Father Diogo de Sancta Anna was a native of Villa Franca Lampazes in the bishopric of Bragança. He entered the Order of the Augustinians, and died in Goa in 1646. He wrote :

"Verdadeira relação do grande e portentoso milagre que aconteceu em o sancto Crucifixo do coro da Igreja das Freiras de Sancta Monica de Goa, em 8 de Fevereiro de 1636."

(A true account of the great and portentous miracle which happened to the Holy Crucifix in the choir of the Church of the Nuns of St. Monica of Goa, on the 8th. of February 1636).

It was published in Lisbon by Manuel de Sylva in 1640.

Father Antonio Pereira.

Father Antonio Pereira was a Dominican missionary in the East; besides being Vicar-General, he was a Deputy of the Inquisition of Evora, in which position he served for many years after his return from India. He was a native of Aveiro and appears to have been born about the year 1640, seeing that he joined Dominicans in 1657. He is said to have died in the beginning of the 18th. century. He wrote :

"Sermão do auto da fé, contra a idolatria do Oriente, pregado na cidade de Goa a 27 de Março de 1672 ".

(A Sermon of the Profession of Faith against the idolatry of the East, preached in the city of Goa on the 27th. of March 1672).

It was published in Lisbon by Miguel Deslandas in 1685. This sermon is very rare. Unfortunately, there are only forty-eight pages of this work, in which almost the whole sermon itself is lacking, having only a few dedicatory passages.

Father Fernão de Queyroz, a Jesuit, was a native of the town of Canavezes in the bishopric of Oporto. He embarked with twenty-two other Jesuits in the ship 'Almirante', and arrived at Cochin on the 26th. of November 1635. He became the Rector of the College of Tana and Baçaim, and was also appointed a Deputy of the Inquisition of Goa on the 29th. of October 1659. He died in College of St. Paul on the 12th. of April 1688, and was buried in the "Casa Professa" of Goa. Amongst other things he wrote :

Father Fernão de Queyroz.

"Conquista temporal e espiritual de Ceylão ordenada pelo F. Fernão de Queiroz da Companhia de Jesus, da provincia de Goa".

(Temporal and spiritual conquests of Ceylon ordered by Father Fernão de Queiroz of the Company of Jesus in the province of Goa.)

The dedication is dated the 1st. October 1687. It was published in Colombo, in 1916.

The learned Portuguese Orientalist, Francisco Maria Esteves Pereira in his introduction to the "Bhagvat-Gita," Coimbra, 1922, p. 6, attributed to the said Fernão de Queiroz the authorship of the following translation of this sacred book of the Hindus :

"Tradução em summaria do livro, que os gentios chamam Bagavota Guita, que se compoem de dezouto capitulos, dando nelles preceytos em que trata respectiva a outava Encarnação do Crusna filho de Deos, e sobre os preceytos que impoz ao Pandovo Arzun, como seu estimado servo, hum dos sinco irmaons ditos Pondovos, de que atras falamos."

(Translation in summary of the work which the gentios call Bhagvat-Gita, which is composed of 18 chapters, giving, in them precepts which treat of the 8th. Incarnation Krishna, son of God, and about the precepts which he imposed on Pandav Arjun, as his esteemed disciple, one of the five brothers of the Pandavas, of whom we spoke before).

This translation remained unpublished till 1922 in the Public Library of Evora. To the same Father Fernão de Queiroz, the above-mentioned Portuguese Orientalist attributed the authorship of the following two Portuguese treatises on Hindu mythology :

1. "Breve relação das escrituras dos gentios da India Oriental, e dos seus costumes."

(A short account of the writings of the gentios of India, and of their customs).

2. "Noticia summaria do gentilismo da Asia."

(A short account of paganism in Asia).

Comparing the brief translation of the Bagavat Gita contained in the manuscript in the public library at Evora, with the two treatises previously mentioned, Esteves Pereira thought that the summarised translation of the Bagavat Gita was a sequel to those treatises and was written by a Father of the Company of Jesus who lived in Portuguese India in the beginning of the seventeenth century. The erudite Portuguese Orientalist concludes in this way: "This summarised translation represents the first attempt made to translate a work written in Sanscrit into the language of one of the peoples of Europe (Portuguese) and preceded by more than a century, the translation of Charles

Wilkins, published in 1875, which, as is known, was the first complete translation of a work written in Sanscrit."

Professor Pissurlencar, however, is of opinion that the same summarised translation which Esteves Pereira published in 1922 at his suggestion and which for many years was kept in manuscript in the Public Library at Evora (twenty eight folios, 4to.), dates from the time after 1761 in which the third battle of Panipat, so celebrated in the history of the Marathas was fought and to which one may find an allusion in the same translation (1). This allusion is as follows:—

> " em Cruxetra, distante de Astanapur seis dias de caminho, onde tambem nos annos passados o exercito dos Mogoles derão cabo do numeroso exercito dos Marathas."
>
> (in Kurushetra, distant from Hastinapur, six days' journey, where, also in past years, the army of the Mogols destroyed the large army of the Marathas.)

The two treatises referred to were translated into Dutch in 1915, and the erudite translator concluded that the first treatise was written between 1646 and 1680, and the second in 1774.

Thus the conjecture of Esteves Pereira was incorrect with respect to the authorship of the two treatises, just as it was incorrect with respect to the date of the first Portuguese translation of the same Bhagavat-Gita.

Father Antonio da Silva.

Father Antonio da Silva—a Jesuit and a Master of Theology and Classics—was a native of Aveiro. He died at the age of sixty-one on the 16th. of April 1666 in the College

(1) Vide Pissurlencar's "Aspectos de Civilização de India Antiga", 1925, p. 52, and "A Antiguidade do Crixnaismo."

of his Order in Santarem. He wrote a eulogy on St. Francis Xavier entitled:

> "Sol do Oriente, São Francisco Xavier da Companhia de Jesus ... no qual como en breve Mapa descreve os des annos de sua milagrosa vida no Oriente."
>
> (Sun of the East, St. Francis Xavier of the Company of Jesus ... in which he briefly describes the ten years of his miraculous life in the East).

It was published in Lisbon in 1665. The book contains 562 pages, exclusive of prologue, index, &c.

Father Antonio da Trindade.

Father Antonio da Trindade, a member of the Order of Minores of the province of Madre de Deos of Goa, wrote:

> "Relação da Provincia da Madre de Deos de Goa".
>
> (An account of the Province of Madre de Deos of Goa).

Father Diogo Monteiro.

Father Diogo Monteiro, a theologian and moralist, was a native of Lisbon, but the dates of his birth and death are not known. He wrote a compendium called:

> "Compendio da vida, virtudes e milagres do B. P. Francisco Xavier, apostolo da India Oriental."
>
> (A compendium of the life, virtues and miracles of the Blessed Father St. Francis Xavier, Apostle of East India).

It has been published by Antonio Alvares, and translated into Spanish by Father Thomas of Castim.

João da Costa.

We do not know anything about the birthplace and life of João da Costa, but, from a note published in the Bibliotheca Oriental, Volume I, col. 58, of Antonio de Leon Pinelo,(1) 1737, Madrid, we know that he wrote:

---

(1) See also Christovão de Nazareth, "Mitras Luzitanas", Part III, page 152.

"Relação dos Reynos, e Senhorios da India quais são de mouros, quais de gentios, e de seus costumes."

(An account of the Kingdoms and Dominions of India, belonging to the Moors and to the Gentiles, and of their customs).

It was translated into Spanish in 1624.

Father Antonio João de Frias.

Father Antonio João de Frias was a native of Talaulim, a suburb of Goa, where he died on the 25th. of June, 1727, at the age of 63. He was the first son of Goa, who wrote in Portuguese and his example was followed by the author of the "Promptuario das Definições Indicas."(1) Frias wrote a treatise called :

"Aureola das Indias e Nobiliarchia Bracmana. Tractado historico, genealogico, panegyrico e moral". Fol. XXVI, Lisbon 224, M. Deslandas, 1702.

(Glory of the Indian and the Brahmanic Nobiliarchy, a historical, genealogical, panegyrical and moral treatise). Fol. 26, 224, Lisbon, 1702.

He wished to prove the superiority of the Brahmans whereas the author of the "Promptuario" tried to prove the superiority of the caste "Chardo", one of the castes of the Goanese Christians. (2)

João Ribeiro.

João Ribeiro was a soldier in India and in the island of Ceylon, about 1681. He wrote :

"Fatalidade historica da Ilha de Ceylaõ. Dedicada a sua magestade D. Pedro II, rei de Portugal."

(A historic fatality of the island of Ceylon. Dedicated to the King Dom Pedro II of Portugal.

---

(1) Rev. Leonardo Paes, a Goanese.

(2) See "Goanese Castes", by Saldanha (Bramana, Chardo and Sudra). P. Pissurlencar, "O Elemento Hindu da Casta Chardó." Nova Goa, 1936.

This work which consists of two parts, the first, of twenty-four chapters and the second, of ten chapters, was kept for many years in manuscript, and was for the first time printed in Volume V of the " Collecção das Noticias para Historia e Geografia das nações ultramarinas."

Domingos Affonso.

Domingos Affonso, an inhabitant of Goa, has left us a work on fireworks called :

" Artificios de fogo que fez na India no anno de 1684."

(Fireworks made in India in the year 1684.)

Antonio de Fonseca Osorio.

Antonio de Fonseca Osorio was a native of Lisbon. He went to India as a soldier and lived there for many years. He travelled in many different parts of the world, both by land and sea, undergoing many hardships which he recorded in his book entitled :

" Peregrino Oriental ; de varias cousas, e successos da India ."

(Oriental pilgrim ; about many things and incidents concerning India.)

The work is in manuscript and is praised by Jorge Cardoso in his book " Advertene ", Vol. I, page 2.

Father Francisco de Sousa.

Finally, we have a work which is very well-known in Indo-Portuguese historiography. It is the work of Father Francisco de Sousa, a Jesuit who died in Goa in 1713, when he was over 81 years of age. He wrote :

"O Oriente conquistado a Jesu Christo pelos Padres da Companhia de Jesus da Provincia de Goa."

(The Oriente conquered for Jesus Christ by the Fathers of the Compauy of Jesus of the Province of Goa.)

The first part is a description of the first twenty-two years of the Company in the Province. It was published in Lisbon, 1710.

The second part contains an account of work done from the year 1564 till 1585.

The third part of the history was never published. The complete work is neither more nor less than a chronicle of the deeds of the Company of Jesus in the various parts of India.

CHAPTER III.

The French or Arcadian School, 1706-1826.

Continuation of literary decadence.

The first part of the eighteenth century resembled the last part of the preceding one in the affectation and bad literary taste of its writers. Their works were notable for exaggeration, disproportionate phraseology and artificiality, and no one belonging to this part of the literary period, can be said to be entirely free from these faults.

Establishment of Academies for literary reform.

In the second part of the century, there was an intellectual movement towards the purification of the style and language, a renascent wave which passed over other parts of Europe at the same time. All eyes were attracted to France by the brilliancy of her writers whom every one wished to imitate. Following her example, Academies for the purpose of literary reform were established in Portugal, amongst which were numbered the Academia Real da Historia Portuguesa, the Academia Real das Sciencias de Lisboa [1] which still exists, and the Arcadia Ulys-

---

[1] It was founded in 1710 by the second Duke de Lafões and to it we owe many publications of works on India. It had usually the favour of the State.

Of. Fidelino Figueiredo, "Historia de Academia Real das Sciencias".

It was this Academy which published nineteen volumes

siponense or Lusitana. A reaction in favour of the study of the Classics was soon initiated by this last named Society. It created a new intellectual atmosphere, further promoted by the infiltration of French ideas and phrases into the language and Portuguese literature began to show fresh signs of expansion and new culture. This society held its own during twenty years at the end of which time it disappeared to be reborn under the name of Nova Arcadia in 1719. One of the brilliant members of this Academy who wrote about India, was the lyrist Bocage who, after Camões, is the most popular Portuguese poet.

Poets of the 18th. century who wrote on India. Bocage.

Manoel Maria Barbosa du Bocage, 1765-1805, (1) known by the nom-de-plume of Elmano Sadino, like Camões, went to India in 1786 when he was only twenty one years old, as a government official, with the Governor, Francisco da Cunha e Menezes. In 1789, he was appointed by the same Governor for service in Damão, and he took up his post there in March of the same year. But two days after his arrival, he suddenly disappeared without giving any reason, though the following lines give us the true explanation of his disappointment and disillusionment in India: "Of the Albuquerque, of the Castros and of

---

under the title: Monumentos ineditos para a historia das conquistas dos Portuguezes", viz:

"Lendas da India", 4 vols.
"Subsidios para a Historia da India", 3 vols.
"Decada XIII de Bocarro", 2 vols.
"Cartas de A. de Albuquerque", 5 vols.
"Documentos Remettidos", 4 vols.

(1) Mendes dos Remedios' "Historia da Literatura Portugueza", p. 432, and "Historia Comparativa da Literatura Portugueza" of Barbosa de Betencourt, p. 327, give the date of birth as 1735, which must be a typographical error.

the Gamas, not a shadow ! They were all blotted out in the twilight of a progressive decadence. Those seas, the theatre of the prowess of Duarte Pacheco and so many captains to whom the fear of the conquered had given the name " Lions of the Seas ", were almost deserted by Portuguese ships ; and the heroic war was changed into a series of disputes and petty quarrels between the rulers and the ruled. Things and men in Asia had lost their epic grandeur. The vanity of the noblemen, the venomous plots of the indigenous races and the literary barbarity of a perfect bazaar of merchants and pilots replaced the virtues and the wit of the first epoch of the conquest. The degeneration of the ancient race went on still more rapidly than Diogo de Couto had predicted. " (1)

Some time after, it was known that Bocage had gone to Macao from which place he returned to Lisbon in 1790. Either going to or coming from Macao, he was shipwrecked, like Camões, saving his poems while swimming to land. (2) It is said, however, by Teophilo Braga that Bocage went to Goa and from there to Portugal. Ismael Gracias is also of the same opinion that Bocage was in Goa more than once, perhaps in the end of the year 1789 or in the beginning of 1790. However, no document or trace of one can be found with respect to this second visit of Bocage to Goa. (3)

Both in Lisbon and in India, Bocage led a wild life ; he associated with companions who had coarse

---

(1) " Poesias de Manuel Maria de Barbosa du Bocage " by I. F. da Silva, containing :
" Estudo Biogaphico e Litterario ", by L. A. Rebello da Silva, Lisbon, 1853, Vol. I, p. 27.

(2) " Estudo Biographico e Litterario ", by L. A. Rebello da Silva, Lisbon, 1853, p. 30.

(3) " T. Braga ", " Bocage, Sua Vida e Epoca Literaria " Porto, 1902, p. 86 ; and Ismael Gracias, " Bocage na India " Nova Goa, 1917, p. 60-61.

low tastes. In consequence of his predilection for such company his beautiful productions are interspersed with obscene verses, and like many poets of his time, he revelled in satires and coarse jokes which he wrote in the form of sonnets. He was admired more for his ready wit and sarcasm than for his higher mental qualities. The following anecdote is an illustration of his gift for repartee :— One evening Bocage was seated in the balcony of the upper story of his house when a Bohemian friend passed by with a bottle of wine under his arm. Bocage at once leaned forward and asked for the wine. His friend retorted playfully : "Give me a rhyme for India and you can have it." Like lightning came the answer : "Então, guindia". (Then hoist it up). He has become a traditional figure to whom a thousand and one anecdotes have been rightly or wrongly attributed.

But in the midst of his collection of rhetorical compositions and ignoble sonnets, there are a few works which reveal the man himself to be full of originality and poetic genius, immeasurably above the society he frequented. There is a page in the life of Bocage, which, when understood, explains why his lyric poetry always wakes a responsive chord. It was the pure, true love that he felt for Maria Vicencia, the daughter of Antonio Marçal Leite whose guest he was for a time, which influenced him. When he was imprisoned on the charge of being a revolutionary, it was not difficult to persuade the mother of the girl that she should not permit her daughter to marry him. On her death-bed, she made Maria swear to give him up. And thus, his unrealised love dream inspired the poet to sing enchanting strains, the sincerity of which can be felt in every line.

Through the noble sentiments which pervade his verses, and his indignant protest against the moral and political decadence of his time, now taking the form of ridicule or satire, now of direct attack and invective,

"Bocage", (1) says Professor Mendes dos Remedios with reason, "shines in the gallery of poets as a star of the first magnitude."

He had no rival in improvisation or in the use of satire and his sonnets excelled the best of Camões in that style. (2)

In the words of Theophilo Braga, Bocage was "the most inspired and unfortunate genius that the Portuguese had yet seen." (3)

Through his satirical talent, he naturally created many enemies, especially amongst the grave and learned members of the Academy. The following epigrams give an idea of the rapier-like thrusts which were exchanged between them :

Epigram of Domingos Caldas Barbosa to Bocage :

" De todos sempre diz mal
O ímpio Manuel Maria
E se de Deus o não disse
E' porque o não conhecia. "

(Of all he ever spoke ill,
The impious Maria Manuel,
If he spoke not thus of God 'twas
For he did not know Him well.)

Immediately Bocage retorted :

" Dizem que o Caldas glotão
Em Bocage aferra o dente
Ora é forte admiração
Vir um cão morder na gente ! "

---

(1) Mendes dos Remedios' "História da Literatura Portuguesa", 5th. edition, Lisbon, 1921, p. 433.

(2) Mendes dos Remedios' "História da Literatura Portuguesa", 5th edition, Lisbon, 1921, p. 433.

(3) Quoted in Ismael Gracias ' " Bocage na India ", p. 43.

(They say that the glutton Caldas
From Bocage has taken a bite;
To see a dog bite people
Is indeed a wonderful sight.)

One of his greatest enemies was Father José Agostinho de Macedo who is one of the most fertile writers of the epoch. For him, Bocage was an author without method or sequence of ideas, incapable of symmetry and ignorant of all the laws of rhetoric. In reality Father Macedo, with all his technique, could never equal the art, emotionalism and spontaneity of Elmano to whose poetry the verses of Boileau are applicable :

Un style impetueux souvent marche au hasard :
Chez lui un beau desordre est un effet de l'art.

His enemies increased so greatly that more than once his life was in imminent danger while in Goa, and in this there is still one more similarity between his life and that of the unhappy Camões. Bocage himself says:

" Camões, grande Camões, quão similhante
Acho teu fado ao meu, quando os cotejo. "

(Camões, great Camões, how similar
I find your fate to mine, when I compare them !)

In India where he was for less than three years, he gave free rein to his humoristic vein and his poetic productions written in the shade of the palm trees of Goa are well known, where he praises the beauties of the Orient and satirises the customs of the society in which he lived. It will not be irrelevant here to give a brief review of the impressions of Goa and its inhabitants which the famous poet has left us in his poetic compositions. He was attracted in the first place to India through the spirit of adventure which had led the first Portuguese to seek glory and fame far from their paternal firesides :

"…. Um vivo ardor de nome, e fama
A' nova região me atrae, me chama."

(An ardent desire for name, and fame
To a new region, attracts me, calls me.)

He went to Goa full of pride based on the past glory of his country, but he was soon disillusioned by the life he found there:

"Por terra jaz o emporio do Oriente,
Que do rigido Afonso o ferro, o raio
Ao gran filho ganhou do gran Sabaio,
Envergonhando o deus armipotente;
Caiu Goa, terror antigamente;
Do Naire vão, do perfido Malaio,
De barbaras nações !...Ah, que desmaio
Apaga o marcio ardor da lusa gente ?
O' seculos d'herois; Dias de gloria !
Varões excelsos, que apesar da morte,
Viveis na tradição, viveis na historia !
Albuquerque terrivel, Castro forte,
Menezes e outros mil vossa memoria
Vinga as injurias, que nos faz a sorte."

Soneto, 158, vol. I.

(Low lies the emporium of the Orient
Which the iron of the stern Afonso, the flashing steel
Of the great son gained from the great Sabaio,
Shaming the God of War;
Goa has fallen ! the former terror
Of the proud Nair, of the perfidious Malay,
Of barbarous nations ! Alas what weakness
Damps the martial ardour of the Lusitanians ?
Oh centuries of heroes ! Days of glory !
Superior beings who in spite of death
Live in tradition, live in history !
Oh terrible Albuquerque, strong Castro, Menezes and a thousand others, your memory
Avenges the injuries which Fortune does us.)

He wrote four sonnets about Goa, the most characteristic of which perhaps, is the following:

"Das terras a peor tu es, ó Goa,
Tu pareces mais ermo, que cidade ;
Mas alojas em ti maior vaidade
Que Londres, que Paris, ou que Lisboa.

A chusma de teus incolas pregoa
Que excede o gran Senhor na qualidade :
Tudo quer senhoria ; o proprio frade
Allega, para tel-a, o jus da coroa !

De timbres prenhe estás ; mas ouro e prata
Em cruzes, com que d'antes te benzias,
Foge a teus infanções de bolsa chata :

Oh que feliz, e esplendida serias,
Se algum fusco Melim, que faz bagata,
Te alborcasse a pardaus as senhorias!"

(Of all the lands, the worst art thou, O Goa !
Thou seemest much more wilderness than city ;
In thee lodges greater vanity
Than in London, Paris or even Lisbon.

The multitude of thy inhabitants proclaim
That they excel the great Turk in quality.
All desire power : the monk himself,
To gain it, pleads a royal right.

With blazoned crests thou teemest, but get gold and silver
With which before thou blest thyself in Crosses,
Now fly to the empty purses of the noble ladies.

Oh how happy, how radiant thou wouldst be,
If some dark Merlin, who knows black magic
Would barter thy dominions for pardaus.)

And in truth when the poet arrived in India, the capital of the great Portuguese empire was in a sad state of decline, politically, economically and socially ; only the remembrance of its former grandeur remained. Bocage knew merely the city ; he probably never saw the villages of Bardez, Salsete and Pondá, where the better classes had gone to seek refuge from plague and other pestilences found in the city. He speaks of the river Mandovi; he did not know the Zuari, which is the legendary Goanese Ganges. Nothing pleased the poet in Goa to which he refers in these lines:

" Terra sem lei, madrasta de poetas,
Estuporada mãe, de gentes baças."
(A land without law, stepmother of poets,
Unworthy mother of swarthy sons.)

He was in Goa during the time when some persons were accused of forming a conspiracy against the government in 1787, with the object of forming an independent republic (1) and Bocage refers to this in his " Epistola a Josinho " as " recent news", which ends in this fashion:

" Eis que perfida mão cabal ruina
(Sepultando o dever no esquecimento)
A todos nos prepara, e nos destina;
Rasgado o peito co'um punhal cruento.
Ia baixar o teu choroso amigo,
Qual vitima innocente, ao monumento:
Uma alma infame, um barbaro inimigo

---

(1) C. Rivara, " A Conjuração de 1787 em Goa "; Bruto da Costa, " Goa sob a Dominação Portuguesa ", pp. 77-85. Pe. G. Saldanha, " História de Goa ", 1925, pp. 225-231.

In this conspiracy was implicated the celebrated L'Abbé Faria, the romantic hero of Monte Cristo of Dumas. He emigrated to France when the news of the conspiracy arrived in Lisbon, where he was at the time with his father. This Abbé Faria is justly considered the father of hypnotism. Vide:

(a) " De la Cause du Sommeil Lucide, ou " l'Étude de la nature de l'homme " par l'Abbé Faria, Brahmine, docteur en Theologie: Paris, (First edition in 1819; second edition, with an erudite introduction by Dr. G. Dalgado, in 1906).

(b) Dr. D. G. Dalgado, " Memoire sur la vie de l'Abbade Faria ", p. 56 and following.

(c) Egas Moniz, " O Abade Faria".

(d) P. Pissurlencar, " Aspectos da Civilização da India Antiga ", 1925, pp. 79-81.

Da fé, das leis, do trono, um desumano,
Credor de eterno, de infernal castigo,
Tendo embebido seu furor insano
Na falsa gente bracmane inquieta,
Que amaldiçoa o jugo lusitano,
Contra nós apontava a mortal seta ;
Mas estorvou o inevitavel tiro
A mão divina, poderosa, e recta;
Desenvolveu-se o crime, inda respiro ;
E, já destes, o' reus de atroz maldade,
Em vis teatros o final suspiro.
Eis, amigo, a recente novidade,
Que de remota Goa ao Tejo envio
Nas murchas, debeis asas da Saudade."

(Lo ! by the perfidious hand a perfect ruin
(Burying duty in forgetfulness)
Is prepared for all of us and is destined for us :
With the breast torn by a cruel dagger
Your lamented friend, an innocent victim
Was to be brought to the grave :
A base soul, a barbarous enemy
Of the faith, of the laws and of the crown, an inhuman creature
Deserving of eternal and hellish punishment,
Having imbued with his insane frenzy
The false turbulent, Brahmin people,
Who curse the Lusitanian yoke,
Pointed the mortal arrow against us ;
But the Divine Hand, powerful and good,
Stayed the inevitable arrow in its flight ;
The crime was discovered, I am still alive
And the criminals of this terrible plot
Have already paid for it with their last breath.
Here you have, friend, the latest news
Which I send from remote Goa to the Tagus
On the faded, feeble wings of Remembrance.

The latest trace of Bocage's stay in India was his poem, "A Manteigui", a composition satirizing in an unrestricted manner the love affair of the Governor of Goa, Guilherme de Sousa. (1)

---

(1) See "Bocage na India", by Ismael Gracias.

In August, 1790, he again reached his birthplace at the age of twenty-five, without a post or the means to live. "Incapable of existing in one country only", as he himself said, he had seen with his own eyes those climes through which Camões had passed, partaking of the same cup of bitter misfortune which both poets had prepared for themselves.

He spent the last years of his life in Lisbon where he continued to write. Besides his sonnets on Goa, he wrote a part of a tragedy entitled "Vasco da Gama", or "A Descoberta da India pelos Portugueses," of which only two scenes of the first Act are published, though the Act seems to have been completed by the author. The scene is passed in Calicut in the place of the Samorim, having for the personages, the Samorim, Vasco da Gama, a Portuguese official called Ataíde, Haril, Prince of Cochin, Alaida, daughter of the Samorim, a Brahmin, &c. As the subject is purely imaginary, and has no interest from the Indian historical point of view, we merely mention its existence.

Some little time before his death, Bocage had a premonition of the coming end, and in some exquisite lines, full of infinite regret, he takes leave of the beautiful Portuguese country in which sonnet he also shows his sensitive horror of the idea of dissolution :

> "Não mais, o Tejo meu, formoso e brando,
> A margem fertil de gentis verdores,
> Terás d'alta Ulyssea um dos cantores,
> Suspiros co'o aureo plectro modulando.
> Rindo não mais verás, não mais brincando,
> Por entre as nymphas e por entre as flores,
> O coro divinal dos nus amores,
> Dos Zephiros azues o affavel bando.
> Co'a fronte já sem myrto, e já sem louro,
> O arrebata de rojo a mão da sorte,
> Ao clima salutar, a margem de ouro.
> Eil-o em fragas de horror, sem luz, sem morte
> Toa d'aqui, d'alli, paido agouro :
> Sois vós, desterro eterno, ermos da morte !"

(No more lovely Tagus, so clear and smooth flowing,
On thy banks, mossy covered, with green-shaded sward,
From high Lusitania, the full throated bard,
Will modulate his sighs to his lyre golden glowing.
No more wilt thou see there, laughing and dancing,
Amidst elf-like Dryads and between sun-kissed flowers,
The heavenly chorus of Love's happiest hours,
The band of blue zephyrs in merriment glancing.
His brow without myrtle, no laurel adorning,
Reluctant, is dragged by the stern hand of Death
To the health-giving clime at the brink of the dawning,
Here horror confronts him, without light, without death.
Here and there sound murmuring forebodings of
mourning :
O Solitude Eternal, hermitage of Death !) (1)

Father José Agostinho de Macedo.

Another poet to write on Indian topics was Father José Agostinho de Macedo, 1761-1831, the implacable enemy of Bocage, who was, in spite of his great intelligence and vast erudition, much below the level of his competitor. He wished to supplant Camões and for this reason took up the subject of the Lusiadas and wrote a poem first called "Gama" (2) and afterwards renamed by him " O Oriente ". In this poem he attempts to show how he thinks that Camões should have presented his subject, and his poem is without

---

(1) This translation was published in " The Poetry Review", Vol. XVII, No. 6, 1926, in an article on " The Poetry of Portugal" by the author.

(2) P. José Agostinho de Macedo, Orth : Eremitarius S. Augustino, author of :

1. " Gama. Poema Narrativo ", 8.° Lisbon, 1811. cf. Estudos, p. 40.
2. " O Oriente. Poema ", 2 volumes, 8.°
   " " " Lisbon 1814.
   " 1827.
   " " " Porto 1854.

life, colour or poetry. (1)

Effect of the disastrous wars with the Mahrattas on the literature.

The decline of the Portuguese power in India which Bocage had noticed with such regret, continued till the Mahrattas who were in constant struggles with the Portuguese, demonstrated the superiority of their forces and seized the dominions of Baçaim and a part of the province to the north of Goa, comprising the island of Salsette and some fortified places besides, on the 16th. May, 1739. There was little left to Portugal except Goa, Damão, Diu and the factory of Surat.

Prose writers who wrote on the wars.

The Portuguese possessions in India were now reduced to their smallest proportions and literature on this subject could only be an account of disasters, as is shown in the following manuscript:

> " Rellação da guerra que o Inimigo Marata fez no Estado da India, e dos progressos della desde o dia seis de Abril de 1737 thé os primeiros de Janeiro de 1745 com algũas noticias das antecedencias e principios; em que teve origem a mesma guerra."
>
> (An account of the war which the enemy Mahratta made in the State of India, and its progress, from the 6th. of April, 1737, till the first days of January 1745 with some news of what preceded the war and its beginnings ; how the same war originated.)

This manuscript is in the Biblioteca Nacional, Lisbon, (Overseas section), and which has recently been included in the " Portugueses e Maratas " by P. Pissurlencar.

In the same Library there is also another manuscript on the same subject which was published by the same writer in " Portugueses e Maratas " IV.

---

(1) " Estudo Biographico e Litterario ", by L. A. Rebello da Silva, p. 26.

"Relação dos successos acontecidos no estado da India desde 17 de Outubro de 1733, em que principiou a governar o mesmo Estádo o vice-rei Conde de Sandomil até 13 de fevereiro de 1740, que durante o mesmo governo se expediu para o reino a nau Nossa Senhora da Conceição, com a origem e motivos que deram ocasião a guerra presente de Maratta."

(An account of the events which took place in the State of India from the 17th. of October 1733 when the Viceroy Conde de Sandomil began to govern the said State, till the 13th. of February 1740, who during the same governorship sent to the Kingdom the ship Nossa Senhora da Conceição with a pretext and motive which gave rise to the present Mahratta war.)

A slightly different version of the same "Account" is found in the above mentioned Library of Lisbon (Reservados section).

In the library of Ajuda, Lisbon, amongst its precious manuscripts, is one relative to this subject entitled :

"Relação sumaria dos successos de Goa com guerra do Maratta, escripta, com a individuação de algumas particulares circumstancias que não são a todos manifestas." 1739.

(The summary account of the events in Goa of the Mahratta war written with the details of some particular circumstances which are not manifest to every one.)

As one may see by the titles of the "Accounts" referred to, the subject matter of each one of them is connected with the celebrated Luso-Mahratta War, in which the Portuguese lost the fortress of Baçaim, with its dependencies, resulting in the treaty, signed between the two ruling powers in 1739, the copy of which as well as other documents connected with the same treaty, may be found in the Archives, of the Government of Goa, (Livro das Monções, No. 110), or in the Biblioteca Pública of Evora (Portugal). Ismael Gracias, a scholar of Goa, published the documents which he found on the subject in Goa, in the Oriente Portuguez, Volumes III and IV, the aforesaid documents of Evora still remaining unpublished, as well as that one which has for its title:

> "Conta que o general marata Chimanagi Apa deo ao seu Rey Xahu da conquista da Praça de Baçaim do Norte no anno de 1740."
>
> (Account which the Mahratta general Chimanagi gave to his King Shahu of the conquest of the Fortress of Baçaim of the North in the year 1740.)

It is in the Biblioteca Nacional of Lisbon. This "Account" covers only nine pages and was sent to Lisbon from Goa, being translated by the Portuguese interpreter of the District Bogona Camotim, on the 8th. April, 1740. The original letter of Chimanagi Apa, written in Marathi and addressed to Shahu on the date, the 22nd of May 1739, was lost, and we believe that a copy of this "Account" fell into the hands of the Portuguese authorities of Goa, probably through the medium of Naro Ramo, Minister of Shahu, with whom the same authorities kept up friendly relations, as we found making investigations in the Historic Archive of Nova Goa, in 1924.

Besides the above-mentioned works, there are various Accounts of this war of the Mahrattas with the Portuguese, in the Bibliotheca Nacional of Lisbon.

Diogo da Costa. With reference to this period, there is a book written by Diogo da Costa, entitled:

> "Relação das guerras da India desde o anno 1736 até o de 1740."
>
> (Account of the wars in India from the years 1736 to 1740.)

This "Account" published in Lisbon in 1740, consists of twenty pages, and does not present any facts other than those which are generally known, except in the part referring to the naval battle of the Portuguese with Sambhaji Angria (pp. 19-20) about which there is also an "Account" in the Biblioteca Publica of Evora entitled :

> "Relação da batalha naval que a nau Nossa Senhora da Victoria teve na costa do Sul contra o pirata Sambagi Angria."
>
> (An account of the naval battle which the ship "Nossa Senhora da Victoria" had on the south coast against the pirate Sambaji Angria.)

and which is still unpublished.

Diogo da Costa also describes the above-mentioned naval battle which took place between the Portuguese and the pirate Sambaji Angria :—

"When the struggles between the Portuguese and the Mahrattas were going on, the latter had agreed with the Angria, that the same Mahrattas, together with Bounsulo should make war against the Portuguese by land, and the Angria by sea, giving the principal duty to the Angria that he should await a Portuguese ship which had gone to bring supplies to the South. In order to carry out his part, the fleet of the Angria left the port of Griem, duly prepared, to await the Portuguese ship which was called "Nossa Senhora da Victoria." The ship had come out from the harbour of Goa on the 8th. February 1739, leading in its train forty-seven trading ships, which were laden with salt, and was going to bring, on the return, rice of the south coast from the ports of Canara. The same ship left the port of Mangalore on the 2nd. of March and returned with the trading ships laden with rice and met the seven ships (palas) and ten warships (galvetas) of Sambaji Angria, entering into combat which lasted till night-fall, at which time the Angria gave up the contest and withdrew.

In the morning of the following day, the Angria

again attacked the Portuguese ship, persisting until one o'clock in the afternoon, and then withdrew, the ship being victorious". "From this encounter resulted great credit to the Portuguese nation", says Diogo da Costa.

Jacinto Machado de Sousa.

Jacinto Machado de Sousa has also written an account of this war and the victories of the Conde de Ericeira :

> "Nova Relação das importantes vitorias que alcançaram as armas Portuguesas na India, e da gloriosa paz que se ajustou, logo que chegou o vice-rei do Estado, o Exmo D. Luiz de Menezes, Conde da Ericeira, até 1742."

> (New Account of the important victories which came to the Portuguese arms in India, and of the glorious peace which was arranged as soon as the Viceroy the Most Excellent D. Luiz de Menezes, Conde de Ericeira, arrived, till 1742.)

With the arrival of the new Governor, the Marquis of Louriçal, the province of Goa, Bardez and Salsette were won back from the Mahrattas under Bounsulo in 1742 ; and during the rule of his successor, the Marquis of Castello Novo, afterwards the Marquis of Alorna, was reestablished the prestige of the Portuguese arms through his victories of Alorna, Bicholim, Avaro and Reddi. The news of these victories aroused in Portugal the greatest enthusiasm and a number of poems were written in celebration of these events, among which were the following by Antonio de Meirelles :

Poem by Antonio de Meirelles on the victories over the Mahrattas.

> "Poema heroico, marcio, historico, da gloriosa e immortal victoria que contra o inimigo Bounsulo alcançou o Illmo. e Exmo. Sr. D. Pedro Miguel de Almeida e Portugal, Marquez de Castello Novo, vice-rei da India, &c. na tomada de Alorna, Bicholim e Sanquelim, no anno 1746." Lisbon, 1747, 39 pages.

> (A heroic, martial, historical poem of the glorious and immortal victory which D. Pedro Miguel de Almeida e

Portugal, Marquez de Castello Novo, Viceroy of India, won against the enemy Bounsulo, at the capture of Alorna, Bicholim and Sanquelim in the year 1746.)

" Poema heroico, ou metricas proesas de Morte, executadas pelo Exmo. Sr. Marquez de Castello Novo, &c. na continuação das conquistas das terras do Bounsulo até a praça de Rarim ".

(Heroic poem or the metrical deeds of Death, performed by the Most Excellent Sr. Marquis of Castello Novo, &c. in continuation of the conquests of the lands of Bounsulo up to the fort of Rarim.)

" Applausos metricos ao Exmo. Sr. D. Pedro Miguel de Almeida e Portugal, Marquez de Castello Novo, &c. pelos felices successos e victorias que tem conseguido na India contra o inimigo Bounsulo ", Lisbon, 1747.

(Metrical applauses to the Most Excellent Sr. D. Pedro Miguel de Almeida and Portugal, Marquis de Castello Novo, &c. on account of the fortunate successes and victories which he accomplished in India against the enemy Bounsulo.)

Prose account by the same author.

The same author, Manoel Antonio de Meirelles, wrote an account in prose of the conquests of the Marquis of Alorna called :

" Relação da Conquista das Praças de Alorna, Bicholim, Avaro, Morly, Satarem, Tiracol e Rarim pelo Illustrissimo e Excellentissimo Senhor D. Pedro Miguel de Almeida e Portugal, Marquez de Castello Novo, Conde de Assuncar, do Conselho de Sua Magestade, e do Conselho de guerra, Vedor da Casa Real, Mestre de Campo General de seus exercitos, Director General da Cavallaria do Reyno, e Capitão General da India Port. " Lisbon, 1747.

(An Account of the conquest of the Forts of Alorna, Bicholim, Alvaro, Morly, Satarem, Tiracol and Rarim, by the Most Illustrious and Excellent Senhor D. Pedro Miguel de Almeida and Portugal, Marquis of Castello Novo, Count of Assuncar, of the Council of His Majesty, and of the Council of War of the Royal House, Master of the Camp, General of his Armies, Director General of the

Cavalry of the Kingdom and Captain General of Portuguese India.)

Another historical Note on the subject was published in Lisbon in 1746 with the following title :

"Epanaphora Indica na qual se dá noticia da viagem que o Illustrissimo e Excellentissimo Senhor Marquez de Castelo Novo fez com o cargo de Vice-Rey ao Estado da India e dos primeiros progressos do seu governo ; e se referem tambem os successos da viagem, do Excellentissimo e Revmo. Senhor D. Fr. Lourenço de Santa Maria, Arcebispo Metropolitano de Goa, Primaz da Azia Oriental; sua chegada entrada e suas funcções archiepiscopaes." Escrita por J. F. M.M.

(Epanaphora India in which news is given of the voyage of the Most Illustrious and Most Excellent Senhor Marquez de Castelo Novo made when he came out as Viceroy of the State of India and the first steps of his government, and it refers also to the events of the voyage of the Most Excellent and Most Reverend Senhor D. Father Lourenço de Santa Maria, Metropolitan Archbishop of Goa, Primate of Oriental Asia ; his arrival, entrance and his archiepiscopal functions.) Written by J. F. M. M.

This work is divided into five parts and in them they treat of the struggles of the Portuguese with the Mahrattas, Bounsulo and Angria which took place during the period of the Viceroyalty of the Marquez do Castelo Novo. Besides these five parts, the sixth part of the same work 'Epanaphora' was published in Lisbon in 1753, and concludes with the end of the Viceroyalty of the same Marquez.

In this last part, we find the name of its author, José Freire de Monterroyo Mascarenhas instead of his initials as in the first five parts. It is a work which throws much new light on Mahratta History. We examined a copy of this book in the Biblioteca Nacional of Lisbon.

Felix Feliciano da Fonseca.

In Lisbon an "Account" was published in 1743, entitled :

"Dos Felicissimos successos obrados na India Oriental em o Vice-Reinado do Illustrissimo e Excellentissimo Marquez de Tavora."

(About the most fortunate events which took place in Oriental India during the Viceroyalty of the Most Illustrious and Most Excellent Marquez de Tavora.)

Its author was Felix Feliciano da Fonseca. It treats of the war of the Sundas with the Portuguese.

Instructions of the Marquis of Alorna and the Marquis of Pombal.

The brilliant governorship of the Marquis of Alorna was brought to a close in September 1750. The Instructions which he left to his successor about the political, social and economic government of India are widely known. They were published in Goa in the year 1836 by F. L. Cabreira and reprinted with 380 Notes by F. N. Xavier in 1856. These Instructions are so important for the history of India that they are worth translating into English: They are known as:

"Instrucção dada pelo Exmo. Marquez d'Alorna ao seu successor no governo deste Estado da India o Exmo. Marquez de Tavora."

(Instruction given by the Most Excellent Marquis of Alorna to his successor in the government of India, the Marquis of Tavora).

Other instructions which are equally important were those given by the Marquis of Pombal to the Governor and the Archbishop of the Orient in 1774. They are as follows:

"Instrucções com que El-Rei D. José I mandou passar ao Estado da India o Governador e Capitão General e o Arcebispo Primaz do Oriente no anno 1774."

(Instructions which the King D. José I had ordered to be sent to the State of India, the Governor and Captain General and the Archbishop Primate of the East in the year 1774.)

These instructions were for the administration of the civil, political, military, financial, judicial and ecclesiastical departments, and comprised a document which showed the breadth of the vision and encyclopaedic knowledge of the Marquis of Pombal. "One would say on reading the instructions", wrote Lagrange, "that the Marquis had visited India and had not only an exact knowledge of the topography of the country, but also of the particular needs of each village in the remedies he suggested."

In these instructions, the Marquis refers to the Bishop of Halicarnasso, a romantic figure in the historical scene of India of that time. (1) This bishop was a friend of Hyder Ali and for this reason the biography of Hyder Ali, written by him, has some historical importance.

One of the Viceroys whose name is connected with the history of the Mahrattas was the Conde de Alva. There is in Portuguese about his deeds in India an Account consisting of twenty-one pages entitled :

> "Relação dos successos prosperos e infelizes do Illmo. e Exmo. Sr. D. Luiz Mascarenhas, Conde de Alva, Vice-Rei dos estados da India, referida a todo o tempo do seu governo, &c. Lisbon, 1757."
>
> (An Account of the successes and misfortunes of Sr. D. Luiz Mascarenhas, Conde de Alva, Viceroy of the States of India, with respect to the whole time of his governorship).

The author of this "Relação" is Joseph Roger. The description is touching which the author makes of the death of the Viceroy, Conde de Alva, when he went in 1756 to attack the fortress of Pondá which belonged to Sunda, fearing that it would come to fall

---

(1) See Ismael Gracias' "O Bispo de Halicarnasso", Nova Goa.

Eduardo de Noronha's "O Bispo de Halicarnasso". Caetano Gonçalves' "O Oriente Portugues", 1905.

into the hands of the Mahrattas and thus become a dangerous neighbourhood for the Portuguese.

In the same year in which the Viceroy, the Conde, de Alva died on the field of battle in Pondá, was printed in Lisbon :

" Relação ou noticia certa dos estados da India."

(An Account or true Historical Note about the States of India).

It contains eight pages in which it refers to the progress of the Portuguese arms against the Peshwas and Bhonsule.

On the same subject was published in Lisbon in 1751, another "Relação" which is found in the Biblioteca Nacional of the same city.

In the same Library there are other Accounts of a few pages each narrating the victories of the Portuguese against Bhounsule :

"Annal Indico-Lusitano.

Dos successos mais memoraveis e das acçoens mais particulares do primeiro anno do felicissimo Governo do Illustrissimo e Excellentissimo Senhor Francisco de Assis de Tavora, Marquez de Tavora, Conde de S. João, do Conselho do Estado de S. Magestade, Fidelissimo Vice-Rey e Capitão General da India. Em que se acharão embaraçadas as Naçoens Europeas com alguns Principes, Potentados da Asia, desde o primeiro de Janeiro de 1751 até ao ultimo de Dezembro do mesmo anno: e se referem ás exequias que na Cidade de Goa se fizerão na morte do Senhor Rey D. João V e o Auto de Juramento com que na mesma cidade foy acclamado Rey de Portugal, Fidelissimo Senhor D. Joseph I, Nosso Senhor. Escripto e oferecido a Illustrissima e Excellentissima Senhora D. M. Anna Bernarda de Tavora, Condessa de Athouguia. Por Francisco Raymundo de Moraes Pereira, Desembargador da Casa da Supplicação de Goa, Lisboa. Na officina de Francisco Luiz Ameno, Impressor da Congregação Camararia da Santa Igreja de Lisboa. 1753".

(Annal Indico-Lusitano.

Of the more notable events and the detailed deeds of the first year of the most fortunate rule of most Illustrious and Most Excellent Senhor Francisco de Assis de Tavora, Marquez de Tavora, Conde de S. João of the Council of the State of His Majesty, Most Faithful Viceroy and Captain General of India, in which is given news of the wars with which the European nations found themselves involved with some princes and potentates of Asia from the first of January of 1751 till the last of December of the same year; and it refers to the ceremonies which they performed in the City of Goa on the death of the King D. João V. and the oath which the same city took in the acclamation of the King of Portugal, Most Faithful Senhor D. Joseph I, our Lord. Written and offered to the Most Illustrious and Most Excellent Senhora D. Maria Anna Bernarda de Tavora, Condessa de Athouguia. By Francisco Raymundo de Moraes Pereira, Desembargador de Casa da Supplicação de Goa, Lisbon. In the office of Francisco Luiz Ameno, Printer of the Congregação Camararia of the Holy Church of Lisbon. 1753).

It contains eighty-nine pages and is found in the book entitled: "Obras Varias", H. G. No. 15217 P. Biblioteca Nacional of Lisbon. Page 6 refers to the attempt which Bounsulo, helped by the Mahrattas, made to retake his old forts, in which attempt he was repulsed by the Portuguese.

In page 16, we read of the same enemies (Bounsulo and the Mahratta) laying siege to the Fortress of Nautim, and being victoriously repulsed by the Portuguese.

And here it will not be out of place to mention the writings of the Bishop of Halicarnasso, otherwise known to history as Father Antonio da Purificação, who was born in Goa Velha on the 14th. July 1720. His life and career are well delineated by Ismael Gracias in his book: "O Bispo de Halicarnasso." (See pp. 1-5). Gracias tells us of him that he went to St. Thomé where he came in contact with Madame Dupleix, a Portuguese lady (formerly Madame Vincens), the daughter of one of those

Bishop of Halicarnasso

families who are descendants of Portuguese noblemen and Indians born in the country. She had a profound knowledge of the Indian languages. Knowing Dupleix for years before her husband died, she married him in 1741, two years after her husband's death. Father Antonio wished to rise and he knew that there was no better way than through a woman. For this he trumped up a relationship of cousin with Madame Dupleix which both she and her husband accepted ; for Dona Joanna, revered by the Hindus as Jan Begum, dominated her husband and allowed herself to be convinced of a false relationship through her vanity (1).

In 1747, D. Fr. Antonio de Purificação succeeded the Bishop of Halicarnasso in the Cathedral of Meliapor. The Marquez de Alorna knew him through Padre Lucas da Costa Cravo, to be dishonest and licentious, and had three sittings of the Council of the Missions in 1747 and 1748 about Father Antonio de Purificação. The meetings of the Missions decided against him and he was being recalled to Goa, when Dupleix was given thirty villages around Pondicherry by the Nawab of Arcot in reward for help he had given him. Then Dupleix asked of the Nawab that the government of St. Thomé and its villages should be given to Father Antonio, which was done. The latter wrote to Marquis Alorna telling him of his good fortune. The Marquis congratulated him and accepted his proposals, but did not forbear to say in the end of his letter that Father Antonio had now a chance to wipe off the stain on his reputation. However, in the end of August 1749, Dupleix had to give up Madras to the English. Boscawen took St. Thomé for the English as well, and imprisoned Father Antonio. He was sent to Portugal

---

(1) Cf. Yvonne Gaebele's "Créole et Grande Dame" (Johanna Begum Marquis Dupleix, 1706-1756).

where he fell in with the Marquis of Pombal and afterwards wrote against the English and against the Jesuits, which documents were published by Cunha Rivara in "O Chronista de Tissuary". He died on the 7th. of February 1776 on his return from Panjim in his carriage, after having dined with the Governor, D. José Pedro da Camara.

In the Library of Manisola, belonging to the Visconde da Esperança, is a work by the Bishop of Halicarnasso, called:

(a) "Deducção chronologica de algumas infracções dos tratados da paz, praticados pelos inglezes no Estado da India, desde o ano de 1748 até o de 1769, pelas quaes se prova serem formalissimos infractores dos mesmos tratados, por factos decisivos, superiores a toda a contestação."

(Chronological deduction from some infractions of the treaties of peace, practised by the English in the State of India, from the year 1748 till that of 1769, by which they are proved to be explicit breakers of the same treaties, through decisive facts, beyond dispute).

It consists of one volume in 4.° which is followed by:

"Manifesto apologetico, e critico, (em defensa da Deducção)."

(Apologetic and critical manifesto in defence of the Deduction.)

(b) "Systema Marcial Asiatico."

(Asiatic Martial System.)

There are three volumes, each volume 530 pages containing coloured pictures of Goa and other countries of India.

The first chapter contains: "Brief news of Goa, its situation, forts and fortifications. Also the plans and perspective of the city of Goa, its islands and adjacent provinces, and the forts of the neighbouring enemies of the State of India". The second chapter relates the various events which combined to bring about the decadence in Goa, and of its inhabitants.

Sr. Barata seems to think that the "Systema" as well as the "Deducção Chronologica" was written by the Bishop of Limoeiro.

(c) "Memorial historico da vida do regulo chamado Adyar Aly Naique".

(Historical memoir of the life of the soldier called Hyder Ali Naik).

Published in "Chronista de Tissuary", Vol. I, pp. 260-266 and pp. 288-294.

(d) "Narração recopilada da cidade de Santo Thomé de Meliapor e das suas aldeias."

(Account compiled in the city of St. Thomé of Meliapor and of its villages).

It discusses the right of the Crown of Portugal to these lands and of the injustice of England in taking possession of them.

It is in the "Biblioteca Publica" Eborensa, Cod. CXVI/2-9.

(e) "Allegação dos serviços prestados á Nação Portuguesa."

(Statement of the services lent to the Portuguese nation.)

In the "Biblioteca Nacional, Lisbon.

Indian languages. In the meantime scholars had turned their attention to the study of Indian languages and it was during the Arcadian period that three grammars were published through the Jesuits, one about Mahratti called:

> "Gramatica Marastta a mais vulgar que se pratica nos Reinos do Nizamxa e Idalxa offerecida aos muito reverendos Padres Missionarios dos ditos Reinos. Em Roma, 1779."
>
> (Mahratti Grammar of the most ordinary language used in the kingdoms of the Nizam Shah and Adil Shah, offered to the very reverend Missionary Fathers of the said kingdoms. In Rome 1778.)

It was published in Lisbon in 1805.

In the same year—1805—was published in Lisbon a Grammar of the Urdu language named :

> " Gramatica Indostana a mais vulgar que se pratica no Imperio do gram Mogul."
>
> (Hindustani Grammar most commonly used in the Empire of the Great Mogul). 150 pages.

A copy of this rare work is in my possession.

Another Grammar on Bengali forms part of the

> " Vocabulario em idioma Bengalla e Portuguez. Dividido em duas partes dedicado ao Exmo. e Revmo. Senhor D. Frei Miguel de Tavora, Lisboa, 1743."
>
> (Vocabulary in Bengali and Portuguese. Divided into 2 parts and dedicated to D. Friar Miguel de Tavora, Lisbon, 1743).

There are two copies of this last mentioned grammar in the British Museum. It is astonishing that the first grammar of that important Indian language Bengali was written in Portuguese.

Various other Indian languages have their grammars in Portuguese also. (1) The reason for this is obvious : when foreigners study a language, they require the grammar of that language which is not the case with those for whom it is the mother tongue.

---

(1) P. Pissurlencar's "Notas Bibliographicas", Provincia, 14th. June, 1926.

CHAPTER IV.

The Romantic School & Contemporary Writers.— 1826 to the present day.

Literary position of Portugal with reference to India.

In the beginning of the nineteenth century, a literary movement began in Germany which spread all over Europe. It was known as the Romantic Movement and represented the reaction against the rigidity of the classic style which had so long influenced European writers. In Portugal, the founders of this school were Garrett, Herculano and Castilho. Many enthusiastic disciples followed their example, who were more or less faithful to the Romantic style. In the list of the more notable of the Romantic writers, besides those already mentioned, we find the names of João de Lemos, Antonio Augusto, Soares de Passos, Francisco Gomes de Amorim, José da Silva Mendes Leal, Thomas Antonio Ribeiro Ferreira, Bulhão Pato and others. Only a few of these have written on India. Not one of the three famous writers, Garrett, Herculano and Castilho, wrote on this subject, for the Romantic movement absorbed all their interest. The glories of Portugal as a colonial power had passed away and the Portuguese writers of the day had little interest in India or the colonies as a subject. If any author wrote on India at all, it was merely in continuation of the history of Portugal as in the works of Bulhão Pato, (1) José

(1) Bulhão Pato, (1829-1912), "Os Portugueses na India", Lisboa, 1883.

Maria Latino Coelho, (1) M. Pinheiro Chagas, (2) Oliveira Martins, (3) Camillo Castello Branco, (4) Lopes de Mendonça, (5) Conde de Ficalho and others. (6)

But in Portuguese India itself, a school of literature was created which is to-day productive, especially with regard to history, poetry and science.

In Portugal, Sanscrit Indology, as it was termed, began to be cultivated after the establishment of a professorship of Sanscrit, and the first Professor to be

---

(1) José Maria Latino Coelho, (1825-1891) wrote :
a. "Luiz de Camões", one volume, 1880.
b. "Vasco da Gama", two volumes, 1884.
c. "Fernando Magalhães", published in 1917.

(2) Manuel Pinheiro Chagas, (1842-1895) wrote :
a. " História de Portugal, 8 volumes.
b. " A Joia do Vice-Rei (trata da vingança de D. Francisco de Almeida contra os Rumes que mataram o seu filho D. Lourenço de Almeida).
c. " A descoberta da India, (Contada por um marinheiro), Lisboa, 1891.
d. " Migalhas da História Portuguesa ".
e. " Os Portugueses na Africa, Asia, América e Oceania", Lisboa, 8 volumes.

(3) Joaquim Pedro de Oliveira Martins, (1845-1894), " História de Portugal " e " Portugal nos mares."

(4) Camillo Castello Branco, (1826-1890) poet, dramatist, novelist and critic. He made extensive researches in history, writing dozens of novels and historical romances. He wrote : "Doze Casamentos Felizes"; Lisbon, 1915. (5th. edition). (The Twelve Happy Marriages). The Ninth Marriage speaks of the story of the King of Meale.

(5) António Pedro Lopes Mendonça, (1826-1865). In 1860 he was nominated Professor of the chair of Modern Literature, but he could not take up the post because he became insane. Of him Bulhão Pato wrote : " He had on his forehead the seal of genius and misfortune." He was the author of the monograph " Damião de Goes. Inquisição", which work has the merit of calling the attention of the public to the chronicler of Dom Manuel.

(6) Conde de Ficalho wrote : " Garcia da Orta e seu tempo."

appointed was Vasconcellos d'Abreu 1842-1906, an orientalist of great erudition who has left some most important works on the Sanscrit language and literature. (1)

Indologists and Historians. Cunha Rivara.

One of the most distinguished Portuguese Indologists was Joaquim Heliodoro da Cunha Rivara, a native of Arrayolos, Portugal, who came to Goa in November of 1855 as Secretary General of Portuguese India. When in Portugal he had already given proof of possessing exceptional talent in History, Archaeology and Literature, both by elaborating the interesting "Catalogo dos Manuscriptos da Bibliotheca Publica Eborense" (Lisbon 1850, Vol. I, pp. 450), so useful to Indian scholars, and by writing numerous instructive articles on history, literary criticism and philology.

Very praiseworthy indeed were his labours with regard to studies relating to India where he found a vast field for historico-archaeological investigations. "About Cunha Rivara", says J. A. Ismael Gracias, (2) "it is impossible to write without a feeling of reverence; he is the most learned European amongst those who have been here in the nineteenth century. An erudite antiquarian who spent the greater part of his day shut up in the Libraries and Archives, a humanist and paleographist, he left a large number of contributions for Luso-oriental history and also guided with a firm

---

(1) Vascencellos d'Abreu was the author of :

a. O Sanscrito como base da glottologia Arica, 1878. (Sanscrito as the base of Aryan languages)

b. Summario das Investigações em Sanscritologia desde 1886 até 1891. (Summary of the Investigations in Sanscritology from 1886 to 1891.)

(2) M. J. Gabriel de Saldanha "História de Goa", Vol. I. 1925, "Carta Prefacio", p. 7.

and benevolent hand the young minds that developed under his paternal direction, exercising an efficacious and salutary influence on the mental and literary evolution of Goa... with equal facility he wrote in Portuguese, Latin, French and English. He tried with great assiduity to revive Konkani, having been the first to compose a historical essay and to have some ancient didactic works in that language printed".

The many services Cunha Rivara rendered to the State and the studies which he initiated on his arrival in India, won him the nomination by the King to continue the historical work of Barros and Couto on the conquest and rule of the Portuguese in Asia. In the discharge of this commission, Cunha Rivara travelled over the greater part of India, from Diu to Cape Comorin, and from the coast of Malabar to that of Coromandel in order to see the more important places where in times gone by the Portuguese flag had once floated. The notes which he collected during these excursions are by no means few. Cunha Rivara also collected notes from the Archives of the Portuguese Government of India, [1] which were examined by him most attentively and patiently as is proved by the numerous documents extracted by him from this rich mine and published for the satisfaction of the curiosity of the public, separately in various volumes and in small articles inserted in the "Boletim do Governo", in the "Chronista de Tissuary" and other periodical publications.

Archives of Goa.

And here it will not be out of place to refer, even though only summarily, to the historical Archives of Goa, of which Rivara and various Indo-Portuguese research workers have availed themselves as the principal sources of

---

(1) About the Archives of Goa, vide T. de Aragão "Descripção das Moedas de Goa", Vol. III, Introduction.

their historical productions.

The creation of the historical Archives in Goa goes back a long time. Towards the close of the sixteenth century, the chronicler, Diogo de Couto, asked permission to utilise for the writing of his history the old papers which were in the office of the Secretary to the Government of Goa and with those documents and others from the different administrative departments, to organize in the capital of Goa a "Tôrre do Tombo", where such important material should be collected for the history of the Portuguese in the Orient. His request was granted and in 1595 the chronicler of India received in his charge the documents which he required. He chose a room in the "Palacio da Fortaleza" for the Archives whose custodian he became with an annual salary of 300 pardaos.

The Portuguese Government, however, in 1774, sent for all the books, registers and ancient documents to be found in the Secretariat of the Government, and also for the papers relating to the correspondence of Goa, the administration of the first Archbishopric, the papers in the possession of the Missions, the Municipal laws, etc., leaving only the letters and treaties with the Kings and Princes of Asia, as they might still be found necessary for administrative purposes.

In virtue of this decision, the documents of the ecclesiastical departments of India, including those of the religious orders, were sent to Portugal in 1775. On the part of the Secretariat there was greater delay for they had to make a careful selection of the papers and it was only in 1777 that the boxes said to contain sixty volumes, but in reality sixty-two, left for Portugal.

In 1778, the Governor General of Portuguese India was ordered to suspend the despatch of the books from the Archives and it was promised that those already sent would be returned. This promise was never redeemed, for the books are still in the Tôrre do Tombo,

Lisbon, having as their title "Documentos remettidos da India", some of which, however, have already been published by the "Academia das Sciencias" of Lisbon. (Four volumes appeared at Lisbon, 1889).

Cunha Rivara lived in Goa twenty-two years, and studied closely not only the Archives in his charge, but also those of the 'Relação' of the old Senate of Goa, of the Revenue Department and others. In 1857, he began the publication in the "Boletim do Govêrno do Estado da India", of the documents which he found, printing them in separate volumes as well as under the title of "Archivo Portuguez Oriental". Up till 1877 he succeeded in publishing six small collections and supplements, forming in all ten volumes in octavo containing royal letters to the City of Goa, to the Viceroys and Governors, and many other documents from the sixteenth to the eighteenth century. In Volume V there are important documents relating to Bijapur. Tolbort, Hunter, Danvers and others have spoken, and with reason, in praise of this work which is the *magnum opus* of Rivara.

Besides this precious work, Cunha Rivara enriched the country with various works of recognized merit, such as the "Chronista de Tissuary", 1866 to 1869 [1] and contributed to various periodicals and almanacs as well as to the "Instituto Vasco da Gama", 1872 to 1875, and the "Boletim do Govêrno". In this last periodical were published by him the treaties made between the State of Portuguese India and the neighbouring Kings, and an important series of documents pertaining to the Mogul Emperor Adil Shah, the Mahrattas, Nizam Shah and others, which were made use of by Judice Biker

---

(1) "A India Portuguesa", Part II.

"A Evolução do Jornalismo, by António Maria da Cunha, p. 542.

in his famous "Collecção dos Tratados da India", published in Lisbon in fourteen volumes.

The Archives of the Secretariat of the Government are among the most important in Goa, but even so there are large breaks in the records, principally in the documents of the sixteenth century. Cunha Rivara used from the Archive of the Relação of Goa (Administration of Justice), the documents of the Red book No. 1, belonging to the sixteenth century, for his "Archivo Portuguez Oriental". In 1872, the judge of the same tribunal, Abranches Gracias, commenced a special publication of documents dating from 1601, with the intention of continuing it till the end of 1836. This work was never completed, however, as it contains only the documents up to No. 881, of the year 1700.

The Archive of the "Camara Municipal" of Goa is also important; its documents date from 1529 to 1728; a part of these have been published by Cunha Rivara in the "Archivo Portuguez Oriental".

In the Archive of the Revenue Department, several antique books about the Convents, Pagodas, Communities, &c. are also kept. Amâncio Gracias published many of these documents in the review, "O Oriente Portuguez" and in his interesting work on the economic history of Goa, which is very valuable for those who wish to know the origin of old duties, not only of Portuguese India but also of Bijapur.

The remains of the Ecclesiastical Archives were reviewed by Father C. C. Nazareth in his work "Mitras Lusitanas no Oriente", an important repository of facts relating to the history of the Portuguese religious missions in India.

Besides the works referred to, Cunha Rivara published amongst other things, the following studies which should interest Indian scholars:

1. Brados a favor das Communidades das aldeas do Estado da India. (A book in favour of the communities of the

villages of the State of India). Nova Goa, 1870 (pp. 102).

2. Cruzamentos entre os Portuguezes e as Mulheres Naturaes, (The marriages between the Portuguese and the indigenous women), published in the Almanack Litterario of Goa for the year 1866, by A. J. F. Gonçalves de Figueiredo, p. 36.

3. O dente de Buddha na Ilha de Ceilão, (The tooth of Buddha in the island of Ceylon), in the " Boletim do Governo", 1858, No. 88.

4. Documentos para a historia da medicina empirica na India, (Documents for the history of experimental medicine in India), in the " Jornal da Pharmacia e Medicina da India Portugueza", by G. Roberto, 1866, p. 67.

5. Noticia dos Reis de Goa da dinastia Cadamba, (News of the Kings of Goa of the Cadamba dynasty), in the "Instituto Vasco da Gama", 1872, p. 255.

6. Autoridades para a historia dos Portuguezes na India (Authorities for the History of the Portuguese in India), by T. W. H. Tolbort, translated from the English and annotated, in the " Instituto Vasco da Gama," 1874, pp. 107-184.

7. Escravidão entre os Portuguezes na India, (Slavery amongst the Portuguese in India), in " Imprensa " of Ribandar, 1871, No. 20.

8. Peças de artilheria da invenção de Wienholtz, que davam 21 tiros por minuto, (Pieces of artillery invented by Weinholtz which could fire 21 salutes per minute), in " Imprensa " of Ribandar, 1871, Nos. 29-33 & 35.

9. Ultimas palavras sobre as peças de artilheria da invenção de Weinholtz, (Last words about the pieces of artillery invented by Weinholtz), in " Imprensa " of Ribandar, Nos. 39 & 40.

10. As Missões do Canará no século XVII, (The Missions of Canara in the 17th. century), in Boletim do Governo, 1860, No. 68. (1)

11. Apontamentos para a historia da Pharmacia e Medicina

---

(1) For his long Bibliography, vide Miguel Vicente de Abreu, " Noção de Alguns Filhos Distinctos da India Portugueza", 1874, pp. 82-161.

Portugueza na India, (Notes for the history of Pharmacy and Portuguese Medicine in India), in the Journal de Pharmacia e Medicina", 1804, pp. 20, 46 & 160 ; 2nd. year 1865, pp. 165 & 252 ; 3rd. year, 1866, p. 36 ; 6th. year, 1869 pp. 37 & 51.

12. Memorias sobre |as possessões Portuguezas na Asia escriptas no anno de 1823, por Gonçalo de Magalhaẽs Teixeira Pinto, publicadas com breves notas e additamentos por C. Rivara 1859, (Memoirs on the Portuguese possessions in Asia, written in the year 1823, by Gonçalo, published with brief notes by C. Rivara, 1859).

13. A Conjuração de 1787 em Goa, Memoria historica, 1875, &c. &c. (The Conspiracy of 1787 in Goa, Historical Memoir, &c. &c.)

On his return to the metropolis in 1877, Cunha Rivara took with him valuable manuscripts, some finished and others to be completed, which after his death in 1879, his widow offered to the Public Library of Evora, amongst which "Historia da India no Seculo XVII" is very interesting.

Besides the above-mentioned historical writings referred to, Cunha Rivara published most valuable works on the mother-tongue of Goa, –Konkani. We shall mention the principal ones :

1. Gramatica da lingua Concany, composta pelo Padre Thomas Estevam e accrescentada por outros padres da Companhia de Jesus.

(Grammar of the Konkani language, composed by Father Thomas Estevam and added to by other Fathers of the Company of Jesus), which is preceded by an introduction called "Memoria da distribuição geographica das principais linguas da India", by Sir Erskine Perry and "Ensaio Historico da lingua Concani", by the Editor (Rivara), 1857, pp. 254.

2. Gramatica da lingua Concany no dialecto do Norte, composta no seculo XVII por um Missionario Portuguez.

(Grammar of the Concani language in the dialect of the North, composed in the 17th. century by a Portuguese Missionary), published for the first time. 1858, 184 pages.

3. Diccionario Portuguez-Concany, composto por um Missionario Italiano e publicado por C. Rivara, 1868, pp. 280.

(Portuguese-Concani Dictionary written by an Italian Missionary and published by C. Rivara, 1868, 280 pages).

Cunha Rivara wished also to publish the "Diccionario Concany-Portuguez" which was in manuscript and was the work of the Jesuits; but he could not realize his wish.

Besides Cunha Rivara, various other scholars distinguished themselves by their investigations carried on in the Archives of the Secretariat of the Government of Goa, to-day a part of the administrative Department of the Privy-Council of the same Government.

Amongst these, the most important was the indefatigable Indian writer, Filipe Nery Xavier, who was an untiring investigator of all that was written with respect to Portuguese India. His work is vast and meritorious, and we are able to say to-day, according to Ismael Gracias, that he was one of the most prolific indigenous Portuguese writers. He left valuable works of historical interest, such as:

Filipe Nery Xavier.

1. "O Gabinete Literario das Fontainhas".

(The Literary Cabinet of Fontainhas").

Volume I, 1846, 228 pages.
do. II, 1847, 298 „
do. III, 1848, 286 „

2. "Esboço de um diccionario historico-administrativo' (Sketch of an administrative-historical dictionary), 1850, 288 pages.

3. "Bosquejo historico das Communidades das aldeas dos Concelhos das Ilhas, Salcete e Bardez, 1852", (Historical sketch of the Communities of the villages in the districts of the islands, Salsette and Bardez, 1852).

4. "Collecção dos Facsimiles das assignaturas e rubricas dos Vice-reis e Governadores geraes do Estado da India, 1853", (Collection of the Facsimiles of the signatures of the Viceroys and Governor-Generals of the State of India, 1853).

5. "Instrucção do Exmo. Vice-rei Marquez de Alorna ao seu successor o Exmo. Vice-rei Marquez de Tavora", (Instructions of His Excellency the Viceroy, Marquis of Alorna to his successor His Excellency the Viceroy, Marquis of Tavora), new edition, 1856, revised and enriched with numerous historical notes based principally on official documents which makes it a precious source for the history of India, especially with regard to the Mahrattas.

6. Resumo historico da maravilbosa vida, conversões e milagres de S. Francisco Xavier, 1861.

(Historical Resumé of the marvellous life, conversions and miracles of S. Francis Xavier, 1861).

7. "Descripção do coqueiro, arequeira, arroz e moedas de Goa, 1866", (A description of the cocoanut tree, areca tree, rice and coins of Goa, 1866). This is a very important work, on account of the study of pre-Portuguese Indian numismatics.

An earnest defender of the 'Communidades', he wrote about those most ancient institutions a bcok called: "A Defesa dos direitos das gãocarias, gãocares e dos seus privilegios", (Defence of the rights of the gãocarias, the gãocares and of their privileges).

With equal zeal, he wrote as well about various branches of local administration.

Another writer who also undertook the work of publishing the documents of the Archives of the Secretariat, was the Chief Secretary, Eduardo de Balsemão, whose work "Os Portuguezes no Oriente", besides being a valuable source for the study of the Portuguese period of Indian history, also throws much light on the history of the Mahrattas, especially on the history now hardly ever studied, of the maritime life of the Mahrattas from the time of Kanogy Angria, and contains useful information about the various Kingdoms of Canara.

Eduardo de Balsemão.

Eduardo de Balsemão is also responsible for the publication of various other Portuguese documents belonging to the Archives of the Government of Goa, in the "Boletim do Governo" of Nova Goa, such as :

1 "Descripção do assedio de Goa pelo Idalcão em 1571" (A description of the siege of Goa by Adil Shah in 1571), in the Almanac published by A. Y. de Figueiredo, 1868, 96 pages.

2. "Uma amostra dos antigos Sagoates (presentes do estado aos regulos e dominantes visinhos)" (A list of the ancient Sagoates - presents of the State to the petty neighbouring princes and rulers). Ibid. 1868, p. 128.

3. "Descripção da Conquista da Fortaleza, de Piro denominada "Pillgoddo", e depois "Sadassiva Goddo". (A description of the Conquest of the Piro Fortress, first called "Pillogoddo" and after "Sadassiva-Goddo"), in the Almanac published by A. F. Pereira, 1869, p. 98.

Teixeira d'Aragão is the first Portuguese research worker who wrote about the coins of Portuguese India in his book entitled "Descripção Geral e Historica das Moedas Cunhadas em Nome dos Reis, Regentes e Governadores de Portugal", (General and historical description of the coins struck in the name of the Kings, Regents and Governors of Portugal), three Volumes. Imp. Nacional, Lisbon, 1880.

Teixeira d'Aragão.

The first Volume, published 1874, Cota 72, B. N. L., contains a historical description of ancient coins and famous Portuguese collections of coins from the time of D. Afonso Henriques up to D. Fillipe III. It also contains nine Documents relating to the subject, an alphabetical Index and twenty-nine engravings of coins. The second Volume published 1877, Cota 72, contains the historical description of the coins from the time of D. João IV till D. Luiz I. One finds also tables of weights and measures and values of gold coins, together with one hundred and ninety-eight confirmatory documents, statistics about coins, thirty-three engravings of coins and an alphabetical Index. The third volume Cota 73, B.N.L, contains a preliminary study on the discovery of the way to India by the Portuguese, the customs of the Indian races, documents relating to the subject and a description of the coins of Portuguese India. 405 pages.

The book also contains forty-seven pages about Moçambique, one hundred and fifty three pages of documents, an alphabetical Index and fifteen engravings of coins. The work is based, not only on the documents of the Archives of Goa, but also on many unpublished ones of Portugal. Teixeira d'Aragão was in Goa in 1871, and from his magnificent production one can see that he had done much useful research in Goa during the few months of his stay.

Lopes Mendes.

The work of Lopes Mendes "A India Portugueza", two volumes, Lisbon, 1886, is appreciated chiefly on account of the engravings of the convents, churches and other Indo-Portuguese buildings, many of which have since been completely destroyed.

Herculano de Moura.

Herculano de Moura wrote the "Historia de Dio" (History of Diu). Only six copies have been published of this book whose value is considerable for it contains all the documentary historical evidence regarding this early period of the history of Diu, which is unedited and in the Archives of Portugal.

Fr. Casimiro Christovão de Nazareth.

Father Casimiro Christovão de Nazareth wrote many books but his principal work is:

> "Mitras Lusitanas no Oriente. Catálogo dos Prelados da Egreja Metropolitana e Primacial de Goa e das Dioceses Suffraganeas com a Recopilação das ordenanças por elles emittidas e sumario dos factos notaveis da historia ecclesiastica de Goa."

(Lusitanian Mitres in the East. Catalogue of the Prelates of the Metropolitan Church and Bishoprics of Goa and of the Suffragan Dioceses, &c., with the compendium of the orders issued by them, and the summary of the notable facts of the Eclesiastical history of Goa). Part I, Nova Goa, 1887, 180 pages. Parts I and II reprinted forming one volume XXIV, 640 pages. Lisbon, 1897; Part III, Bombay, 1888, 261 pages, and Second Edition, Nova-Goa, 1924, 512 pages.

It gives an account of the introduction and development of the Roman Catholic religion in India, dividing that account into 19 periods, from 1501 to the 30th. June, 1878.

It contains biographical notes of all the Bishops who governed the diocese in the period indicated, information about the parishes, circulars, etc.

It is a work which has interest only for the historians of Christianity in India; but still for the writers of the history of India, it is a source full of historical facts, about things which though they pertain to the Church in the Orient, are closely connected with the glorious cycle of the Portuguese conquests.

Equally worthy of note are the books about the Portuguese in India of Miguel Vicente d'Abreu, Fredrico Diniz d'Ayalla, A. A. Bruto da Costa, Cristóvam Pinto, Constâncio Roque da Costa, António Francisco Moniz and J. A. Ismael Gracias.

Amongst all these writers, it is necessary to treat more fully of the last named who has left various original works on the archaeology and history of India.

Ismael Gracias.

The following works are worthy of mention:

1. "A Imprensa em Goa nos Seculos XVI, XVII & XVIII,—1880," (Printing in Goa in the 16th, 17th. & 18th. centuries).
2. "Catalogo dos livros do assentamento da gente de guerra que veio do reino para a India desde 1731 até 1811, existentes na Biblioteca Publica de Nova Goa, 1893."

(Catalogue of the registers of the soldiers who came from Portugal to India between 1731 and 1811, in the Public Library of Nova Goa—1893).

3. "O Bispo de Halicarnasso", (The Bishop of Halicarnasso), 1903. (1)

4. "Uma Dona Portuguesa na Côrte do Grão Mogol, 1907" (A Portuguese lady in the court of the Great Mogul, 1907). (2)

---

(1) See chap. III.

(2) Uma Dona Portugueza na Côrte do Grão Mogol", by Ismael Gracias.

Various writers have referred to two ladies, Portuguese Christians, in the Moghul Court, one being in the Court of Akbar and the other in the Court of Aurangzeb, Bahadur Shah, Jehandar Shah and Farrukhsyer. About the first, history keeps absolute silence; "A person", says Heras, "mentioned neither by the contemporary Mahomedan historians, nor by the Jesuits at the Imperial Court, nor in Portuguese documents, nor by the early European historians, nor by contemporary travellers". (a) Hence the learned author supposes that this woman never existed. (b)

Concerning the other lady, it is a historical fact, though it is not mentioned in "Sair Mutaqherin", and other contemporary Mussalman chronicles. (c)

It is, however, confirmed by Colonel Gentil, whose account is also confirmed by Portuguese documents. Ismael Gracias' book is a collection of Portuguese letters in which this second lady Dona Juliana, appears as a sort of ambassador of the Portuguese Viceroy, who uses her power as favourite at the Court for the solution of diplomatic negotiations. (d)

(a) "The Writing of History", 1926, page 113.

(b) See Heras "The Story of Akbar's Christian Wife," in the Journal of Indian History, III, pgs. 218-255.

(c) Father Hosten "The Family of Lady Juliana Dias da Costa," in the Journal of the Punjab Historical Society, VII, pp. 8949.

Father Heras—Journal of the Bombay Historical Society, Vol. I, No. I, pp. 93-97.

(d) Sir Evan Cotton—The Memoirs of Colonel Gentil, in Bengal, Past and Present, Vol. XXXIV, pp. 77-87.

5. " India em 1623 e 1624—Excerptos das memorias do Viajante Pietro della Valle, 1815", (India in 1623 and 1624—Extracts from the memoirs of the traveller Pietro della Valle,) 1915.

6. " Bocage na India ", (Bocage in India), 1917.

Besides these and other similar works and papers, Ismael Gracias published various articles, chiefly in the " Oriente Portuguez", an important review of which he was the Director and principal collaborator for many years. His articles about the " History of Bassein " which were published in this Review, will always be read with great pleasure. Their value would have been enhanced still further if he had also made use of the numerous existing sources for the writing of Mahratta history in dealing with his subject " Porque se perdeu Baçaim ? " (Why was Bassein Lost ?)

Among the research workers who are continuing investigations in this Archive, is Professor P. Pissurlencar who, besides studying the Portuguese sources, is also studying the documents written in Indian languages and those which are found in the foreign Archives and Libraries, in order to fill up the gaps to be found in the Portuguese documents. He thus proposes to write besides other books, the history of the Mahrattas with respect to their relations with the Portuguese, about which his first five monographs are already published.

Overseas section of the Archives of Portugal.

But the number of documents on India in Goa is is a mere nothing in comparison with those existing still unpublished in the Archives and Libraries of Portugal.

In the Overseas Section (Secção Ultramarina) of the Biblioteca Nacional, Lisbon, are one hundred and forty one bundles of papers which are divided in the following way :

Correspondence of the Governors :

D. Pedro de Mascarenhas, Conde de Sandomil (1735); Luiz de Menezes, Marquez de Louriçal (1741), Luiz de Mascarenhas, Conde de Alva ou Flor (1755-1756); Manoel da Saldanha de Albuquerque, Conde da Ega (1758-1762); Internal Government (1765-1766); D. João José de Mello (1770); D. José Pedro da Camara (1778-1779); D. Federico Guilherme de Souza (1780-1786) ; Francisco da Cunha Menezes (1787-1794) etc.

Correspondence of the Secretaries to Government :

Antonio Brito Freire (1745-1748); Francisco Ramos Nobre Mourão (1782-1784) ; Sebastião José Ferreira Barroco (1791).

Correspondence of the Prime Ministers:

João de Sousa de Menezes Lobo (1758-1762) ; José Baptista Vas Pereyra (1765) ; José da Rocha Dantas e Mendonça (1788-1812).

There is also much correspondence from the Inspectors of Revenue, the Archbishop Primate, from the Bishop of Cochin and the Government of Damão, and there is much material on religious subjects, missions, the army, and about questions respecting tobacco, agriculture and so on.

The following are some of the important documents in Lisbon :

1. "Resolução que se tomou em Conselho sobre a successão do cargo de Vice-Rei, a favor de Martim Affonso de Sousa e contra D. Estevam da Gama."

(Resolution which was taken in Council about the succession to the post of Viceroy, in favour of Martim Affonso de Sousa and against D. Estevam da Gama). 22nd. January. 1544. Page 445. (B 17-5).

2. "Carta de D. João III a D. João de Castro sôbre coisas da India. 1546."

(Letter of D. João III to D. João de Castro about Indian things. 1546).

(Copy in folio. fls. 9. Y-5-78. No. 3).

3. "Governo de D. Pedro de Mascarenhas, resposta que da parte d'El Rei lhe foi dada, sôbre a provisão que pediu para se poder retirar do governo, quando lhe aprouvesse."

(The rule of Dom Pedro de Mascarenhas, the answer which was given by the King about the provision which he asked for in order to be able to retire from the government when he wished to), 20th. of March, 1554, pages 818-886.

4. "Provisão para que os reis christãos e os gentios que favorecerem a christandade, nas partes da India possam navegar de umas partes para outras."

(Act declaring that those Christian Kings and the heathen who favour Christianity in different parts of India could navigate from one part to the other). Cintra, 20th. of September, 1570, fls. 142. B. 14-46.

5. "Capitulações das pazes com o Hidalcão em 1571".

(Terms of peace with Adil Shah, 1571). fls. 133-8290.

6. "Noticias varias, desde 1575, enviadas pelos Jesuitas".

(Various items of information from 1575, sent by the Jesuits). See "Noticias" which the Father Provincial of Goa sent to the Academy. fls. 42. 176.

7. "Emprestimo de Cochim para socorro de Malaca. 1587 a 1598".

(Loan in Cochim for aid of Malacca, 1587-1598). 2 Volumes, 6-5, 6, 7.

8. "Successos de 1594. Noticias de 1595".

(Victories of 1594. Items of news of 1595). See "Annaes e Poematicos", fls. 74-75. 8570.

9. "Socorro de dinheiro, no governo de D. Francisco da Gama".

(Help with money during the rule of D. Francisco da Gama). Vol. II, F. 5-11.

10. "Roteiro da navegação de Goa a Diu".

(Log-book of navigation from Goa to Diu). See D. João de Castro, 8033.

11. "Apontamentos varios e documentos sobre o Estado da India".

(Various notes and documents relating to the State of India). Fol........Vol. I., G., 5-1.

12. "Extracto das cousas pertencentes ao governo da India tirado das cartas dos Padres Geraes para os Provinciaes".

(Extract relating to Government of India affairs, taken from the letters of the Fathers Superior to the Fathers Provincial). T-7-39.

13. "Itinerario da India a Portugal, de Fr. Tristão da Cunha. (Seculo XVIII)".

(Itinerary by Father Tristão da Cunha from India to Portugal. (18th. century).

14. "Missões Augustianas nos seculos 16.° e 17.°".

(Augustine Missions in the 16th. and 17th. centuries). By Father Antonio de Moraes.—A. 2-59.

15. "Vantagens alcançadas pelos Hollandezes sobre os Portuguezes até a paz de Munster".

(Advantages gained by the Dutch over the Portuguese till the peace of Munster). (1617-1648) fl. 1-v, 599.

16 "Viagem da armada de Nuno Alvares Botelho, desde Lisboa.

Voyages of the fleet of Nuno Alvares Botelho, from Lisbon (1624-1625). Fl. 61.

17. "Governo de Nuno Alvares Botelho. Suas Victorias. (1631)".

(Rule of Nuno Alvares Botelho. His victories. 1631). Fl. 3-7640.

18. "Naus que invernam no caminho chegam tão desmanteladas, que para nada servem. (1631)".

(Ships which pass the winter on the way, arrive so dismantled that they are good for nothing. 1631). fl. 1.

19. "Relação sobre algũas cousas que sucederão nestas partes da India desde o anno de 1636 que V. M. dilhas partio athe este prezente 1638".

(Account of some things which happened in these parts of India from the year 1636 that V. M. left the islands. till the present time. 1638).

20. "Treslado do Caderno geral que o Senhor Almirante Visorei da India mandou fazer de todas as rendas e foros que sua Magestade tem nesta cidade e ilha de Goa e adjacentes, e as terras de Salcete e Bardez, no qual mandou

assentar declarar todas as religiões, Prelados, Ministros de S. Officio, Rellação e Contos e mais pessoas que tem ordens, ordinarias e tenças por assentamento nos livros da fazenda, matricula e fronta da Ribeira e das ditas terras de Bardes e Salcete ... "

(Transcription of the general Memorandum which the Count Admiral Viceroy of India ordered to be made of all the rents and tenures which his Majesty has in this city and island of Goa and the adjacent ones, and the islands of Salcete and Bardez, in which he ordered to be noted and declared all the religions, Prelates, Ministers of the Holy Office and supreme Court of Justice and Exchequer, and all persons who have orders, monthly allowances and pensions to sign in the books of the Revenue Register and declaration of Ribeira and the said lands of Bardez and Salcete).

21. " Hollandezes em guerra prejudicam as possessões Portuguezas ".

(The Dutch in war harm the Portuguese possession). (1631-1640). fl. 3. 7640.

22. " Malaca abandonada por morte de Nuno Alvares Botelho) ". 1632.

(Malaca abandoned by the death of Nuno Alvares Botelho). 1632. 7640.

23. " Ceilão restaurada em 1632. Noticias ".

(Ceylon restored in 1632. Information ". fl. 17, 18. 7640.)

24. " Ceilão e a fortaleza de Columbo arrazadas por tempestade ". (1633).

Ceylon and the Fortress of Colombo ruined by storm ". (1633). fl. 66. Doc. 22.

25. " Relação breve e geral das principaes cousas que suceder am em a India no ano de 1633 ".

(Brief and general account of the principal things which happened in India in the year 1633).

Among the descriptions of important facts which occurred in India in that year, we find a historical note about the peace and the services of the Viceroy. Cod. Y-2-53, Doc. 20, fl. 60-62 v.

26. "Bengala invadida pelo Mogol, que mata todos os Portugueses". 1633.

(Bengal invaded by the Mogol, who kills all the Portuguese). 1633. fl. 66. (Doc-22).

27. "Situação melhorada com as pazes da Inglaterra em 1634".

(Situation bettered by the peace with England in 1634). fl. 93. Doc. 35.

28. "Breve de Urbano VIII° sobre o real d'agua ou imposição na carne e no vinho para o socorro da India. 1635".

(Papal letter of Urban VIII about the *pie* of water or tax on meat and wine in aid of India. 1635). In fol. No. 39. C. 79.

29. "Goa attacada pelos Hollandezes". (1636-1637).

(Goa attacked by the Dutch. 1636-1637. fl. 141-150. 7640.

30. "Relação do succedido desde a morte do Vice-Rei Pedro da Cunha em 1639, dezembro de 1640".

(Account of what happened from the death of the Viceroy, Pedro da Cunha in 1639 till December 1640). Fls. 147.-191. Doc. No. 61 and 66.

31. "Instrucção secreta ao Conde d'Aveiras para o Governo da India. 1640".

(Secret order to the Conde d'Aveiras for the Government of India. 1640). 4180.

32. "Regimento sobre a entrega de Bombaim aos ingleses: dado em Pangim a 14 de Janeiro de 1665".

(Act about the giving of Bombay to the English drawn up in Pangim on the 14th. January 1665). Copy. Manuscript in folio, bought by the heirs of Judice Biker, with copies of other documents about the transaction. 8548.

33. "Relação verdadeira do que sucedeo no Estado da India desde dous de Janeiro de 1683 athe vinte e sinco de Janeiro de 1684".

(True account of what happened in the State of India from the 2nd. January 1683 till the 25th. January 1684).

34. "Successos desde 2 de Janeiro de 1684".

(Successes from 2nd. January 1684). True account. fl. 70. 465.

35. "Registo das cartas do Governador D. Rodrigo da Costa. 1686-1688".

(Registry of letters of the Governor, D. Rodrigo da Costa 1686-1688). Letters of the period. 1 vol, in fol. of 218 pages bound. (Heirs of Judice Bicker). 8538.

36. "Papeis do governo de D. Rodrigo da Costa".

(Papers of the Government of D. Rodrigo da Costa). (1686-1688). 8538.

37. "Noticias varias, dos Sec, XVII e XVIII".

(Various news of the 17th. and 18th. centuries). Letters of the period. 1 vol. in fol. of 191 folios bound. B-6-17).

38. "Fala que Novicão fez ao Xaidalcão, pedindo lhe este seu parecer sobre a guerra que queriam fazer os Portuguezes").

(Conversation which Novi Khan had with Adil Shah asking him for opinion about the war that the Portuguese wished to make). fl. 35 v. B. 17-6.

39. "Possessões adquiridas no vice-reinado de D. Luiz de Menezes".

(Possessions acquired during the vice-royalty of D. Luiz de Menezes). 1493.

40. "Regimento do governador da India, Antonio de Melo e Castro, para o Padre Manuel Godinho, quando o mandou a Lisboa por terra sobre as insolencias dos inglezes contra os Portuguezes na India e sobre a entrega de Bombaim áqueles que pede escusa de fazer".

(Act of the Governor of India, Antonio de Melo e Castro, for Father Manuel Godinho, when he sent him to Lisbon by land about the insults of the English to the Portuguese in India and about the giving over of Bombay, to those who did not want to do it). Fol. 161. do vol. B. 6-17.

41. "Bramanes de Salsete convertidos".

(Brahmans of Salsete converted). fl. 45. 7540.

42. "Cartas dos Padres Jesuitas".

(Letters of Jesuit Fathers) 7640.

43. "Cartas regias ao vice-rei D. Francisco da Gama com as respostas do mesmo".

(Royal letters to the Viceroy D. Francisco da Gama with answers to the same) in vol. 4. in fol. (F.C. 12-15).

44. "Ceilão, Noticia desta ilha".
(Ceylon, News about this island). fls. 440. B. 12-5.

45. "Ceremonial de que usavam os Vice-Reis quando escreviam aos principais indigenas".

(Ceremonial forms which the Viceroys used when they wrote to the important Indians. 6-43. fol. 150. 257.

46. "Desvantagens que traz ao paiz o haver inquisição n'ess colonia".

(Disadvantages which are brought to the country by. having the inquisition in that colony). 6-21. fls. 98. 235.

47. "Documentos relativos a Bombaim, Diu, etc. Dos sec XVII e XVIII".

(Documents relating to Bombay, Diu, etc. belonging to the 17th. and 18th. centuries). Copies in Mss. in-fol. belonging to the heirs of Biker. 8548.

48. "Parecer que D. João de Mascarenhas deu ao Infante D. Luiz sobre as cousas da India".

(Note that D. João de Mascarenhas gave to the Infant D. Luiz about Indian affairs). Copy in fol. 6 fls. Y-5-70. No. 8.

49. "Noticias diversas enviadas da India a Manuel Severim de Faria. 1625)"

(Different Notes sent from India to Manuel Severim de Faria. 1625).
See Father Luiz Fernandes. No. 32.

50. "Noticias diversas em cartas de P. P. Jesuitas".

(Different Notes in letters of the Jesuit Fathers). 17th. century. c. 29.

51. "Relação da India, cidades, portos, fortalezas, governadores, vice-reis, desenhos coloridos".

(Account about India, cities, ports, fortresses, governors, viceroys, with coloured drawings).

52. "Registo da correspondencia do vice-rei D. Rodrigo da Costa. 1710-1712).

(Registry of the correspondence of the Viceroy D.

Rodrigo da Costa. 1710-1712). Registry of the original. 1 vol. in fols., 220 fls., enc. Oriental. 8529.

53. " Listas das respostas de Vasco Fernandes Cesar de Menezes na monção de 1713 ".

(Lists of the answers of Vasco Fernandes Cesar de Menezes during the monsoon of 1713). Mss. in fol. 220, fl. Bound in red Indian leather, belonging to the heirs of Biker. 8529.

54. " Victoria naval dos Portuguezes em Surrate, sendo Vice-rei Vasco Fernandes Cesar de Menezes. 1714 ".

(Naval Victory of the Portuguese in Surrat, the Viceroy being Vasco Fernandes Cesar de Menezes, 1714).

55. " Successos de 1714 a 1733 ".

(Successes of 1714 to 1733 by Conde da Ericeira Fls. 90-98. 465.

56. " Noticias desde o fim do governo do Vice-Rei Vasco Fernandes Cesar de Menezes ".

(Notes from the end of the government of the Viceroy Vasco Fernandes Cesar de Menezes). (1717-1733 .) fl. 98. 465.

57. " Noticia do estado do reino de Maysur ".
(Note about the state of the Kingdom of Mysore). 1724-1725. Letter of the period. (A-5-2). 178.

58. " Tomada de Bicholim ", 1726.

(Taking of Bicholim, 1726). 712.

59. " Viagens das armadas de Antonio de Brito Freire. 1727 a 1758 ".

(Voyages of the fleets of Antonio de Brito Freire 1727-1758) by Antonio de Brito Freire. 485-486.

60. " Carta do Arcebispo Primaz de Goa enviando a Academia Real de Historia, noticia de umas laminas de cobre em que está escrita a doação de um pagode transformado depois em egreja de N. S. de Guadalupe, Goa ".

(Letter of the Archbishop Primate of Goa sending to the Royal Academy of History news about some sheets of copper on which is written the gift of a Pagoda transformed into the Church of Our Lady of Guadalupe, Goa). 13th January 1729. fls. 149. 712.

61. "Descripção de Bengala, usos e costumes, ceremonias religiosas, brahamanes, etc. Costa de Coromandel".

(Description of Bengal, habits and customs, religious ceremonies of the Brahmins etc. Coast of Coromandel), 1738. Original 175 folios. 550.

62. "Guerra do maratha". (1739-1740).

(Maratha War. (1739-1740). See Summary Account of the incidents of Goa. 660.

63. "Guerra dos marattas. 1740".

(Mahratta Wars. 1740) See Summary Account of the incidents of Goa. Cx. 3.

64. "Guerras dos Maratas, 1740-1745".

(Mahratta Wars. 1740-1745). See Father Francisco Alvares, 4179.

65. "Cartas (2) do Conde Sandomil, governador da India, sobre assuntos do seu governo" (1740-1749).

(Two letters of Conde de Sandomil, Governor of India, about things pertaining to his rule 1740-1749). Copies in H-5-45. Nos. 28-29.

66. "Guerra do Marata 1741".

(Mahratta War, 1741). See "Noticias de Goa". fls. 12. 465.

67. "Colecção de Manuscritos, sendo grande parte originais acerca do Estado da India e suas Fortalezas, entre os anos de 1741 e 1750".

(Collection of manuscripts, being in great part the original ones about the State of India and its fortresses, between the years 1741-1750) Manuscripts bound in white, 163. 4179.

68. "Noticias extraidas de cartas do Vice-Rei, Marquez de Louriçal. 1742".

(Notes taken from the letters of the Viceroy Marquez of Louriçal. (1742). A-1-38. C. 2.

69. "Decadencia do comercio na Asia e meios de o levantar, 1743".

(Decadence of the Commerce in Asia and the means to revive it, 1743). fls. 235. 675.

70. " Derrota da costa n. e s. de Goa, 1744 ".
(Description of the voyage along the coast north and south of Goa, 1744). 617.

71. " Guerra. Victorias do Marquez de Castello Novo, 1746.
(War. Victories of the Marquis of Castello Novo, 1746). See " Account of Victories ". No. 1, Box 13.

72. " Marquez d'Alorna Governador, reprehendido por extorsões. 1747 ".
(Marquez d'Alorna, Governor, reprimanded for extortions, 1747). fls. 21. Letter 13a. 7663.

73. " Instrucções do Marquez de Tavora ao Conde de Alva, Vice-Rei, 1754 ".
(Instructions of the Marquez de Tavora to the Conde of Alva, Viceroy, etc). B. 7-38.

74. " Missões de Chorão, Rachol, etc. noticia de 1760 ".
(Missions of Chorão, Rachol, etc. Information of 1760). See Jacinto Manuel de Rego. fl. 160, 177.

75. "Mapa d'artilheria do Piro e do exercito terrestre destinado a expugnar a mesma praça em 5 de Abril de 1768 ".
(Plan of the Artillery of Piro and of the infantry army destined to empty the same fortress on the 5th. April 1768). p. 160. 553.

76. " Plano e perspectiva do sitio da Praça de Piro, Abril de 1768 ".
(Plan and perspective of the site of the Fortress of Piro. (April 1768). Pen drawings. p. 161. 553.

77. " Petição dos Mazanes de Diu, dirigida a Junta do commercio, expondo os fundamentos da ruina desta communidade ". De Diu, 21 de Dezembro de 1773.
(Petition of the Mazanes of Diu directed to the Board of Commerce setting forth the rudimentary causes of the ruin of this community). From Diu, 21st. December 1773. Original with autographed Oriental signatures and respective translations). 8841.

78. " Instrucção que em 1774 levou o governador D. José Pedro da Camara ".
(Instruction which in 1774 the Governor, D. José Pedro da Camara received). See " Instrucção com que El-Rei ". a 6-16.

79. "Posses e previlegios que os Mogores de Delhi concederam a Nação portugueza em Bengala, em uma representação a S. Mg. Rainha D. Maria I dirigida por Georges Gearmain. De Calcutta aos 31 de dezembro de 1784".

(Rights and privileges that the Moguls of Delhi conceded to the Portuguese nation in Bengal in representation to Her Majesty the Queen D. Maria I, led by Georges Gearmain from Calcutta, 31st. December 1784).

In original with autographed signature. In fol. of 27 fls. 8841.

80. "Carta de Francisco da Cunha Menezes a Antonio Vicente Rosa sobre a protecção pedida pelo rei de Cochin, China. 1789".

(Letter of Francisco da Cunha Menezes to Antonio Vicente Rosa about the protection solicited by the King of Cochin China, 1789). No. 17. Box 41.

81. "Praça do Piro, 1790-1793".

(Fortress of Piro, 1790-1793.) See "Negociações que discorreram". p. 49. 4401.

82. "Conquistas e campanha contra o Bounsulo".

(Conquest and campaign against Bhonsle.) 8803-8805.

83. "Campanha do Bonsalo e conquista de Alorna, etc. Festejos dos Jesuitas".

(Campaign of Bhonsle, and conquest of Alorna. Feasts of Jesuit Fathers).

84. "Derrota de Goa a Moçambique e vice-versa, com o Marquez de Castello Novo".

(Description of the voyage from Goa to Moçambique and vice-versa by the Marquez de Castello Novo).

85. "Disposições da guerra do Angria".

(Results of the war of the Angria). Mss. in [illegible]ol. Coll. p. 114. 8548.

86. "Gentios de Goa, pedem licença para celebra[illegible] o dos seus ritos".

(The Hindus of Goa ask permission for the celebration of their rites). See "Portaria de 24 de Março de 1781". fls. 37. B. 16-16.

87. " Lutas com holandezes ".

" Struggles with the Dutch ". Various news of the 17th. and 18th. centuries. 465.

88. " Malabar, descripção do Reino e da Christandade de S. Tomé ".

(Malabar, description of the Kingdom and of the Christianity of St. Thomas). See " Historia verdadeira da Christandade ". (a. 2.–33, 34-36).

89. " Maratas e turcos no reino de Madurey ".

(Mahrattas and Turks in the Kingdom of Madura) See " Relação das guerras dos turcos ". 4179.

90. " Guerras no sec. XVIII ".

(Wars in the 18th. century) ". E-5-18.

91. " Reino, situação, forças, etc.".

(Kingdom, situation, strength, etc.). See " Notice of the Kingdom, situations, etc.". 7247.

92. " Guerra contra o regulo Bounsolo ".

(War against the small king Bhonsle). fl. 133. E. 4-17.

93. " Guerra do marata e Bunsolo. (Sec. XVIII).

(War of the Mahratta and Bhonsle. (XVIII century). fl. 384. 4530.

94. " Missões e conventos ".

(Missions and convents). Ecclesiastical History. See. Memoirs for the Ecclesiastical History of Goa.

95. " Missões dos Agostinianos ".

(Missions of the Augustinians). See the Memoir of Father Antonio de Moraes. 745.

96. " Provisões, alvaras e Cartas de oficio por D. Francisco da Gama, 4.° Conde da Vidigueira ".

(Provisions, documents and official letters for D. Francisco da Gama, 4th. Count of Vidigueira). See " Livro da Chancellaria ". G-5-2.

97. " Noticias do Reino de Malabar ".

(News about the kingdom of Malabar). 536.

98. " Noticias ecclesiasticas de Goa ".
(Ecclesiastical Notes on Goa).

99. " Noticias historicas do Ceilão ".
(Historical notes on Ceylon). See João Ribeiro.

100. " Registo das Ordens do dia do Governador do estado 1827-1833 ".
(Registry of the Order for the day, of the Governor of the Estate. 1827-1833). See " Registo das Ordens do dia ".

In the Biblioteca Nacional de Lisboa :

" Memorias para a Historia Ecclesiastica do Arcebispado de Goa e seus suffraganeos ".

(Memoirs for the Ecclesiastical History of the Archbishopric of Goa and its dependencies). Mss. 176 (A-44) by Henrique Bravo da Moraes. Good copy with coloured pen sketches. One volume of 307 fol. Bound.

It is divided into 12 chapters as follows :

1. " Descobrimento da sepultura do Apostolo S. Thomas na India, 1538 ".
(Discovery of the grave of the Apostle St. Thomas in India, 1538). (Copy of the 18th. century).

2. " Sobre as tribus do Brazil."
(About the tribes of Brazil).

3. " Noticias do Arcebispado de Goa ".
(Notes on the Archbishopric of Goa). Copy of the 18th century. Fol. 9.

4. " Breve e verdadeira noticia dos termos e procedimentos entre os Illmos. Arcebispo Primaz da India e Bispo de Malaca nas controversias da conversatoria dos Religiosos da companhia de Jesus, 1731 ".
(Brief and true Note about the terms and procedure between the most illustrious Archbishop Primate of India and the Bishop of Malaca in the controversies of the department of the brothers of Jesus. 1731). Letter of the period. 25 fol.

5. " Cartas de Henrique Bravo de Moraes á Academia Biblioteca da Historia, acerca da sepultura de D. Gaspar de Ornellas, 1.° Arcebispo de Goa, etc.".

(Letters of Henrique Bravo de Moraes to the Royal Academy of History about the grave of D. Gaspar de Ornellas, 1st. Archbishop of Goa, etc.) Goa. 1726-1727. Original, Fol. 25 and 41).

6. "Materias ecclesiasticas succedidas em Goa no anno de 1677 e 1678".

(Ecclesiastical matters which happened in Goa in the years 1677 and 1678). Copy of the 18th. century. Fol. 37.

7. "Noticias que o Padre Provincial da Companhia de Jesus da Provincia de Goa manda á Real Academia de Portugal, começadas no anno de 1585, em que o Padre Francisco de Souza acabou a 2.ª parte da sua historia intitulada "Oriente conquistado".

(Notes that the Father Provincial of the Company of Jesus of the Province of Goa sends to the Royal Academy of Portugal beginning with the year 1585, in which Father Francisco de Souza finished the 2nd. part of his history entitled "Oriente conquistado".) Letter of the 18th. century. fls. 42.

8. "Progresso e memoria das noticias que El-Rei ordena se dê á Academia Real da Historia Portugueza dos cartorios e archivos desta nossa Santa Provincia da madre de Deos dos Reformados de S. Francisco nesta India Oriental. 1726."

(Progress and Memoir of the notes which the King orders to be given to the Royal Academy of Portuguese History about the Archives of this our Holy Province of Madre de Deos dos Reformados de S. Francisco in this Oriental India. 1726). Good copy with pen and ink designs, fl. 79.

9. "Noticia de como e quando se erigio a cathedral de Goa, e dos Bispos, Arcebispos que nella houve. 1722."

(Historical Note of how and when the Cathedral of Goa was built and of the Bishops and Archbishops who were in it. 1722). Original signed by Henrique Bravo de Moraes. With the coloured insignia of the Archbishops. Fls. 79.

10. "Noticias ecclesiasticas de Goa, etc.

(Historical Ecclesiastical Notes of Goa, etc.
Various notes written in the 18th. century. fl. 252.

11. "Relação dos progressos da Missão de Ceylão, casos prodigiosos nela acontecidos desde 1720 a 1722."

(Account of the progress of the Mission of Ceylon and some important cases which happened there from 1720 to 1722). Original signed "Gabriel de Sá for the Congregation". fl. 297.

12. "Relação verdadeira, mas breve do insigne milagre do apparecimento e visão de Cristo crucificado na Cruz, que está no monte da Boavista desta cidade de Goa no anno 1619."

(True account, but brief, of the notable miracle of the apparition and vision of Christ crucified on the Cross which is on Mount of Boavista of this city of Goa in the year 1619). Catalogue of the works of the Library of the Convent of Santa Cruz of Miracles." Copy belonging to the 18th century.

A manuscript of fls. 43-64, XVII century gives brief biographical notes of sixty-two Fathers of the Company of Jesus who died in the Province of Goa, from 1st. February 1625 till 12th. November 1688.

Another manuscript, fls. 65-71, has a note at the end about some extraordinary Images (Imagens prodigiozas) which the Fathers of the Company had in some Churches and Chapels in the Province of Goa in India, and a brief narration of some more recent miracles. It refers to the Images of the Child Jesus in the Church of the "Castelo de Rachol" and of the Virgin, "Our Lady of Grace", "Our Lady of the Mountain".

Fols. 71-72 v contain descriptions of notable relics which are found in the sanctuaries of the Fathers of the Company of Jesus in the Province of Goa in India.

Fols. 73-75 speak of the Sepulchres, which are found in some Churches and Chapels of the Jesuit Fathers in the Province of Goa.

In fols. 75-76 we read about books which some priests of the Company of the Province of Goa wrote, a number of which were printed in the "Castelo de Rachol" with Portuguese characters, but in the language of the country; for some of the most illustrious of the

Fathers wrote in Latin, others in Portuguese, some in Spanish and others in the language of the country and in Persian script. They dealt with different subjects according to the part of the country in which they found themselves. The names of some of the authors are not declared because they themselves tried to hide their identity; even the nationality of some of the older writers is not stated.

Fols. 77, 78 and 78 v. contain a note on the houses and schools of the Jesuit Fathers in the Province of Goa in India.

In the " Biblioteca do Ministerio da Guerra " :—

1. " Cartas (2) de Francisco de Lucena, sobre negocios da India, 1633-1635 ".

(Two letters of Francisco de Lucena about Indian transactions (1633-1735). Original.

2. " Documentos (nominações etc.) relativos a historia da India e Oriente ".

(Documents (appointments etc.) relating to the history of India and the East) 17th. and 18th. centuries. Original.

3. " Relação das bullas, breves, etc., que estão na Torre de Tombo, a que se referem as dioceses da India Portugueza ".

(Accounts of bulls, Papal letters, etc., which are in the Torre do Tombo in which they refer to the dioceses of Portuguese India). In fol. No. 10.

The investigator of Indian history has also material in the Portuguese documents in the libraries and Archives of Paris, London, Spain, etc. The documents in the British Museum were catalogued recently by the Count of Tovar in one volume. See Catalogo dos Manuscritos Portugueses, List 1932.

The works on the study of Konkani initiated by Cunha Rivara, bore good fruit, for they resulted in the

Monsenhor S. R. Dalgado

studies of Monsenhor Sebastião Rodolpho Dalgado who published two important dictionaries Concani-Portuguese and Portuguese-Concani, besides a Concani

Grammar with explanations in Portuguese which still remains unedited, and "Florilegio dos proverbios Concanis" which was published by the "Academia das Sciencias" of Lisbon.

Influence of the Portuguese language on the Oriental languages and vice-versa.

Monsenhor Sebastião Rodolpho Dalgado, a native of Goa, was nominated in 1907 as Professor of Sanscrit in the University of Lisbon. After he went to Portugal, his literary labours were extraordinary and his talent as a philologist became more and more evident. He adopted as the subject of his research work, the reciprocal influence which existed between Portuguese and the Oriental languages. The intercourse of the Portuguese with the various peoples of India, as a result of the discoveries must have influenced their language greatly. The Portuguese navigators, traders warriors and priests, who were so to speak constantly travelling about the country, made use of many of the words, both in writing and speaking, which they heard in the Orient; in the same way, their mode of speaking and their intonation and not a few terms in use in Portuguese, were communicated to those with whom they lived in India.

All this, without doubt, Monsenhor Dalgado observed, to which we owe the greater part of his productions, and as he advanced, the field of his research work became wider, as his works clearly show.

Thus were published successively various studies on the different dialects of the Portuguese spoken in Indian regions: that of Ceylon (1) and Goa in 1900; in 1903, that of Daman; in 1906, that of the North, that is Bombay.

(1) The following is a prayer for the King in the Indo-Portuguese dialect of Ceylon in use there to-day. And below is a poem called "Christmas Greetings" in the same dialect. It is interesting to note the similarity between this dialect and modern

Taking as the basis of his investigations the languages spoken in India and in the rest of the Orient, in 1913, he gave us :

" A Influência do vocabulário Português em línguas Asiáticas", (the Influence of the Portuguese vocabulary on Asiatic languages), which treats of about fifty languages. The theme of the laborious work is the individual and systematic examination of the Portuguese works, introduced into the languages of Asia, spoken

---

Portuguese. The words foreign to Portuguese have notes attached.

(a) Oração por o Rey, a Rainha, o Prinspe de Wales, o Reyal Familho, o Governador, &c.

" O Omnipotente e moito gracioso Deos e Pai, noste ruga com Ti per misericordioso sobre nosse Sinhor Soberano Rey Edward VII, a Rainha Sinhora Alexander e Prinspe de Wales e todo o Reyal Familho, e sobre o alto Courto de Parliamento (1) e aqui ne Ceylon nos te ruga per o governador e Conselhe, Julgadors e todos em authoridade baiso de nosso Rey, que ellotros podi ordena todos cousas ne cizo (2) justicia e misericordia, per a honra de Teu Santo Nome e per o bem de Teu Igreja e povo, per meyo de Jesus Christo, Nosso Sinhor, Amen ".

(From " Oriente Portuguez "
B. C. Tavares de Mello).

Prayer for the King, the Queen, the Prince of Wales, the Royal Family, the Governor, &c.

Oh omnipotent and most gracious God and Father, we ask thee for mercy on our Lord Sovereign, King Edward VII, the Queen Lady Alexandra, the Prince of Wales and all the Royal Family, and for the High Court of Parliament, and here in Ceylon we pray thee for the Governor and his Council, for our Judges and all in authority under our King that he may be able to order all things for others with prudence, justice and mercy, for the honour of Thy Holy Name, and for the good of Thy Church and people, through Jesus Christ, Our Lord, Amen.

---

(1) **Courto de Parliamento : Casa de Parlamento.**

(2) **Ne ciso : Tino, prudencia.**

by the peoples with whom the Portuguese came in contact more or less intimately and directly from the time of the discoveries and conquests, that is, from the 15th. century to the present time. One concludes from this work that the number of Portuguese words adopted in the Indian languages is considerable.

(b) Hum bom entrago de Natal 1907 (1)

Bom entrago de Natal nos disija,
Per todos Nossas am'zades e estranheiros,
O bomzido Salvador quem isti dia nace,
Tem leste (2) este dia per todos par benze.

Alleluia, alleluia, Jesus tem nacido
De hum Virgin e santo Mai
Ne cidadi chomadi Bethlehem,
Enter anjo-chusmos (3) tambem.

Natal, o nacemento de Sinhor,
Par bensas per nos proclama,
Ne terra paz, bom vontade per gentes
Salutacan glorioso de Anjos.

Dia de Natal, que allegroso
Par nos Christãos de boa intendimento
Juntamus cambrados amoroso
Com allegria e amor ispantoso.

Vi Christãos allegra o bonansa
Que Jesus nacido per nos trize (4).
De pecados reconsiliação,
E per todos eterno salvação.

Nan desse (5) por isto nehum pecado
Este dia allegroso ti danifica
Mas perdam e paz elle agor offerece
Sem dineiro, livremento ricebe.

---

(1) Feliz entrada ou boas festas do Natal de 1907.
(2) Tem leste: Está prompto.
(3) Enter anjos-chusmos: Entre os coros dos anjos.
(4)—Trize: trouxe.
(5)—Nan desse: não deixe.

"The introduction of Portuguese words" says Dalgado, (1) "in the Asiatic languages, has for means of transmission, either separately, or simultaneously, (a) the direct rule, (b) commercial intercourse, (c) political influence, (d) the neighbourhood of Portuguese colonies, (e) religious propaganda, (f) the proximity of many vernacular languages in certain cities, (g) the indirect influence of the language which had already introduced Portuguese words, (h) the co-existence of Indo-Portuguese, and (i) Indo-English."

CHRISTMAS GREETINGS, 1907.

Good greetings for Christmas we wish
For all our friends and strangers.
The blessed Saviour Who this day was born
Is ready this day to bless every one.

Alleluia, alleluia, Jesus is born
Of a Virgin and Holy Mother,
In the city called Bethlehem
Amongst a chorus of angels also.

Christmas, the birth of the Lord
Who proclaims blessings for us,
On earth peace, goodwill to men,
The angels gloriously sing.

Christmas Day, how happy
For us, Christmas of good will!
We unite in loving fellowship
With wonderful love and joy.

O Christians! see the joy of goodness
That Christ being born has brought us,
Forgiveness of sin,
And for all, eternal salvation.

Do not for this permit any sin
To spoil this happy day.
The pardon and peace He now offers
Without price, freely receive.

---

(1) "Influencia do Vocabulario Portuguez nas linguas Asiaticas". Introduction, p. xxciii, Dalgado.

In his work "Glossário Luso-Asiático", in two volumes, Dalgado shows, with the corresponding words, the numerous words which the Portuguese took from the Orientals, specially from India, in the "Journal of the Royal Asiatic Society of Great Britain and Ireland", April 1921, pages 263-267. Mr. Longworth Dames makes a criticism of the work which he signalises as admirable.

But, besides these studies, Sanskrit never failed to win the attention and love of Monsenhor Dalgado which we can see in the versions published by him in 1897 and 1916 under the titles of "Hitopadexa" and "História de Nala e Damayanti", and from the compendium which he published in 1920 with the title of "Rudimentos da lingua Sanscrita". During the same time, some works on Indology were published in Portugal by G. Vasconcelos d'Abreu (1), Francisco Maria Esteves Pereira (2), Candido de Figueiredo (3), Ansur (4), and Bernardino Gracias (5), and in Goa

---

(1) a. "Investigações sobre o caracter da Civilização Arya-Hindu, 1873.
b. O Sanscrito como base da glottologia Árica, 1878.
c. Summario das Investigações em Sanscritologia desde 1886 até 1891.
d. Curso de Litteratura e Lingua Sanscrita Classica e Medica.
e. Os Contos, Apólogos, e Fabulas da India; influencia indirecta em Gil Vicente.
f. A literatura e a religião dos Arias na India, 1885.
g. A origem do povo Indo-Arico, &c. &c.

(2) See Yugavarga no Boletim da classe da 2.ª Academia das Sciencias de Lisboa, Vol. XII.
"A conversão dum Rei da India ao Cristianismo".
"A Lenda de Barlaam e Josaphat em Portugal", etc.

(3) A penalidade na India segundo o código de Manu.

(4) Perolas do Ramaiana.

(5) "Xacuntala and Maghaduta", translated into Portuguese.

by Panduranga Pissurlencar ([1]), Mariano Saldanha ([2]), Bragança Pereira ([3]), Amâncio Gracias ([4]) and recently António M. da Cunha ([5]).

Indo-Portuguese poetry.

Portuguese poetry had many worshippers to keep the vestal fires burning and the poetry produced in India was deeply imbued with Indian sentiment and enriched and beautified with Indian terms.

Thomas Ribeiro.

When Thomas Ribeiro, ([6]) 1831-1901, the celebrated Portuguese poet who was in India for some time, founded in 1872 the Instituto Vasco da Gama, he wrote: "The land of India is the land for literature". From his pen we have two expressive poems, one called "Velha Goa", the other entitled, "Sino d'Oiro" which is written about the bell of the Cathedral in Goa. The latter was published in the "Almanack Annuario Recreativo" for the year 1898, and contains the following beautiful lines :

---

(1) "A Antiga India e o Mundo Externo" and "Aspectos da Civilização da India Antiga" are two works of P. Pissurlencar in which are summarized the last results of investigations made by European and Indian Orientalists on the history of Ancient India.

(2) Translation into Portuguese of Meghaduta.

(3) O Sistema das Castas. "A Ethnografia da India Portuguesa".

(4) Subsídios para a história económico-financeira da India Portugueza. Nova Goa. 1909.

(5) "A India Antiga e Moderna".

(6) He also published as a result of his journey to India his prose writings called "Do Tejo a Mandovy" and "Entre Palmeiras", "As Novas Conquistas", and "Jornadas".

É noute lobrega ! O Sino
O Sino d'oiro da Sé
Dá badaladas soturnas
Chamando às preces nocturnas.

•

Tange, sino d'oiro, tange
Na velha torre da Sé !
Que o teu convite inda abrange
Um grande império onde há fé.

•

A tua voz ainda soa
Desde às ruinas de Goa
Até as flores do Japão ;
Desde Ormuz ao Guzerate,
Desde Timor a Pekim,
Desde Ceylão a Surrate,
Desde Cambaya a Cochim,
Soa sempre e só desmaia
Nas planuras do Hymalaia.

(Dark night has fallen ! the bell,
The golden bell of the Cathedral
With sullen strokes
Calls to evening prayers.

•

Ring golden bell, ring
In the old Cathedral tower ;
For thy invitation is still sufficient
For a great empire where there is faith.

•

Thy voice is yet resounding
From the ruins of Goa
To the flowers of Japan ;
From Ormuz to Gujerat,
From Timor to Pekin,
From Ceylon to Surat,
From Cambay to Cochin,
It resounds always and only dies away
In the plains of the Himalayas.

One of the poets who shows in his work the deep influence of Indian inspiration is Fernando Leal. Born in Portuguese India where the traditions of Indian civilization have been fused with those of the Portuguese, Fernando Leal tried to restore those ideals which in former times had so ennobled India, the cradle of the literature which represents in some respects the highest spiritual development of the human race, Maria Amalia Vaz de Carvalho observes about his poetry: "Indian inspiration explains the dazzling profusion of its imagery, the mysterious sweetness of its legends, the infinite calm sadness of its nights, its inexhaustible goodness, its capacity for filling the world with its myths and its sacred symbols".

Fernando Leal.

Writing equally well in Portuguese and French Fernando Leal was an incomparable translator of some of the most beautiful verses of Victor Hugo which are given in his book "Reflexos e Penumbras". His small poems referring to India are "Novembro", and "A Reconquista de Goa", in which he celebrates the deeds of Portuguese arms. "O Rei de Benares", a paraphrase of a story from the Mahabharata, is a tale for children and is inserted in his "Livro da Fé", Nova Goa, Imprensa Nacional, 1906:

Num dos reinos indianos
Foi pois que isto sucedeu
Há não sei quantos mil anos
Num poema antigo o li eu
Dêsse reino além dos mares
A capital foi Cashi
Que hoje se chama Benares.

(In one of the Indian kingdoms
I know not how many thousand years ago
This is what happened;
In an ancient poem I read it.
It was about that kingdom beyond the seas
Whose capital was Kashi
Which to-day is called Benares.)

And here follows the story of a dove, which being pursued by a falcon, alighted on the hand of the king of Benares. The king promised the falcon his treasures if the falcon would not molest the dove, but the falcon answered :

Os falcões querem sòmente
Pombas de carne macia.
....
E se tens tamanho dó
Dessa pomba tenra e bela,
Quero a tua carne só
Mas em peso egual a dela.

(Falcons only desire
Doves with tender flesh,
And if you have such pity
For this dove so young and beautiful,
I desire from your flesh
Just an equal quantity.)

The King of Benares cut off a piece of his own flesh to give to the falcon ; but no matter how much he cut off, the dove weighed still more and so his whole body was thrown into the scales :

Porque se uma pomba é leve,
É muito mais leve um santo ;
Pesar por isso não deve
Mais que uma pomba nem tanto.
Sendo a pomba uma inocente,
Nunca faz mal a ninguém ;
Mas um homem que é clemente
Não só não faz mal, faz bem.

(Because if a dove is light,
A saint is still lighter ;
And so he should not weigh
Even as much as a dove.
As the dove is an innocent creature,
It never does harm to any one ;
But a man who is merciful
Not only does not do harm but does good.)

The heavens, jubilant over this proof of goodness and sacrifice on the part of the king of Benares

Transportaram-no em victória
Brandamente pelos ares.

(Transported him in triumph
Softly by the winds.)

The little poem ends with this advice to the children for whom it was written:

Dentro d'alma erguei-lhe um templo
E se um fraco vos pedir
Protecção buscai seguir
Aquele sublime exemplo.

(In your soul raise him a temple
And if a weak person asks you
For protection, try to follow
That sublime example.)

This poem is also published in "Relampagos", Porto, 1888.

The later works of Fernando Leal, who was a contemporary of the great Portuguese literati, Antero do Quental, Eça de Queiroz, Oliveira Martins, Moniz Barreto and others, are lacking in the beauty which characterized the verses of his youth.

Manoel Salvador Sanches Fernandes.

Manoel Salvador S. Fernandes has written a short poem called "A Lyra da India", published in Bastorá, by Rangel, in which the author in Alexandrines, expresses the past splendour of India:

Brahma! Vishnu! Shiva! a trimurti potente!
Eis! as grandes criações d'uma época esplendente
Que, na India, desfraldou o seu pendão de Luz
Antes da lei boudhaica e antes da lei da Cruz.
E essa época doirada, d'essa época gigante
Que exige as vibrações de uma lyra possante
Da theorba viril, que ruge furibunda

O canto dos Heroes e nas almas diffunda.
Sê tu o ardente arauto anunciando sonora
A Poesia sublime, a Poesia da Aurora.
A India seja o teu deus, seja a lyra o teu templo
Que de bela oração saia de ti o exemplo.
Olha ! Vês essa Sé donde há pouco eu sahi ?
Ei-lo ! O rico Pantheon, o grande capitólio
Onde Maggh, Zenabay, Kalidass, Valmiki,
E cada obreiro tem um luminoso sólio.

(Brahma ! Vishnu ! Shiva ! the powerful trinity !
Behold the great creations of a brilliant epoch
Which in India unfurled its banner of light
Before the Buddhist law, and before the Law of Christ.
It is that golden epoch, it is that gigantic epoch
Which calls for the vibrations of a powerful lyre
Of the virile lute which resounds wildly
With the song of the heroes and diffuses it in the souls.
Be thou the ardent herald, sonorously announcing
Sublime poetry, the Poetry of the Dawn.
May India be thy God, may the lyre be thy temple
May the model of a beautiful prayer issue from thee.
Look ! dost thou see that cathedral from which
A little time ago I came forth ?
Behold it ! the noble Pantheon, the grand capitol
Where Maggh, Zenabay, Kalidas, Valmiki,
And each labourer has a luminous throne.)

The author who was confined to bed for many years through a persistent illness, lives in a land of dreams at the edge of a Golden Vision created by Indian environment. He hears :

... hinos magistraes, cantos de ouro e de Luz
Do Telanga, Muchtabai, Crisnaji, Tucaramas
Que se ergueram ao céu das sublimadas famas
Nas azas desse ideal que a tua alma seduz.

(... majestic hymns, songs of gold and light
Of Telanga, Muktabai, Krishnaji, Tucaramas
Who soared heavenwards through their sublime works
On the wings of that ideal which enchants thy soul.)

And when he wakes a wave of pessimism born of

illness overwhelms him and the poet says in discouragement :

E lento se esfumou esta Visão doirada ;
Fanou-se alto o Panteon ; vaporaram-se os mythos
E ante a Vida Real e ante a branca Alvorada
A minha alma chorou saudosa do Infinito.

(And slowly was blurred this Golden Vision ;
The Pantheon on high disappeared ; the myths melted away ;
And standing before the Royal Life and before the White Dawn,
My soul wept with longing for the Infinite.)

R. B. Barreto Miranda.

R. B. Barreto Miranda has amongst other poems one called "Velha Goa", which was published in the Annual Review, "Republicas", Ortigas, Margão, 1894, in one volume. He has also a short poem entitled "Um feixe de flores silvestres para a coroa da glorificação centenal de Felipe Nery Xavier", 1901. (A bunch of woodland flowers for the crown of the centenary celebration of Felipe Nery Xavier), dedicated to that Indo-Portuguese historian ; and he has a third poem named : "Portugal na India—Epopeia do Oriente—No Jubileu do centenário 1498–1898", (Portugal in India, Epic Poem of the Orient—Centenary Jubilee of 1498-1898).

J. F. da P. Soares.

J. F. da P. Soares has written the "Melopeias Indianas", published in Bastorá, by Rangel, 1898. This volume is a collection of poetry containing an interesting little poem in roundelays called "O joven Sardessae". "Aos martyres de Cuncolim", and a legend called "O fantasma de Narola", are poems written in correct rhymed verse.

Leandro Xavier Pereira.

"Primeiros Versos", Bastorá, Rangel, 1899, is a collection of poems by Leandro Xavier Pereira of which the only one of Indian interest is "Velha Goa".

L. F. da Costa.

"Sangue e Redempção" is a little poem by Leopoldo Francisco da Costa, alluding to the revolt of Satary, 1897.

José Joaquim Fragoso.

José Joaquim Fragoso is the author of "Sivaji Maharaja, Vencedor de Abdul Khan", published by Bragança & Co., Nova Goa, 1921. It is full of Indian terms and is followed by a prose work entitled: "Traços genealógicos do Maharaja" in which the author wishes to prove that Sivaji had Portuguese blood in his veins, which fallacy has been ably demonstrated by Professor Pissurlencar in his Monograph "Sivaji com sangue Português?".

Florência de Moraes.

Florência de Moraes, a Portuguese lady living in Goa, wrote a volume of verses entitled: "Vozes da India", which was printed by Casa Luso-Francesa, Nova Goa, 1907. The book contains many verses referring to India. In a sonnet descriptive of the dream of Portugal, India is called the 'Bride of Heroes'.

In a part of the book entitled "Ideal" the little poem, VII, is an invocation to the Portuguese spirit which pervaded India from Ceylon to Diu, as well as to the Far East. The section named "Amor" contains three sonnets which sing of Indian nights and, immediately following, there is a small poem in praise of India:

> A India é fonte sempre viva e perturbante
> Como os beijos da primeira amante.
>
> (India is a source ever as vivid and perturbing
> As the kisses of the first lover).

The last sonnet of the part entitled "Redempção" contains two references, one to the Indian sun and the other to the Ganges "which passes lamenting and without comfort like a dethroned king".

Mariano Gracias.

The best verses of Mariano Gracias which have reference to India are found in his book: "Terra de Rajahs", 1925, Bombay. They are inpregnated with profound lyrical beauty and so interspersed with oriental terms that the author thought it necessary to add an explanatory glossary of the Indian words. In the poem called "O Génio da Raça", the poet sings of India:

Foi a India de luz berço lendario
Da civilização. Extraordinario

Paiz de sonho e lenda! Um povo ideal
De immenso genio e altissima moral!

Terra de Sabios, de immortaes poetas
Philosophos, videntes e os ascetas.

Valmiki, Somadeva, e Kalidassa,
Buddha, Manu, Pannini e Wyassa,

Durgavaty, Maytreyi e Kalinatha
Dvantary e Soma e Aryabratha.

Kaverajah, Jayadeva e o Vedanta,
E tanto genio, tanta gloria, tanta!

Bharata, Wishwakharma e Xancara,
E tanta gloria de grandeza rara.

Sutras, Kalpas, Purannas, Karmas, Shastras,
Kawyas, Zamans, Nirvannas, Dharma Shastras,

Jatakas, Itihassas, e Dharshanas,
Yogas e Mantras ... Cousas sobrehumanas!

E o Genio da Raça—clarão belo
Qual proprio Surya ou Tchandra ou Setestrello.

E foi esse clarão, grande e profundo,
Onda de ouro rolando sobre o mundo.

Que alagou com a sua claridade
As vindouras nações—a Humanidade.

(India was the legendary cradle of the light
Of civilisation. Extraordinary

Country of dream and legend ! An imaginative people
With great genius and the highest morals !

Land of Sages, of immortal poets,
Philosophers, prophets, and ascetics :

Valmiki, Somadeva, Kalidassa,
Budha, Manu, Pannini and Vyassa.

Durgavati, Mayetri and Kalinatha,
Davantri and Soma and Aryabharata.

Kaviraj, Jayadeva and the Vedanta,
So much talent and so much glory !

Bharata, Vishvakarma and Shankarya,
And so much glory of rare greatness.

Sutras, Kalpas, Puranas, Karmas, Shastras,
Kavyas, Shamans, Nirvanas, Dharma-Shastras.

Jatakas, Itihasas, and Darshanas,
Yogas and Mantras—things superhuman !

It is the genius of the race—the beautiful reflection
Of the Sun itself or of the Moon or of the Seven Stars

And it was this reflection strong and penetrating,
A wave of gold rolling over the world,

Which flooded with its brightness,
The future nations—Humanity).

The Sonnet "Sardessay" is descriptive :

Um belo tipo de oriental beleza
Opulencia, vigor, graça, nobreza !
Deviam ser assim os meus Avós.

A beautiful type of Oriental beauty
Opulence, vigour, grace, nobility !
My ancestors must have been like that.

The "Oração ao Surya" is an ode not devoid of beauty :

Surya ! meu lindo sol esplendido do Oriente
Oh grande Surya, eu te saudo reverente !
Eu te ergo, meu bom Sol, e de bruços no chão
Na fé dos meus Avós, a minha saudação.
Arya do Antigo rito, Arya de velha lenda,
Aqui te ergo do humbral da minha pobre tenda
Como ao meu deus Krisna, Vishnu, Shiva ou Brahma
O' Ananta Supremo, o meu alto Salama.

O' fecundante Sol ! O' Creador sublime
Embaixador de Deus que em todo o ser imprime
A chancela de luz ! tu que doiras e aqueces
O homem, a fera, a flor, a pedra, a planta, as messes,
A miseria, a velhice, agasalhando os nús
Bendito sejas tu, Ó grande deus de Luz.

Surya ! Ó minha alegria e meu velho brazeiro
O teu ardente beijo é que me fez trigueiro,
Da tua luz, do teu calor, da tua graça
E' feito o meu Paiz, é feita a minha Raça
E a minha amada, e a minha irmã, e minha mãe
Foram feitas por ti trigueirinhas tambem.

(O Sun ! my beautiful glowing Sun of the East
O great Sun ! I salute thee reverently
I raise to thee, my good Sun, prostrate before thee
In the faith of my ancestors, my salutation .
Aryan of the ancient rites, Aryan of old legend
Here I raise to thee, from the threshold of my humble tent,
As to my god Krishna, Vishnu, Shiva or Brahma,
Oh Supreme Ananta, my highest salutation.

Oh life-giving Sun ! Oh sublime creator
Ambassador of God Who in all thy being hast impressed
The seal of light ! Thou who gildest and warmest
Man, beast, flower, stone, plant, the harvest,
Misery, and old age, clothing the naked,
Blessed be thou, Oh great god of Light.

Oh Sun my joy ! Oh ancient brasier !
Thy ardent kiss has bronzed my cheek,
Thy light, thy heat, thy influence
Has made my country, has made my race,
And my beloved, and my sister and my mother
Were also tanned by thee.)

The " Metempsycose " is perhaps one of the most beautiful lyrics of the poet and is steeped in oriental legend; the worm, not resigned to its fate of being a crawling miserable creature, asks Brahma to transform it into a flower and Brahma turns the worm into a flower and the flower says: 'I am beautiful and I have perfume and all admire me, but I am fastened to a branch. How I wish I could have my liberty !'

Quem me dera subir ao azul, erguer o vôo
Qual leve borboleta !

(If I could only rise into the sky, spread my wings
As the butterfly does !)

And Brahma transforms the flower into a butterfly. But the butterfly not content with its fate says :

Triste destino o meu voar de rosa em rosa
E eternamente muda, ouvir os passarinhos
Sempre a cantar, talvez saudades dos seus ninhos.

(O sad destiny which forces me to fly from rose to rose !
And eternally dumb to listen to the little birds
Always singing, perhaps of fond remembrances of their nests.)

The butterfly is transformed into a bird, the bird

wishes to be an eagle and the eagle wishes to be a star. And the star sighs :

Oh poderoso Brahma ! Oh Brahma complacente
De que serve esta luz sem a do sentimento
Sem o grande clarão da Luz do Pensamento !
Dae-me pois essa luz que só de Vós dimana.

(Oh powerful Brahma ! Oh complacent Brahma !
What is the use of having light without the light of feeling
Without the great reflection of the light of thought ?
Give me then that light which only from thee emanates.)

And Brahma transforms the star into a human soul. Dissatisfied and exhausted in its search for perfection, the soul addresses him in sad discouragement :

Mas que aguda tortura a dôr do Pensamento !
Antes eu fosse um verme, um simples infusório,
E da Dôr não subir o grande promontório !
Sofri, lutei ... Não há nada que me conforte !
Hoje só ambiciono a santa paz da morte.
Ah pudesse eu dormir na funda treva muda !

(But what acute torture is the pain of Thought !
I would rather be a worm, a simple worm
And not rise to this great height through pain.
I suffered, I struggled ... there is nothing which comforts me !
To-day I desire only the holy peace of Death.
Oh if I could but sleep in the deep still darkness !)

Brahma is not moved.

Mais eis que surge Budha,
O grande pensador de larga fronte calma
E com o seu Nirvanna aniquilou a Alma.

(But here Buddha rises,
The great thinker with the broad, calm forehead
And with his Nirvana he annihilated the soul.)

There is profound beauty in this thought. We do not know if the author had gleaned it from purely eastern sources or from the school of oriental thought developed by the French poets belonging to the School of Beaudelaire, Theophile Gauthier and Jean Lahor.

In all the other smaller poems of this book, the Indian influence predominates. In "Merenda" he describes the fruits of India, in "Cortejo Real", "Bailadeira", "Rajah de Godwara", and "Saguate" he portrays Indian customs. The "Dança de Bailadeiras" is a chansonette which is essentially eastern :

Bailae, bailae, bayaderas
Entre pompas e alegria.
A mais linda das chymeras
E' o amor de cada dia.

(Dance, dance, temple girls
Amidst pomp and joy.
The most beautiful of chimeras
Is the love of each day.)

And further :

Bailae, bailae docemente,
Cantae de amor as paixões
Em languida voz dolente
De enfeitiçar corações.

(Dance, sweetly dance,
Sing of the passions of love,
In the sorrowful and languid voice
Which charms all hearts.)

In the "Noivinhos" (Fiancés) in which "she is seven and he is ten", in the "Fakirs e Yogues" in "Sundorem", in "Toilette", in which he describes the adornments of an Indian woman, in the "Lenda dos Abolins" the same spirit pervades, unfortunately not always divested of a sensual tone which takes away a certain dignity from those compositions, some of which as regards rhyme and rhythm, are truly remarkable.

Floriano Barreto, a prose writer and poet who

died at an early age, left various writings about India which were published by the Indo-Portuguese Press. His book "Phalenas", Bastorá, Rangel, 1898, which has a part devoted to Indian subjects, contains various pieces of poetry on Indian themes and begins with the little poem "Sindrimal" which the author describes as :

Floriano Barreto.

... Uma flôr indiatica
Que espaneja ao Sol posto a corolla aromatica
Aos effluvios da noute e encantos do luar
Mas quando o fulvo Sol principia a dourar
O puro azul do céu limpido e transparente
Como urna de cristal,
A delicada flôr fecha suavemente
O calix virginal.

(... An Indian flower
At sunset opens its aromatic corolla
To the vapours of the night and the charms of moonlight ;
But when the resplendent Sun begins to gild
The pure blue of the sky, limpid and transparent
As a crystal urn,
The delicate flower softly shuts
Its virginal calix.)

His rhyme is delicate, but his verse sometimes loses its naturalness and appears studied and monotonous. In his poem "Uma mãe Hindu" (A Hindu Mother), he writes of the offering of her son to the God Jagannath ; the sonnet "Os Parses" is descriptive. "Bailadeira da India" combines the voluptuousness of the Orient with the Portuguese rhythm :

Tilinta os guizos ; tchinn. Saranguis lentamente
Desprendem pelo espaço em languidas doçuras
Harmonias d'amor aveludadas puras
Que embalam a noss'alma em um sonho dolente,
São soluços de amor, são melodias cerulas
Aereas, virginaes, cristallinas, ignotas.
Tilinta os guizos : tchinn. São orvalho de perolas
Que se evaporam no ar em turbilhão de notas,

Bate os guizos : tchinn, e matisa e constella
Com estes finos sons musicaes e sonoros
Caricias ideaes que o sarangui evola,
Que semelham ao longe as Apsaras em coros
Descantando ao luar a volata mais bela
Com a voz doce como um setim de corola.

(The little bells ring : tchinn. Slowly the Sarangis
Disperse into space in long drawn out sweetness
Harmonies of love, velvety and pure
Which lull our soul into a sorrowful sleep.
They are sobs of love, they are cerulean melodies,
Airy, virginal, crystalline, unknown.
The little bells ring : tchinn. They are dew drops of pearls,
Which evaporate in the air in a whirlwind of notes.
Make the little bells dance : tchinn, tchinn, and scatter and adorn
With these delicate and sonorous musical sounds,
Ideal caresses which the Sarangi evolves
Which resemble at a distance the chorus of Apsaras
Singing in the moonlight the most beautiful trills
With sweet voices smooth as the satin of a corolla.)

Then follow five sonnets in rhythmic Alexandrines; then a series of strophes in which the dancing girl is referred to in the same spirit as which Victor Hugo wrote his typical lines :

Oh, n'insultez jamais une femme qui tombe,
Dieu sait sous quel fardeau sa pauvre âme succombe.

Among interesting lyrics in this book are the "Mandos Traduzidos", popular compositions in Konkani, whose translations into Portuguese verse can give the reader an idea of the evolution of lyrical sentiment in that Indian dialect. The little poem "Satti" is the immolation of the widow on the funeral pyre in which the chorus of Brahmins sings :

Acompanha na vida e acompanha na morte
O espôso que baqueou na região do gêlo :
O casamento é nó tão poderoso e forte
Que nem a Trimurti poderia rompê-lo.

(She accompanies in life and accompanies in death
The husband who stumbled into the region of ice :
Marriage is a knot so powerful and strong
That not even the Trimurti could sever it.)

In these lines, written with the licence due to poets we should not seek to explore the ethical mazes of Indian mythology and sociology.

"O coqueiro" is an ode modelled on the "Redondilhas", in which he tells us the uses of the cocoanut tree :

O' rei dos vegetaes, ó elegante palmeira,
Que estendes pelo céu luminoso e fulgente
Esse tufo gentil do teu leque virente
No qual farfalha terna a viração fagueira.

(O King of the vegetable world, O elegant palmtree,
Which stretchest up towards the sky, luminous and sparkling
That graceful tuft of thy green fan
In which the gentle breeze whispers softly.)

O coqueiro é a providência do indio
Ninguém despreza-o, ninguém prescinde-o
Por isso o culto do hindu o consagra
E o considera quási celeste.
Fornece assucar chamado jagra
Limpa, ilumina, embriaga, veste.

Tu queres casa? esta árvore amiga
No tronco dá a ripa, o aguieiro e a viga.

(The cocoanut tree is the Providence of India
No one despises it, no one does without it,
For this the Hindu cult consecrates it.
It furnishes sugar called jagari,
It cleanses, gives light, intoxicates, clothes.

Dost thou desire a house? This friendly tree
Gives from the trunk the rafters, the gutters and the wood.

In this collection of poetry, a number of Indian terms are used which have now become a part of the

Portuguese language, and in the last part names celebrated in Indian history and literature are used in beautiful Alexandrines :

E a tua sombra talvez Vyassa compuzesse
Com a frente vergada ao labutar de idea
Parte do Maha-Bharata—a pujante epopea—
E Valmiki entoasse alçando a fronte ufana
As Slokas musicaes do grande Ramayana.

(It was in thy shade perhaps Vyassa composed
With his brows bent in the effort to shape the idea,
Part of the Maha Bharata, the powerful epic,
And Valmiki entoned, raising up his proud forehead,
The musical strains of the great Ramayana.)

The first part of "Phalenas" entitled "Indianas", ends with an ode to "Velha Goa" in which the poet laments its ruin :

Rainha do Mandovy, ó emporio gigantesco
Que assombraste as nações com o teu esplendor.

• •

Ja não resplende a luz no teu vasto horizonte

•

Sumiu-se para sempre a tua gloria passada
E a fama universal do teu nome temido.

(Queen of the Mandovy, O gigantic emporium
Which overwhelmed nations with thy splendour.

•

Now the light shineth not in thy vast boundary.

•

For ever extinguished is thy past glory
And the universal fame of thy dreaded name.)

Floriano Barreto died in Oporto while still a young man. After his death his admirers in India collected his most beautiful poems and prose-writings in a book called: "Livro Posthumo", Nova Goa, Casa Luso-

Francesa, 1906, in which in the poetry section one will find, besides other verses, the "Indianas" already referred to and some beautiful compositions on "A Cultura do Belo em Goa", (The cultivation of the beautiful in Goa), "Cerâmica em Goa" (The Potter's Art in Goa), "Interiores Domésticos" (Interior of homes), "O Culto da Música" (The Cult of Music), "Pintura" (Painting), comprising a collection called "Arte Goaneza", some descriptions of the habits and customs of Indian Christians under the title of "Instantaneos" (Snapshots) of landscapes under the name of "Aguarellas (Water colours) and three notable aesthetic and critical articles on Christian Dancing entitled "O mandó", which are studies on the art of dancing and the music for this popular Indo-Portuguese recreation.

Paulino Dias.

Paulino Dias is a melodious poet who sings in many and varied harmonies. His verses are to be found in many reviews and papers. Though he has verses which are as fine as those of Guerra Junqueiro, at times his poetry lacks both rhyme and rhythm. In the "Revista da India" which he founded with Adolfo Costa, he published a part of a translation in prose of the "Bhagvad Gita" which was never finished. In this publication we also find his poem in which a Muslim conqueror on a swift charger kidnaps the queen of Udaipur:

Como era muito linda e branca e timorata
Dissera o vencedor. Sob um luar de prata
Hei de cingi-la a sós na linha da cintura.
Estavam mortos os rajas barbados de Udaipura
Quatorze mil ranis, bemfeitas com liras
Se tinham imolado em quatorze mil piras.
Só uma salvou-a, Allah! de sete véus coberta,
Cheia de oiro, a andar a uma morte certa
E a chorar, a chorar que o seu pranto caia
Em perolas na terra enternecida e fria.

(How beautiful and fair and timid she was !
Said the conqueror. Under the silvery moon
Alone I shall encircle her waist.
The bearded Rajahs of Udaipur were dead ;
Fourteen thousand Ranis, slender as lyres
Had immolated themselves on fourteen thousand pyres.
Allah saved only one ! Covered with seven veils,
Full of gold, going to certain death,
Weeping, weeping, so that the tears fell
Like pearls on the pitying cold earth.)

In the desperate flight, the knight missed his footing and almost fell into the abyss, and in the heart of the captive who had been cursing her captor, there surged a feeling of pity :

De repente faltou-lhe a terra ; ahi ao fundo
Um grande abismo e escuro ; o céu profundo.
Allah, Allah, Allah ! Era a ultima ruina ...
Mas de repente à beira escura da ravina
A princeza se ergueu heroica e radiante
E susteve na queda o cavaleiro errante ;
Amparou-o tão bem sobre o maguado peito,
Que ele se desmaiou sobre o macio leito.
E ela levantou os sete véus sorrindo
E envolveu o Raja com um olhar tão lindo !
Bemfeito era ahi. No silencio sagrado
Vinha subindo ao longe o luar imaculado

(All at once he missed his step. Downwards
There was a huge, dark chasm of unfathomable depths.
Allah, Allah, Allah ! It was his inevitable end.
But suddenly at the dark edge of the ravine,
The princess, heroic and radiant, raised herself
And sustained in his fall the knight in danger.
She held him to her sorrowful breast
And sheltered there, he lost consciousness.
And smiling, she raised her seven veils
And cast on the Raja a thrilling glance.
It was a perfect setting. In the sacred silence
The immaculate moon was rising in the distance.)

Whoever is conversant with the Portuguese language and metre, realises that this beautiful poem, like other works of the author, contains flaws of construction and liberties of expression which detract from its value.

His unpublished verses which would make volumes, are in the possession of his family. "A Patria" a modern review, published some productions after the death of the poet. "Tilotoma" is a sonnet where he sketches the profile of the celestial dancing girl who inflames the heart of Indra. "Campestre" is a pastoral in which the author describes the girl who returned from weeding. It is beautifully written :

Rapariga que vens com um feixe de palha
De que varzea quem sabe, e que distante eira
Enches meu coração, o' morena estrangeira
E o teu simples olhar minha alma agasalha.

E eu fui vencer dragões, no topo da muralha
Dos vencidos perdi a mocidade inteira
Vim por lutar sem nome e a noute traiçoeira
Para ver-te voltar com um feixe de palha.

Teu seio oscila alto e eu fico pensativo
Sorris ... não para mim, mas eu fico captivo
— Ai ! que simples tu es que me fazes tão bem.

Quem me dera fugir das vastas derrocadas
Das horas sem alivio, altas noutes cavadas
E como tu voltar duma varzea tambem !

(O girl who comest with a bundle of grass
Who knows from which field or from which distant threshing-floor,
Thou fillest my heart, o dark stranger !
And thy simple glance comforts my soul.

I went to conquer dragons ; on the top of the wall
Of the conquered, I spent my whole youth.
I came without name to fight in the treacherous night
And I see thee return with a bundle of grass.

Thy breast marks the rhythm of thy steps and I am pensive
Thou smilest ... not at me, but I am captivated
Ah ! Thy simplicity does good to me.

How I wish I could escape from the vast ruins of my life !
From the hours without respite, the long nights of toil,
And like thee, return also from a field !)

In the review "Luz de Oriente" of Pondá are various poems by Paulino Dias on Indian themes. These poems are written under the nom-de-plume, Pritidassa, which is sometimes changed into Prithi Das.

In the "Hymno de Gajendra a Vishnu", the profusion of Indian terms can be realised by the following verses:

Tu cuja perfeição o Mahadeva canta,
Tu por quem Xuca geme, Vyassa triste pensa
E por seculos diz Valmiki : Rama, Rama.
O Hari cujo peito o amor dos seus inflama
Ó tu que tens por throno o lotus do Vaikunta
Tu cujo nome o Xastra em balde aos ceus pergunta
Tu cuja forma o sabio e o santo ainda não sabe
Tu cuja perfeição no infinito não cabe
Ó tu que dás o Moksa, o tu que dás o Swarga.
O meu louco pensar, perdida nau sem leme
Apaga-se a teus pés, o eterno Vishvambara.

(Thou whose perfection the Mahadeva sings,
Thou for whom Xuca groans, Vyassa thinks of sadly
And Valmiki for centuries says : Rama, Rama.
O Hari whose breast the love of thine inflames
O thou who hast for throne the lotus of Vaikunta
Thou whose name the Shastra asks the Heaven in vain
Thou whose form the sage and the saint do not yet know.
Thou whose perfection the infinite cannot contain
O thou who givest salvation, O thou who givest Heaven.
My maddening thought, lost ship without a rudder,
Faints at thy feet, o eternal Vishnu.

It was in this review that Paulino Dias published his "Coro a Narayana" which occurs in his poem

"Indra". The writer had a chance of reading it in the manuscript which was lent to her by the family of Paulino Dias. It is a magnificent poem in four cantos in which he gives us a kaleidoscopic view of Indian mythology and the heroic deeds of Indra. In the song of Indra, he sings of victory while in company with Vayu, he watches in the intoxication of triumph, the funeral procession of the beheaded Dasas, Gauras, Bahars and their captive wives. The chorus of priests celebrates the glories of Indra. But the ancient Aryans give praises to Varuna and to Mitra. Indra, haughty and insolent, goes to fight the gods whom he superseded. The second canto portrays Indra with the ancient gods who sing in chorus the praise of Aditi. The act ends with a singular combat in which Indra is almost conquered, but at the order of Diaus Pitara is freed by the strong arm of Mitra :

Diaus Pitara — "Wait, Mitra, wait".
Mitra — "Let me kill him, Father,"
Diaus Pitara — "No."

Não. E' severa
A vontade que vem irrevogavel do alto
Passou por mim alguem que encheu de sobresalto
Minha velhice branca e apagou minha Historia.

No. Severe is
The will which comes irrevocable from on high
Some one passed by me who filled with fear
My white old age and ended my History.

And Indra kills himself on the point of a lance. In the third Canto, Brahma creates a woman, Ahilya, of whose beauty the gods sing praises and Savitri Lacxmi, Devis, Apsaras and the Rishis do homage. This woman wins the love of Gautama who marries her and adores her. In Canto IV, Indra changes himself into various forms and in the end taking the form of a man seduces the beautiful and virtuous Ahilya. Gautama hurls a curse on her and turns her into a stone, but adds :

> Caiste na traição ! Mas ha de vir um dia
> Um deva para ti, da linhagem da Lua
> E tocar-te com os pés, então a imagem tua
> Ha de voltar à vida, ó mulher inocente.

> (Thou hast been betrayed but thou wilt see one day
> A god for thee of the lineage of the Moon
> Who will touch thee with his feet, then thy image
> Will return to life, oh innocent woman.)

His malediction to Indra is irrevocable :

> Pela chaga que abriste em meu peito cavado
> Mil chagas se hão de abrir por teu corpo malvado.

> (For the wound which thou hast opened in my hollow breast,
> A thousand wounds will open in thy wicked body.)

Indra — " Shall I decay irreparably ? "
Gautama — " Thou dost not deserve even one exclamation of pity. "

Purvassa to Indra :

> Tu eras o deus da chuva e a tempestade amarga
> Um nababo como raio, ó Indra, figura oca
> Que adorava a cantar toda a Ariavarta louca.
>
> Não es tu o senhor nos longos horisontes
> Tu não fizeste nunca o vento, o fogo, a aurora.
> E' a natureza, a Mãe, a unica criadora !
> De joelhos ó Indra ! Escutae-me eremitas
> E' tempo de apagar as crenças infinitas
> Sonhos e criações das palidas edades.
> Outras forças se impõem as severas verdades
> As que vejo a vibrar na criação altiva
> São forças naturaes — Brahma, Vishnu, Shiva.

(Thou wert the god of rain and the bitter tempest
A lord with the lightning. Oh Indra, hollow form
Whom the Ariawarta, mad with love, adored in singing.

Thou art not the lord of the distant horizon
Thou didst never make the wind, the fire and the dawn.
Nature is the mother, the only creator!
On thy knees, O Indra, listen, hermits;
It is time to blot out the numberless beliefs,
Dreams and creations of the past ages.
Other forces impose their severe truths.
Those which I see vibrating in the proud creation,
Are natural forces, Brahma, Vishnu, Shiva.)

The seven hermits say:

"Victory to Trimurti and the gods of the future."

Amongst his little poems published in book form, we find one called "Vasco da Gama", Nova Goa, Imprensa Nacional, 1898, which tells of the discovery of the maritime way to India. "A Deusa de Bronze", Imprensa Minerva, Nova Goa, 1909, tells how an Indian courtesan tired of life, falls in love with "Naga", presses it against her breast and dies from the bite of the poisonous cobra. The verses are magnificent and an Indian atmosphere pervades the whole of this beautifuf Beaudelarian poem. The last lines, when the poison takes effect, are as follows:

Venha já sobre mim a noute e o esquecimento
Oh repouso, Oh repouso abençoado e impassivel!
Cobre com aza negra o meu feroz tormento!
Tu es da minha vida a ultima victoria,
Apaga o meu delirio e o agudo sentimento.
Não quero o mundo, a pompa, a tentadora gloria.
Uma lagrima só de palpebra pendida
(e cerrando os olhos lentamente)
Alguem ha de chorar uma mulher perdida.

(Night and forgetfulness already envelop me.
O repose, O repose! blessed and calm,

Cover with thy black wing my fierce torment !
Thou art the ultimate victory of my life.
Blot out my delirium, and acute sense of pain,
I do not desire the world, pomp or tempting glory.
One tear only hanging from an eye-lid
(and closing her eyes slowly)
Someone will weep for a lost woman.

His poem "Vishnulal" signed by the pen-name of Prithi Das, Nova Goa, 1919, expresses in triple rhyme the remorse and expiation of a Brahmin who in a moment of irresponsible hallucination had killed in a mountain hermitage a young, handsome "cudvalina" (1) whose body was then devoured by jackals. The little poem is accompanied by a translation in French verse which the poet writes elegantly. Throughout this poem there is a breath of veiled realism and intense artistic emotion as we find in the works of Anatole France. In this work the influence of the French contemporary school is evident and the French translation is more musical than the original in Portuguese :

Eu sou de longe, eu tenho lembranças funestas.
Escuta, O Vatsura ! um dia entre mangueiras
Eu vi-a no sari e as manilhas de festas,

Os braços lisos como o caule das figueiras.
Eh Madana, Madana, em meu sangue danado !
Ao vê-la no sol posto, a orla das cordilheiras.

Olhos no chão, esquiva e o pescoço inclinado.
Tinha ela o mogrim e o pat sobre o cabelo.
E da aldeia ninguem, nem um pastor com gado.

---

(1) "Cudvalina" has almost the same meaning as Curumbina, that is, it is a word which indicates caste and profession. It is a kind of Goanese servant employed in the fields. Cudvalim is a Konkani word which has been Portuguesised by Paulino Dias and Curumbim is Christian whereas Cudvalim is non-Christian, being Hindu but of very low caste.

Atraz dela só eu como a cobra capelo. (1)

(I belong to a far off country and I have dark remembrances
Listen, O Vatsura ! One day amidst the mango trees
I saw her in sari robed in festal splendour,

Her arms smooth as the stem of the fig tree.
O Madana, Madana, how my blood was on fire,
To see her at sunset at the edge of a mountain.

Her eyes downcast, coy, her head bent.
She had *mogrim* and *pat* in her hair.
And no one was there from the village, not even a shepherd with his flocks.
Only I followed behind her like the hooded cobra.

*

Fui. Num paiz sem nome e os vales ignorados
Vivia um santo antigo em rija penitencia
Suspenso dum pimpal, os dous olhos vasados.

Sei, tu és Vishnulal ! bradou com virulencia,
Sae do paiz sagrado e a benção dos eremitas !
Eu prostrei-me a seus pés com profunda obediencia

Não lanceis Xap, eu vou para terras malditas
Maharaja ... Vishnulal, expia o teu pecado.

(I fled. In the unknown valleys of a nameless country
Lived an old saint in rigid penitence,
Suspended from a peepal tree staring into vacancy.

---

(1) The French verse is still more harmonious as we may see from the following :

Que me veux tu ? je suis des pays étrangers :
Que te dire, oh passant ! du chagrin qui me baigne !
Une femme je vis un soir dans les manguiers.
Avec deux bras luisants, drapée de longue pagne
Eh ! Madana que j'eus le sang bouillant en moi ;
De la voir, sur la brune, au bord d'une montagne
Le cou rouge, moulé, penché d'honte ou d'effroi
Lourde du mogarin la noire chevelure.
Et personne alentour, mais personne, ma foi !
Le desir me tordait comme une corde dure ...

"I know thou art Vishnulal!" he shouted with violence
"Go away from this sacred country and the benediction
of the hermits",
I prostrated myself at his feet in profound obedience.

"Do not curse me, I go to lands which are cursed
Maharajah" ... "Vishnulal, expiate thy sin".

In the work of Paulino Dias there is a profusion of words and neologisms of Indian origin which make his compositions interesting even from the point of view of philology and of the infiltration of Indian terms into the Portuguese language. His short unpublished poems contain them by hundreds. It is a pity these poems are not published as a posthumous volume, annotating in the margin his corrections, in order that we might be able to appreciate the naturalness and artistic emotionalism which characterised him. To the courtesy of his family the writer owes the privilege of being able to read his poems in manuscript. Mention will be made here of some referring to India.

"Zaiu" is a descriptive sonnet the imagery of which is deeply Indian, while "Tara" is a charming pastoral. The sonnet "Bailadeiras" is a poem in which the desire for the redemption of the erring woman has rarely been so nobly expressed by a poet! In the poem "A Pracriti", Indian thought dominates the whole composition.

"Viassa" is an admirable sonnet which is equal to any of the best poems written by the contemporary Portuguese poet, Antero de Quental. Here it is:

Eu tive um sonho, vi o topo do Himalaia
—Picava-o o vento largo! E era um fragor de guerra,
Choques, gritos de leões, clarins, ondas na praia...

— Em volta a Ariavarta, a milagrosa terra—
Escuro. E só o monte a erguer-se de atalaia.
Mas alguem era aí com o escopro, o malho e a serra,

Numa furia que não abate e não desmaia,
A cortar, a ferir os pedaços da serra.

E gritei a tremer, agitado de frio :
—Quem é aí no pavor que amedronta e assombra,
A cortar e a rugir sobre um monte sombrio ?—

Era então o luar um crescente de prata.
E ouvi dizer-me alguem pelo meio da sombra :
—E' Viassa a esculpir o imenso Mahabarata—.

(I had a dream, I saw the top of the Himalayas.
—A great wind was blowing there — And there was a sound of war,
Shocks, roars of lions, bugle calls, waves on the shore ...

And all around, Aryavarta, the miraculous earth—.
Darkness. And only the mountain raised itself as a sentinel.
But someone was there with a chisel, a hammer and saw,
In a fury which never abated or grew fainter,
Cutting and wounding the pieces of the mountain.

I shouted trembling, shivering with cold ;
In fear which terrifies and overcomes,
Who is there cutting and groaning on the dark mountain ?

Then came the light of the silvery crescent ;
And I heard someone say from the midst of the shadow :
It is Vyasa shaping the immense Mahabharata.)

It is impossible to give a complete resumé of all the works of Paulino Dias. Our sincere wish is that they should be published in full to add to the lustre of Indo-Portuguese literature.

We shall conclude this brief sketch of his work with one of his most graceful stories on Indian subjects. The poem is called "A Cobra e O Sapo". (The Cobra and the Toad).

There was a clay modeller whose name was Nanu. He used to model lions, palm-trees, mountains, Indian servants returning from the fountains with water ; the clay became beautiful in his hands. And to his door came half-naked people and beautiful young girls who stood in ecstasies watching him at work. One day in May, Nanu saw a majestic cobra, black and velvety, coiling and uncoiling in the leaves. What a beautiful model it made ! Nanu smiled while he watched the cobra slowly forming and uncurling its rings, while steely glances flashed from its eyes. And Nanu modelled it. He had already formed the head, the tail, the beautiful markings and had begun the hideous poison spots on its head which the cobra slowly waved from side to side, when all at once he saw a poor toad sitting on a stone in the mud. Dumb and motionless, it was looking at the cobra "as one would look at a dear king". The toad saw the velvety spots, the coils, the turns, the fury, the scintillating colours and felt over it its terrible breath, and the toad sobbed. Suddenly the cobra raised itself and like a flash of lightning, killed the poor toad with one stroke of its head. How tragic and how beautiful ! Nanu left his clay to see it lying in death, its little feet stretched upwards and its eyes "still fixed on its dear king." Struck with compassion, Nanu began to make a model of the toad. He formed it beautifully and covered it with gold and precious stones, till it also seemed a king of gold".

E pelo sol poente
Viram todas as gentes extasiadas
Nanu com duas estatuas levantadas,
Uma altiva e sombria,
E outra humilde a seus pés como um farrapo,
E ele ambas adorava tristemente,
Com os seus olhos ambas envolvia
Que a gente não sabia
Se Nanu adorava uma serpente
Ou se adorava um sapo.

(And at sunset
All the people in ecstasies saw
Nanu with two statues raised up,
One haughty and sombre,

And the other humble like a rag at its feet.
And he adored both sadly
And his eyes were cast on both,
So that the people could not understand
If Nanu were adoring a serpent, or if he were
Worshipping a toad.)

Nascimento Mendonça.

Nascimento Mendonça, undoubtedly the most vigorous figure in Indo-Portuguese literature, is the writer who had greatest originality. He possesses the impetuous imagination of the Portuguese combined with Indian sensitiveness.

Unfortunately, the greater part of his work, remains unpublished. Amongst his published poems "A Morta", Tip. Rangel, Bastorá, is an admirable composition with an Indian setting. As we also find in the works of Paulino Dias, the impressions that dominated the poet were so vivid that his verse alone was not sufficient to express either the force of his thought or the vivid colouring in which oriental imagery abounds. For instance, the action in the poem "A Morta" is laid in the court of Ayodhia where Rama laments chaste Sita, who is dead, and whom his pride had caused him to repudiate. Nascimento Mendonça is not content with confining his genius to the writing of wonderful verses, but he also impresses on the mind of the reader the oriental scenery as a background in which the action he describes stands out in clear relief. Thus he tells us before commencing the poem :

"The scene is laid in the wonderful park of the palace of Ayodhia and it is the glorious and tragic hour of sunset. Rama, the invincible hero of Lanka, clasps his hands with a sorrowful gesture and adores the divine sun which is dying. Beautiful in the purple light seems the garden of Ayodhia surrounded by a high wall of the finest marble of Jaipur ...

The impression made on the reader will certainly be much greater when the sonorous verses are united in his mind with scenery which has as its complement the dying sun, "the sorrowful gesture" of the hero "in a garden surrounded by walls of the finest marble".

Rama remembers his lost happiness :

> Meu amor, meu amor foi um sol luminoso !
>
> (My love, my love was a luminous sun !)
>
> Lembrava uma arequeira amoravel e rara
> Que o meu olhar regava e o meu desejo ardente.
>
> (She reminded me of a beetel-nut tree, tender and rare
> That delighted my eyes and my ardent desire.)

A cloud of irreparable disillusionment passes over him ; he succumbs to it exclaiming :

> Como o sonho de amor nos atormenta e illude !
> Traz a morte consigo o sonho loiro e lindo
> Se não ha n'alma um sol que em perfume o transmude.
> Amor, amor, amor ! Astro de oiro fulgindo ...
>
> (How the dream of love torments and deceives us
> The golden beautiful dream brings death with it
> If there is not in the soul a sun which changes it into perfume.
> Love, Love, Love ! Star of gold resplendent ...)

Then a group of faqirs pass singing, at the moment when the despair of the hero contrasts with the glory of the hour in which the last rays of the setting sun are fading in the wonderful garden, where "orange trees grow in the deep silence, palm-trees, figs and aloes,—all the strange and vigorous vegetation that frames the divinely beautiful lake, which, as it caresses the lower branches of the trees, sobs a delicate song of passion and dream."

These two descriptions of the scenery show the poet to be profoundly oriental. In "A Morta," we have the songs of faqirs, the ecstasies of Rishis, the dances of the temple girls, chants of the souls, lakes, lotuses, apsaras and stars, united in a story which is marvellously legendary. The prayer of Botho to the Sun is a gem :

Surya divino e resplendente !
O Sol, doirada mistica urna
Sejas bendito eternamente
Surya que beijas docemente
Minha alma, triste flor nocturna.

O tu que a beijas e a fecundas !
O' luz que es pão, ó luz que es sangue !
Sol que de amor e luz inundas
As almas simples e profundas,
Volve-me em luz est'alma exangue.

Arranca, O Sol, dos corações,
Toda a ruim e rasteira herva
Engr'nalda-os de astros e illusões ;
Enche-os de flor's e de clarões
E nelas só a luz conserva.

(O divine and resplendent Sun !
O Sun, golden and mystic urn !
Be thou blest eternally,
O Surya, who sweetly kisses
My soul, sad nocturnal flower.

Oh thou who kisses it and makest it productive
O light who art bread, o light who art blood,
O Sun who with love and light floodest
The simple, sincere souls.
Bathe my exhausted spirit in light !

Extract O Sun, from the hearts
All the ruinous and noxious weeds ;
Crown them with stars and illusions,
Fill them with flowers and radiance,
And in them keep only the light.)

Rama, mortified and remorseful, tearfully says :

Oh Almas imortaes ouvi ... tende piedade
Que eu não fui nunca um tigre, o whaga sanguinario
Eu amei a beleza, adorei a Bondade
Foi meu algoz o orgulho acre e tumultuario.

Fui o filho do Jangle, impetuoso e heroico
Que ama O Sol, a Luz, a Beleza infinita
Era forte o meu corpo e o coração estoico
E no meu sangue rugia uma lava maldita.

(O immortal Souls, listen... have pity !
I never was a tiger, a blood thirsty lion,
I loved beauty I adored goodness,
My destruction has been my bitter and tumultuous pride.

I was the child of the jungle, impetuous and heroic,
Who loved the Sun, the Moon and infinite Beauty,
My body was strong and my heart was stoic
And in my blood surged a cursed lava.)

Then a mysterious secret voice said :

Sobe na luz pobre alma sucumbida
Sobe na luz do Sol divinamente
Sê o condor audaz, forte e fremente
Que jámais na desgraça cae vencida.

Sobe ao ceu, sobe ao ceu ardentemente
E quando O Sol as azas te queimar
Has de ao nada cair serenamente
Para tornar a amar, lutar, sonhar.

(Rise in the light, poor crushed soul,
Rise divinely in the light of the Sun.
Be the audacious condor, strong and impetuous,
Which never falls conquered by misfortune.

Rise to heaven, rise to heaven eagerly,
And when the sun shall scorch thy wings,
Again shalt thou fall serenely into nothingness
In order again to love, fight and dream.)

Rama says :

Sita-bay, Sita-bay ! ... Quem me dera ve-la !
(Sitabai !, Sitabai, ... What would I not give to see her !)

From the lotus flower sweetly rises, in a deluge of tremulous light, the lovely, sorrowful phantom of

Sita, emaciated and shadowy. And the hero opening his eyes and clasping his hands in adoration laments :

Foste no meu verão a sombra compassiva
No meu inverno triste a luz que me embalava
O pallida Devi de fronte pensativa
Tu eras o luar, eu o sol que escaldava.
Meu amor, meu amor, a lugubre lembrança
Cresta-me o coração num sopro acre de lava.)

(Thou wert in my summer time the compassionate shadow,
In my sad winter, the light which soothed me.
O pale Goddess with pensive forehead !
Thou wert the moon, and I the scorching sun.
My love, my love, the sad remembrance
With a bitter breath of lava burns my heart.)

The phantom trembles, wrings its hands, seems to shudder with the sting of remembrance and Rama reminds it of "Do tigre de Lanka o beijo viperino"

(The venomous kiss of the tiger of Lanka).

The sweet phantom closes its eyes in anguish. Rama continues in the pain of impotent jealousy :

Ah porque não esqueço a clava de Ravana ?
Eu te vejo Rahnin, ai eu te vejo ainda
No lugubre paiz da raça deshumana
Eu te vejo chorar tão desolada e linda
Sob o olhar do Rakxaça apaixonado e lasso
E a minha dôr é como um Smudra que não finda.

(O why do I not forget the club of Ravana ?
I see thee there, I see thee still
In that unfortunate country of merciless people
I see thee weeping, so lonely and beautiful,
Beneath the glance of the Rakshasa, troubled and weary,
And my pain is like a never-ending ocean.)

And Sita's glance speaks of irreparable misfortune, but almost immediately the sweet calmness of grief returns to her and wraps her in a veil of tenderness and melancholy. The hero says passionately :

Sonho ver-te em Lanka, o flor amargurada
Que loucura, que horror assalta me a lembra-lo
Antes me abrisse o peito o fio de uma espada !

(I dream of seeing thee in Lanka, O crushed flower !
What madness, what horror overcomes me when I think of it !
Sooner would I have my breast pierced with a sword !)

And in a wave of tenderness, remorse and intense regret :

E tu foste em Lanka, o fino ser tão puro
Como um sporo de Luz, do divino Surya
Na treva que confrange e o lamaçal impuro
Mas o meu coração foi como um mar em furia.
Foi de pedra Deva ! meu coração violento.

Eu nunca mais amei. Sou o aço d'armadura
Sobre o peito sem luz, de um gigante derrotado
Que se desfaz na dôr de uma lembrança obscura
E eras tu Sitabay, meu amor inviolado
No meu acre verão a sombra de uma palma
Nas areias da Vida o meu sonho doirado
Só tu eras, Sita, a esposa de minha alma.

(And thou wert in Lanka, the delicate being as pure
As a ray of light of the divine Sun
In the tormenting darkness and in the mire.
But my heart was like a raging sea
My violent heart turned to stone, God !

I never more loved, I am the steel of the armour
On the breast already dead, of a defeated giant
Who is broken down with the pain of unhappy remembrance.
And thou wert, Sita Bai, my inviolate love,
In my bitter summer the shadow of a palm-tree,
In the sandy desert of life, my golden dream.
Only thou Sita, wert the wife of my soul !)

And pleading in his immortal and sorrowful desire for her forgiveness, he says :

Fala... da-me o perdão! Que tormentos os meus!

(Speak ... give me pardon. What torments are mine!

All the garden trembles ... and the phantom of Sita, seeing her image tremble in the eyes of the Maharaja like a star lost in a stormy ocean, feels her compassion and pity return for her husband, so unhappy and repentant. He advances as though to embrace her and opens his arms, lacerated with long penances, and she, sad and sweet, light as the vapour in the limpid blue Elysian morn disappears.

The birds sing. The roses bloom. The face of Heaven seems to smile and the great harmonious voice of Life rises sweetly like a cloud of incense saluting the sun.

It is a wonderful composition. Poetry and prose are both full of artistic emotion. In this poem one can detect the influence of Greek tragedy.

In the paper called "Luz d'Oriente" of Pondá under the nom-de-plume, Nitipal, Nascimento Mendonça publised many fine poems on Indian subjects. Here is "Puruxa":

E foi no Mar de Amrita, ardente e esplendoroso
Que eu o vi Madeva—ai que visão sublime!
Sobre as cabeças mil do Xexa poderoso;
E eu tremia de assombro humilde como um vime.

Puruxa, o vencedor dos Seculos e o Espaço
Mil cabeças tinha Ele e mil olhos ardentes
Era luz o seu sangue e o seu corpo era d'aço
Tremiam só de vê-lo os monstros e as serpentes.

(It was in the ambrosial Sea, ardent and resplendent
That I saw Mahadev—O vision sublime!
Above the thousand heads of powerful Sesha;
And I trembled like an osier, humble with fright.

(Purusha, the conquerer of centuries and of space,
Had a thousand heads and a thousand keen eyes

His blood was of light and his body was of steel,
Only to look upon him the monsters and serpents trembled.)

The mythological description continues and then he says :

Ele era o Adhidaiva, o Senhor, o Monarcha
Que creara do Swarga os devas colossaes
E o seu olhar subtil e amplo de partiarcha
Fendia a rocha branca fendia os metaes.

(He was the Adhidaiva, the Lord, the Monarch
Who created the colossal gods of Heaven ;
And his comprehensive subtle glance of patriarch
Would cleave the white-rock and unearth the metals.)

Ele foi o Adhidaiva e foi o Purxotoma
O espirito que é luz e clarão que é Beleza.

Puruxa, Purxotoma, o Vencedor da Terra
O Vyassa Prometheu, Edison, Platão
Nem os devas dirão quantos astros encerra
— Samudra sideral — teu grande coração.

(He was the Adhidaiva, and the Puruxotama
The spirit which is Light, the reflection which is Beauty.

Purusha Purushotoma, O Conqueror of the Earth !
O Vyassa, Prometheus, Edison and Plato,
Not even the gods can say how many stars
Thy great heart,— sidereal ocean—encircles.)

"No Jangle" is a poem in which he prays for the return to simple forest life :

Ergue-te Pardessi ! a Terra é Paraiso
Onde floresce ao Sol, o lotus da Ilusão.

Ah ! Vamos ver surgir das aguas misteriosas
O victorioso sol que fecunda a floresta.
Vamos ouvir cantar nas fontes rumorosas
A alma de Prithivi triumphante e honesta.
Tu vens, oh caminheiro, exhausto e desolado !

A' floresta pedir como um vencido e um crente
Consolação e alivio ao coração golpeado.

(Raise thyself, Pardesi. The earth is Paradise where
The lotus of illusion opens to the Sun.

Ah let us go to see, rising from the mysterious water,
The victorious sun which fills the forest with life.
Let us go to hear in the murmuring fountains
The soul of Prithivi singing triumphant and true.
Thou comest, O Traveller, exhausted and disconsolate,
To ask from the forest, as a vanquished soul and a believer,
Consolation and relief for thy wounded heart.)

In his book of verses "Lotus de Sangue e de Ideal" one finds at each step Indian imagery and Indian ideas. There is not, however, any poem with a purely Indian theme except "Tentação do Vaishya", a harmonious composition in which Vaishya lives happy and humble by the side of his companion who,

Mais esbelta que a palmeira
Cantando embalava os filhos
E aos pés dela o seu desejo
Era um jardim a florir.

E era de graça tranquila
O lume do seu bom lar
Numa lampada de argila
Agni, o deus tutelar,
Mas Nisumba, a feiticeira
Veio um dia á verde serra.

(More graceful than the palm-tree,
Singing, rocks her sons ;
And at her feet his desire
Was as a garden in bloom.

It had a tranquil beauty,
The fire of his good hearth.

In a clay lamp was
Agni, the tutelary god.
But Nisumba, the witch.
Came one day to the green mountain,

And filled the heart of the humble Vaishya with ambition, pride, sadness and bitterness. Vaishya satisfied his ambition with palaces and riches but he never recovered his former happiness.

In the collection entitled "Hervas de Hind", published by Rau e Irmãos, 1921, the Indian subjects and ideas are numerous. In the first little poem called "Invocação" the poet saw the form of Krishna :

... eu vi o Deva
Co'a lua nos cabelos
Eu vi Ananta, os Bhudas, Brahmadeva
Toda a legião que os Saniasis enleva ;—
Bustos de homem ou formas de capelo.

(... I saw the god
With the moon in his hair
I saw Ananta, the Buddhas, the God Brahma,—
All the legion that charms the Sunyasis ;
Forms of men or shapes of armour.)

But nothing charmed him :

Só me prendeu a tua face augusta
O terra, O Prithivi !
O Terra, O Terra, O Noiva enamorada
Arvore, Musgo, Flor, Canção alada
Eu sou uma creança deslumbrada
Ao pé de ti.

(Only thy august face held me
O Earth, O Prithivi !
O Earth ! O Earth ! O beloved bride ! O Prithivi !
Tree, moss, flower, winged song,
I am a child overawed
Near thee.

Nascimento Mendonça died in June 1926, during the time when the writer was in Goa consulting the libraries of that Portuguese province. His was a soul essentially poetic and emotional, and he was a Bohemian at heart. He wrote in English some "Poemas em Prosa" which contain strains similar to those of the "Gitanjali" and "the Gardener" of Tagore. Through the kindness of his son, the writer had the privilege of reading the unpublished works of the great poet.

A book in prose entitled "Os deuses de Benares" is a most beautiful conception in which a Hindu, blasé through scepticism and modern civilization, goes to look for a hermit in the jungle and full of contrition and penitence, seeks the gods of his forefathers. Before his eyes passes the whole of the Indian Olympus, and the devil, like the incarnation of Mephistopheles of Goethe, makes him see the inanity of each one of those old gods. The young Hindu, weeping at each lost illusion, returns disconsolate from the austerity of the hermitage to the luxury of the city, in the profound conviction that the gods are dead. Mendonça's books will appeal to men of letters who care for art and oriental culture.

Amongst his unpublished works which the writer had the honour of reading, there is a collection of Sonnets entitled "Cantico do Vento e da Agua" in which the virile, sonorous verses are pervaded by a wholly Indian atmosphere. Thus in the first sonnet, the image of the monsoon is clear, and only he who has lived by the sea in India can appreciate to the full the beauty of the poetic descriptions :

Oh vento da monsão, dize-me : a que vieste
Com o tam-tam e a voz clangorosa e candente
Rugindo sobre o mar alucinadamente
E povoando de sons a soledade agreste ?
Lembra-me o teu silvar uma cobra que investe
No bruto matagal desolada gente.

(O wind of the monsoon, tell me! thou who camest
With the tam-tam and thy white, hot, clangorous voice
Roaring madly over the sea
And peopling with sounds the wild solitude,
Thy hissing reminds me of a cobra which attacks
Lonely people in the wild jungle.

In the second sonnet he says:

Vento de maio, alvoroçado e veemente
Pastor de nuvens nas planicies de Punjab
Eu vejo o teu rebanho, as ovelhas—quem sabe—
Vão adorar o Deus da minha terra ardente.

O pastor, O pastor, deste claro deus de Hind!
Que importa o Sol? .. Dize aos rebanhos: vinde! vinde!
Na dor e a fome deus a todos agasalha.

(Wind of May, frenzied and vehement,
Shepherd of the clouds in the plains of the Punjab.
I see thy flock; the sheep, who knows?
Go to adore God in my burning country.

Oh shepherd! Oh shepherd! of this clear sky of Ind!
What does the Sun matter ... Say to the flocks "come come."
In pain and in hunger God shelters all!

The sixth sonnet is a song of thanks to the Monsoon which fertilises India:

O vento vae pelo palmar passando
Com voz de mando e o seu clarim de guerra
Dobram-se os robles e sorriem sonhando
Que os rios do ceu jorram sobre a terra.

O lodo é como pedra faiscando
E lume e lava todo o areal encerra ...
Ah! vento da monsão, vai clangorando
Vae ululando pelo mar e a serra.

Dir-se-ia que és a voz de uma desgraça
Ara do mal que sobre o mundo esvoaça
Voz de tigre que os berços sobressalta

E comtudo, meu Deus! é a tua fala
Que na leiva arida a semente embala
No pó hostil a vida imensa exalta.

(The wind passes through the palm groves
With its commanding voice and its clarion of war
The oaks bend and smile, dreaming
That the rivers of heaven are gushing forth over the earth.

The mud is like a flashing stone
And fire and lava cover up the sand,
Ah wind of the Monsoon, go noisily
Howling by sea and by mountain.

One would say that thou art the voice of a misfortune ·
•An evil constellation hovering over the world;
A tiger's voice which awakes the horizons.

And withal, my God, it is Thy voice
Which in the arid clay, rocks the seed.
And raises up teeming life from the hostile dust.)

Nascimento Mendonça is incontestably the deepest and most emotional of the poets who have given to India beautiful verses in the musical Portuguese language.

Adolfo Costa is a lyric poet whose compositions are to be found in various Indo-Portuguese papers. Together with Ana d'Ayala, his wife, he wrote a book "De mãos dadas", Nova Goa, Colonial, Bragança & Co., 1907, where we find with reference to India, a descriptive sonnet called "Aldeas" a poem, "Em Viagem", in which he uses Indian terms and the third, in which he addresses "Velho Portugal":

Adolfo Costa.

Por acaso, na praia solitária
Onde está a fortaleza Gaspar Dias
Outr'ora magestosa e tão lendária
Hoje em destroços e ruinas frias,

Eu escutava o rio socegado
Carpindo soluçante nas areias
Saudades do fortim desmoronado
Sem torres, sem canhões e sem ameias.

(By chance on the solitary shore,
Where is the fortress, Gaspar Dias,
Once so majestic and wrapped in legend,
To-day changed into cold ruins,

I listened to the quiet river
Rippling along, in the sands, sobbing
Regrets of the small tottering fort
Without towers, without cannons, and without battlements.)

And "Velho Portugal" in the form of a troubled exhausted old man, relates his story where the heroes of Portuguese India file past :

Albuquerques, Cabraes, Almeidas, Castros,
Valentes companheiros meus antigos

(Albuquerques, Cabraes, Almeidas, Castros,
My brave old companions.)

He refers to the poet Camões :

Tive um amigo, vate aventureiro,
O bom Camões de celebre renome
Cantou as minhas glorias, foi guerreiro
E morreu no Hospital ao frio e á fome.

(I had a friend, adventurous bard,
The good Camões of renowned fame.
He sang my glories, he was a warrior,
— And died in hospital, of cold and hunger.

The poem ends in the book by the prayer of the poet for Portugal. But in a Soirée d'Art given by an aristocratic family in Goa, when the writer had the opportunity of hearing the author recite the same poem, the poet concluded with a verse affirming his faith in the regeneration of Portugal under the green and red

Republican flag. The poem has since been published with this addition.

Together with Paulino Dias, he founded the Revista da India (The Indian Review), of which only the first volume was published, July 1913—June 1914, where we find two descriptive sonnets of his, entitled " Baguem ", a description, of a dancing girl ; and " Rishi " :

•

Enlevados nos Xastras nobres e altivos

Impassível na dor, como um herói
Êle é no bosque a fôrça que constroi
E a voz que os Vedas místicos proclama.

•

Em sua volta cantam moluonis
Passam na sombra tigres e reptis
E êle só diz baixinho : Rama ! Rama !

(Wrapped in the Shastras, noble and proud,

Impassive in pain as a hero,
He is in the wood the strength which constrains
And the voice which the mystic Vedas proclaim.

Around him sing 'moluonis'
In the shade tigers and reptiles pass
And he but says under his breath : Rama ! Rama !)

He has also given us a touching poem : " O eco das ruinas " which is a review of the past glories of Portugal, in the midst of the present desolation of Old Goa. It ends thus plaintively :

Nesse ruir
Dos velhos monumentos, velhas glórias
Cobriu-se de Luto o anjo das vitorias ;
Um vento mau, um vento de amargura,
Deixou tudo em ruínas ;
Sòmente—mãos divinas !
Afaga-nos a linda Gopacpura,
A velha Goa soluçando endeixas,
Gritos e queixas ;

Ao Mandovi que murmurando, passa,
Das loucuras fatais da nossa raça !

Mas é tempo ; a corneta alvoroçada
Ecoa pelos ares a alvorada
Que à vitória conduz ;
Clarim de Portugal, clarim de guerra
Espalha em vibrações por sôbre a terra
A tua alma de luz !

(In the decay of the old monuments, old glories,
The angel of victory was shrouded in mourning.
An evil wind, a wind laden with bitterness,
Left all in ruins.
Only—hands divine !

The beautiful Gopacpura
Soothes us ; and old Goa sobs laments,
Cries and complaints ;
To the Mandovi, which murmuring, passes,
Of the disastrous folly of our race !

But it is time ; the cornet in transports
Echoes to the zephyrs the morning strain
Which leads to victory ;
Clarion of Portugal, clarion of war !
Thy soul of light is scattered in vibrations
Over the earth !)

The poet has in preparation a book almost ready for the Press, entitled "Euryanas" on Indian subjects.

The Scientific Movement.

The Portuguese contribution to Science with regard to anything concerning India is very small, notwithstanding that chroniclers who accompanied the discoverers of the way to India, left behind them valuable information about the Ethnology, Medicine and Natural History of the lands newly discovered.

It is a pity that this scientific work should not have been continued by the succeeding generations for the sake of the honour of their colonization, already notable from so many different points of view. (1) (2)

One of the earliest writers, João de Barros, describes with exactitude in his "Decadas" the symptoms and gives the cause of Scurvy which began to attack the sailors in the Indian sea.

> "................... Many people ill and some died.
> The greater part had Erysipelas and their gums so swollen that their mouths could scarcely contain them and as the gums grew larger they rotted and were cut away as dead flesh; it was very painful to see; we came to know afterwards that that illness was produced from eating meat, salt fish and biscuits which had become spoiled with keeping too long a time." (3)

This disease of the Indian seas, which developed in that region, due to the want of fresh food during the long period spent in doubling the Cape of Good Hope, drew two expressive stanzas from Luiz de Camões:

E foi de doença crua e feia
A mais que nunca vi, desampararam
Muitos a vida e em terra extranha e alheia
Os ossos para sempre sepultaram
Quem haverá que sem o ver o creia
Que tão desformemente ali lhe incharam
As gengivas na boca que crescia
A carne juntamente apodrecia.

Apodrecia c'hum fetido e bruto
Cheiro que o ar, visinho inficionava
Não tinhamos ali medico astuto
Cirurgião subtil menos se achava
Mas qualquer neste officio pouco instructo
Pela carne já podre assim cortava
Como se fora morta; e bem convinha
Pois que morto ficava quem a tinha.

(Canto V. Est. 81. & 82)

---

(1) "Historia da Colonisação Portuguesa no Brazil", edited by Carlos M. Dias, 1925.

(2) "A Renascença Portuguesa—A Medicina Tropical e a Parasitologia", Lecture by Dr. Carlos de França, Coimbra, 1925.

(3) João de Barros, Decada I, LIV. IV., Chap. III, p. 291.

(A dread disease its rankling horrors shed
And death's dire ravage through mine army spread
Never mine eyes such dreary sight beheld,
Ghastly the mouth and gums enormous swell'd;
And instant, putrid like a dead man's wound,
Poisoned with fetid steams the air around.
No sage physician's ever-watchful zeal,
No skilful surgeon's gentle hand to heal,
Were found; each dreary mournful hour we gave
Some brave companion to a foreign grave.)

(Translation from Mickle)

We have already said that we owe to Gaspar Correa the first European description of Asiatic Cholera. It was the epidemic of 1543, which gave him the desire to study "Morixy". The epidemic was so severe in Goa,

> "that all day long the bells tolled and twelve or fifteen bodies were buried daily; and such was the state of things that the Governor sent an order not to toll the bells in order not to alarm the people." (1)

The illness commenced with a severe pain in the abdominal regions and the patient began

> "to vomit and drink much water with dysentery and cramp which caused the nerves of the arms and soles of the feet to contract with such pain that the patient fell into a comatose state, resembling death."

In order to estimate the spirit of observation which characterised the men of that time, it is enough to say that the Governor, convinced that nothing was known of the nature of the disease, ordered an autopsy to be made—by the way, the first autopsy made in Goa—which revealed

> "........the stomach shrunk to the size of the stomach of a

---

(1) "Lendas da India" by Gaspar Correa.

chicken and wrinkled like leather which had been put in the fire." (1)

Garcia da Orta, the erudite doctor whose work translated by Claudius d'Ecluse, has given us much information regarding the *flora* of India, has also left us an admirable description of Cholera, identifying it with the 'Haiza' of the Arabs, known amongst the Indians by the name of 'Morxi', and translated into 'Mordexi' by the Portuguese. The symptoms he describes are as follows :

> "The pulse is failing, and often cannot be felt, the patient is very cold with cold perspiration, complaining of great heat and constant thirst, the eyes greatly sunken, not possible to sleep, vomiting and purging till the patient becomes too weak to expel anything more ; he has cramps in his legs,..." (2)

It is not astonishing then that the diseases of India and its natural history should have aroused the attention of the new colonists. If after the work of Garcia da Orta, the activity in the study of Botany was limited to a practical field, introducing into India new cultures, the establishment of the teaching of Medical Science in Goa represents a notable chapter of progress in colonial Portuguese history. (3) Its first attempts sketched in 1687 by the Governor, Dom Rodrigo da Costa, resulted in a course of lectures begun in 1691, which was interrupted and again started till, in 1801, it became a course of three years, prescribed by Dr. António José Miranda e Almeida. It was remodelled by Dr. Lima Leitão, in 1819, and eventually became the "Escola Médico-Cirúrgica" of Nova Goa, in 1842.

---

(1) "Lendas da India", by Gaspar Correa.

(2) "Colloquios", by Garcia da Orta.

(3) "A Educação e o Ensino na India Portuguesa," by Meneses Bragança, Nova Goa, Imp. Nac., 1922.

This Medical School is an institution which does much to carry on the benefits of Portuguese culture.

Froilano de Mello.

The present Director is Froilano de Mello.—He founded the "Boletim Geral de Medicina e Farmácia de Nova Goa", which was started in 1911, and the "Arquivos Indo Portugueses de Medicina e História Natural", begun in 1921. The complete list of his works is published in Vols. II & III of the "Arquivos", divided into the following series:

A.— Trabalhos Bacteriológicos (Bacteriological Works).
B.— Trabalhos Protozoológicos (Protozoölogical Works).
C.— Trabalhos Micológicos, (Mycological Works).
D.— Trabalhos Helmintológicos (Helminthological Works).
E.— Trabalhos Entomológicos (Entomological Works).
F.— Miscellaneous Works.

An important publication from which we can form an idea of the Hygiene of Portuguese India is the report on the "Primeira Conferência Sanitária de Goa", (First Sanitary Conference of Goa), Nova Goa, Imp. Nacional, 1914, 2 volumes, edited by the same author.

Alberto C. Germano Silva Correa.

Another man of science is Alberto C. Germano S. Correa who has written some memoirs on Anthropology, Climatology and the History of Medicine in India. (1)

---

(1) "História do Ensino Médico na India Portuguesa," by G. da Silva Correa, Nova Goa, 1920.

He also wrote:

(a) "India Portuguesa—Estudos Anthropológicos e Acli-

Information about the new scientific movement with reference to Indian Parasitology and Anthropology may be found in the "Arquivos da Escola Médico-Cirúrgica de Nova Goa" published in two series.

Dr. Gelásio Dalgado is the author of an important study on the Flora of Goa ([1]) and also of some other Essays, written in French, on Abbé Faria, a Christian Brahman of Goa who became famous in Europe through his practice of Auto-Suggestion. His theory may be found stated in the book "De la Cause du Sommeil Lucide ou E'tude de la Nature de l'Homme, par l'Abbé de Faria", which was published in Paris in 1819, and thanks to Dr. D. G. Dalgado, was re-edited in 1906.

Dr. Gelásio Dalgado.

---

mológicos."
(Anthropological and Aclimological Studies.) 1918.

(*b*) "Colera morbus na India Portuguesa desde a sua conquista até a actualidade.—Estudo nosográfico, epidemiológico e sanitário, 1919."
(Cholera Morbus in Portuguese India from the time of the conquest till the present. A Nosographical, Epidemiological and Sanitary Study, 1919.)

(*c*) "Os Lusos Descendentes da India."
(The Portuguese Descendants in India.)
An Anthropo-Aclimological, Historical and Demographical Study.

(*d*) "O Clima de Goa. Temperatura."
(The climate of Goa. Temperature). 1922.

(*e*) "India Portuguesa: Fisiografia e Clima."
(Portuguese India: Physical features and climate). 1926.

([1]) Gelásio Dalgado has contributed the following important works on the identification and systematization of plants, entitled:

(1) "Classificação botânica das plantas e drogas descritas

To know more of this interesting character, one may read the "Memoire sur la Vie de l'Abbé Faria", which is an explanation of the charming legend of the Chateau d'If, in the romance "Monte Cristo", taken from the Episode "Faria" in "Monte Cristo" by Dr. D. G. Dalgado.

Dr. Egas Monis of Lisbon also produced a learned essay entitled "O Padre Faria na História do Hypnotismo", Lisboa, 1925.

(Father Faria in the History of Hypnotism). It is an analysis of the doctrines of Metaphysical Hypnotism according to the system of Abbé Faria.

---

nos Colloquios da India de Garcia da Orta." Bombaim, 1894.

(Botanical classification of the plants and drugs described in the "Colloquios da India" of Garcia da Orta. Bombay. 1894.)

(2) "Flora de Goa e Savantvadi. Catálogo Metódico das plantas medicinaes, alimentares e industriaes," Lisboa, 1898.

(Flora of Goa and Savantvadi. Methodical Catalogue of the medicinal, alimentary and industrial plants, Lisbon, 1898.)

(3) "Vires plantarum Malabaricarum ou virtudes das plantas do Malabar extraidas do Hortus Medicus Malabaricus de Henrique Van Rheede com classificações das plantas segundo o moderno systema de nomenclatura botânica. Classificação terapêutica das plantas mais úteis de Goa e Savantvadi e apontamentos fisiológicos. (Supplemento ao Archivo Médico)". Bastorá, 1899.

(The virtues of the plants of Malabar taken from the "Hortus Medicus Malabaricus" of Henrique Van Rheede with the classification of plants according to the modern system of botanical nomenclature and the therapeutic classification of the more useful plants of Goa and Savantvadi, with physiological notes (Supplement to the "Archivo Médico". Bastorá, 1899.)

Latest activities. During the past few years, due to a renascent movement which has affected Portuguese India in common with other Portuguese territories, the attention of Government as well as scholars has been given to the revival of culture and important contributions have been made to the study of History, Ethnography, Anthropology and Natural Sciences, in various reviews. Here we should cite the new edition of the "Arquivo Português Oriental", of which two volumes have been arranged and annotated by A. B. de Bragança Pereira, the President of the Archaeological Committee of Portuguese India. It is a repository of old documents referring to political, administrative and social activities of the Portuguese during the early days of their rule in India.

This publication together with the "Oriente Português", to which we have previously referred, and the "Boletim do Instituto Vasco da Gama" forms a rich source for research workers on Indian subjects.

Information about the Ethnography of India is also to be found in the "A India Antiga e Moderna" by Dr. A. M. da Cunha.

Conclusion. The endeavour has been made in this work to estimate the far-reaching effect of the maritime exploits of the Portuguese on their literature which culminated in the brilliant productions of the Classic period when the heroic deeds of the people on sea and land were immortalised by the great Camões and further chronicled by Damião de Goes, João de Barros and Diogo de Couto, at a time when the glory of Portugal had reached its height.

Then followed the decay of political power and the loss of the overseas possessions accompanied by the literary decay, so marked in the Gongoric and Arcadian periods, and the diminution of interest in Indian topics as subjects for literary expression, when only the Jesuits, in the solitude of their cells, continued to inscribe the passing events in documents which have much value from a historical point of view.

It has been shown that owing to the stress of the political situation in Europe and the internal vicissitudes of Portugal, the beginning of the Romantic period marks the cessation, in Portugal, of literary production with India as the inspiring theme. At the same time, the beginning of a new literature was created in Portuguese India itself by Indo-Portuguese scholars who, while imbued with Western culture, were also influenced by Oriental thought and atmosphere.

Indo-Portuguese literature is yet in its initial stage, but its future is most promising and the wealth of historical documents in the libraries and Archives of Portuguese India, offers a vast field for research work to Indologists.

THE END

INDEX

D

E

F

J

K

L

M

N

O

S

T